100 MISTAKES THAT CHANGED HISTORY

100 MISTAKES THAT CHANGED HISTORY

Backfires and Blunders That
Collapsed Empires,
Crashed Economies, and
Altered the Course of Our World

BILL FAWCETT

Berkley Books, New York

THE BERKLEY PUBLISHING GROUP
Published by the Penguin Group
Penguin Group (USA) Inc.
375 Hudson Street, New York, New York 10014, USA
Penguin Group (Canada), 90 Eglinton Avenue East, Suite 700, Toronto, Ontario M4P 2Y3, Canada
(a division of Pearson Penguin Canada Inc.)
Penguin Books Ltd., 80 Strand, London WC2R 0RL, England
Penguin Group Ireland, 25 St. Stephen's Green, Dublin 2, Ireland (a division of Penguin Books Ltd.)
Penguin Group (Australia), 250 Camberwell Road, Camberwell, Victoria 3124, Australia
(a division of Pearson Australia Group Pty. Ltd.)
Penguin Books India Pvt. Ltd., 11 Community Centre, Panchsheel Park, New Delhi—110 017, India
Penguin Group (NZ), 67 Apollo Drive, Rosedale, North Shore 0632, New Zealand
(a division of Pearson New Zealand Ltd.)
Penguin Books (South Africa) (Pty.) Ltd., 24 Sturdee Avenue, Rosebank, Johannesburg 2196,
South Africa

Penguin Books Ltd., Registered Offices: 80 Strand, London WC2R 0RL, England

This is an original publication of The Berkley Publishing Group.

Copyright © 2010 by Bill Fawcett & Associates Inc.
Interior maps provided courtesy of the author. Maps created by James Clouse.
Cover illustrations by Dave Hopkins.
Text design by Tiffany Estreicher.

PRINTING HISTORY
Berkley trade paperback edition / October 2010

Library of Congress Cataloging-in-Publication Data

Fawcett, Bill.
    100 mistakes that changed history : backfires and blunders that collapsed empires, crashed economies, and altered the course of our world / Bill Fawcett.
        p.   cm.
    ISBN 978-0-425-23665-9
    1. History—Miscellanea.   2. History—Errors, inventions, etc.   I. Title.   II. Title: One hundred mistakes that changed history.
    D10.F36   2010
    909—dc22   2010028546

PRINTED IN THE UNITED STATES OF AMERICA

10   9   8   7   6   5

Thanks to researchers Mari Hillburn and Karen deWinter. And special thanks to Tom Colgan for actually letting me have the fun of writing this book.

But the real dedication has to be to the millions of men, women, children, soldiers, sailors, airmen, and even animals that paid such a high price for the mistakes of others from the beginnings of recorded history. And maybe an apology to those who will come after for the mistakes being made now that they someday will have to pay for.

INTRODUCTION

History-Making Mistakes

O r perhaps more accurately "Mistakes Making History." Look around. Do you think the world got this way on purpose? The best-laid plans of mice and men often do go awry, and this book is about the awry part of that phrase. Much of history happened not because of careful planning by great leaders but because of mistakes made by them and others. In this book we take a look at one hundred decisions, actions, and just plain accidents that changed the course of history. To qualify as a mistake, the error has to be something that the person making it knew better or should have known better than to make. Being outwitted is not a mistake; doing something so stupid that any reasonable person would know it would cost you the battle, your kingdom, or your life is a mistake.

Life was not always the same as it is today. We view the past through the lens of today, as modern people looking at it from today's perspective. In ancient Rome, communications between cities could take days, not seconds, and the worldview of a Saxon noble or a Crusader is a far cry from yours or even anything you have seen in the movies. Honor and faith to them were as important as wealth or status is today. Context is important. By necessity, the entries in this book are short. That limits, perhaps mercifully, detailed explanations of the time and attitudes in which the mistake took place. The story of each mistake begins by setting it in context. Because these mistakes were world-changing events, many have books or whole libraries' worth of books written about them. Do seek out books to read further if something really interests you. History becomes more fascinating the deeper you delve into it.

In this age when every sniffle and stutter is recorded and rebroadcast hundreds of times, it is easy to see that no one is perfect, and we are constantly reminded that to err is human. People make mistakes—some of them whoppers—and the great leaders of history managed to be mistaken just as often as are the much-scrutinized politicians of today. Some of those mistakes changed the course of history for the entire world or at least for a continent.

There may be a philosophical message hidden among this survey of the stumbles and missteps on the march of history. Feel free to seek it out. But for the most part, whether in a war or in the bedroom, the great mistakes of the past are fun to read about, and that is the point of this book. It can even be a little reassuring that so many have blundered so often in the past and yet we all survive and even thrive. Looking at the devious route the world took to get here also provides insight into the illogical, often confusing, but always fascinating time we live in now.

1

|||||||||||||||||||||||||||||||||||||||||||||||||||||||||||||||||||||||||||||||

AMBITION

The Mistake That
Made the West

499 BCE

|||||||||||||||||||||||||||||||||||||||||||||||||||||||||||||||||||||||||||||||

I t can be argued that this mistake set into movement the events that created and preserved Western culture as we know it today. This is why it is included here a bit out of chronological order. The world as we know it today all began with a very bad judgment made by the tyrant of the Ionian city-state of Miletus. His name was Aristagoras, and his mistakes began a chain of events that are still being played out today. The city of Miletus was located on the eastern coast of the Aegean Sea, in an area known as Ionia. That entire coast was controlled by Persia, and the tyrant and his city owed both allegiance and taxes to Darius I.

To understand Aristagoras' mistake you need to take a look at the world as it was in 499 BCE, more than 2,500 years ago. The fastest means of communications was a message sent by horseback, and it took weeks for communications from Darius I to reach a distant city such as Miletus. It also took months for Darius to raise an army from the heart of the Persian empire and march it to a distant satrapy, a Persian province, such as those on the Aegean coast. Miletus was in the boonies, the far end of the empire. What this meant in practical terms was that the tyrants, men in absolute control of an area or city for Darius I, operated on their own as kings, called satraps.

There was also a lot of competition among the Persian satraps. Everyone wanted to look good so that they could be promoted to more prestigious and comfortable positions in the capital of Babylon. The problem for this particular satrap was that Greek Aegean cities like Miletus were neither important nor prestigious. Men such as Aristagoras needed to do more than just be competent to get noticed; they needed to do something spectacular that attracted the attention and approval of a distant emperor. Only then were they given more control of a richer and more important satrapy or even a coveted position in the Babylonian court.

Off the coast of Ionia, in the Aegean Sea, is the island of Naxos. This island had on it a city-state in what we would call today the sphere of influence of Persia. Darius had appointed a tyrant to rule in his name and collect taxes. Yes, even at the dawn of civilization it was all about taxes. But being farther from the center of the Persian empire than even Miletus, the men of Naxos felt that they could throw out the tyrant Darius has assigned, and the island was too far from the capital for him to react. So Naxos declared its independence and executed the satrap. Being separate and independent lowered their taxes and gave the city's merchants more freedom to trade where they wanted. Those economic considerations were the more likely source of inspiration for the revolt rather than any philosophical need for freedom or democracy as we think of them today. At the time, the rights of men or the right to rule were vague concepts at best, but self-interest was just as strong a motivator then as now.

Aristagoras saw this nearby revolt as an opportunity. If he could recover Naxos for Persia, that might earn him some real credit with Darius. At a minimum, he could add the island to his satrapy, increasing his own importance and tax revenue. But the tyrant of Miletus had a problem. He could raise an army, but Naxos was an island, and he had no ships with which to transport his men to Naxos. To solve this problem, he cut a deal for the loan of the fleet controlled by the satrap of the larger and richer Lydia. This deal had a double advantage. That satrap, Artaphernes, happened to also be Darius I's brother. His involvement guaranteed that news of Aristagoras' victory would make it to court. Then the tyrant hired one of the top admirals of the day, Megabates. He was an experienced and proven commander for the expedition. It was a good move right up until Aristagoras publicly insulted the seaman. In revenge, Megabates warned the citizens of Naxos that the invasion was coming. The island armed and prepared its defenses and put away food supplies, so that by the time Aristogoras' ships arrived, the islanders were more than ready to deal with the invading soldiers. After four months of frustration and defeat, Aristagoras and his army were forced to retreat back to Miletus.

This created a very serious problem for Aristagoras. In exchange for the use of his fleet, the tyrant of Miletus had promised the brother of the emperor a large portion of spoils from Naxos. He had also agreed that after he conquered Naxos, he would use the same army to assist in the conquest of the city of Euboea and the area around it for the Lydian satrapy. But having failed to conquer Naxos and with his army crippled, Miletus was in no position to conquer anyone else, and he had no loot to divide. This put Aristagoras in a very difficult situation. He had made these promises to Darius' brother, not just another local leader. The probable result of his military failure on Naxos was going to be, at the very least, exile and most likely execution—in a very unpleasant manner.

Aristagoras must have been a tremendously persuasive speaker. Knowing he was going to suffer at the hands of the Persian empire, he convinced the people of Miletus to revolt against Persia. Cultural differences and distance may have helped. The people of Miletus were culturally Greek and had more ties to and trade with the cities of Greece than to distant Babylon. Then the soon-to-be-former tyrant of Miletus was able to convince a few of the other former Greek colonies ruled by Persia, also on the eastern Aegean coast, to join in and follow his leadership. His success in persuasion was even more impressive considering that the whole situation followed from Aristagoras' being unable to crush an identical revolt by the Greek-speaking people of Naxos.

As the new leader of the Greek revolt, Aristagoras then looked for allies. He offered gold and trade rights in order to entice assistance from cities on the Greek mainland. Sparta turned him down, but Athens and Ephesus decided to support the revolt. There had to be some element of pride or financial benefit for this, considering that the Persian empire was unrivaled in power and size at that time. It is the equivalent today of Italy offering military support to the residents of Bangor, Maine, in a revolt against the United States. A tremendous mismatch at best. Still, two of the leading cities of Greece sent ships and soldiers to Ionia.

Even though he wanted to assist his brother, there was nothing Darius I could do quickly. It took time to gather an army and even more time to march it halfway across his empire. A joint Ionian, Athenian, and Ephesian army marched on Sardis, the capital of Lydia, ruled by Artaphernes, the emperor's brother whom Aristagoras had stiffed after his failure. The Greeks and rebels managed to surprise the city and were inside before an effective defense could be offered. Artaphernes and his soldiers retreated into the Citadel, a castlelike area in the center of the city, and held out. The Greek and Ionian army then pillaged the rest of the city. The Greeks set Sardis on fire, and the brother of the Persian emperor could do nothing but watch as his capital burned around him.

Not long after Sardis lay in ashes, Darius I's army arrived to assist his brother. It managed to catch the retreating Greek army and quickly defeated it. They killed or enslaved most of the rebels, including Aristagoras. Only the Athenians were able to escape this fate by hurriedly boarding their boats and sailing back to Athens.

The Persian emperor and his family never forgot what the Athenians did. Up until then, the Greek cities had been considered too poor and too remote to be worth conquering. The burning of Sardis had dramatically demonstrated that the Greeks should be considered a threat to the Persian empire, and the Persian empire could not and did not tolerate threats.

If Aristagoras had not overreached himself, insulted his admiral, and then led a revolt to save his own hide, it is quite possible that Persia would not have paid much attention to the relatively poor and small Greek cities beyond that empire's border. If Athens had not meddled in another country's revolt, then the world would be most different. The mistakes Aristagoras made, from insulting his admiral to starting a self-serving and hopeless revolt, began the Greco-Persian wars that included the Battle of Marathon, the famous stand of the 300 Spartans, and eventually Alexander the Great's conquest of Persia. Without the impetus of the Persian threat, Philip of Macedon might never have been able to unite Greece. Western culture might never have been forced to grow to greatness. The much greater Persian empire could have continued to dominate the Western world for centuries longer than it did, and the world today would look very different. It would have been a world in which the Persian values of subservience to the state and a strong central ruler were more important than the Greek values involving personal rights and pride in individual accomplishments. The world is as it is today all because a local Persian politician, ruling a city at the far edge of the empire, got too ambitious.

2

||||||||||||||||||||||||||||||||||||||||||||||||||||||||||||||||||||||

AHEAD OF HIS TIME

A Pharaoh Goes Too Far

1390 BCE

||||||||||||||||||||||||||||||||||||||||||||||||||||||||||||||||||||||

Some great thinkers are years ahead of their time, whereas others are millennia ahead of theirs. Pharaoh Akhenaten proved to be the latter when he took on Egypt's most powerful icons, the gods. Had he succeeded, the world might have experienced a large-scale movement of monotheism a thousand years before the Hebrew Bible was written. Instead, his overzealous tendencies virtually buried his newfound faith. This was a time when the pharaoh was considered a god, so it took a lot of effort for the Egyptian's living god and messenger to the other gods to alienate almost his entire population, but somehow Akhenaten managed to do just that.

Akhenaten inherited a vast empire when he came to power in 1390 BCE. His father, Amunhotep III, set up diplomatic relations with the surrounding kingdoms and created an era of peace and tranquility. This golden age in Egyptian history gave rise to the cult of Amun-Ra, who was praised above all other gods because he brought great abundance to the Fertile Crescent. As Amun-Ra's status increased, so did that of his priests. They controlled one-third of the country's wealth and soon became as powerful as the pharaoh himself. Amunhotep must have recognized the threat because he started showing interest in the god Aten, and when the pharaoh favors a god, the people generally follow suit. This is probably just what Amunhotep hoped for. Whatever his plan, he would not see it come to light. When he died in 1352 BCE, Akhenaten took up the reins under the name Amunhotep IV; however, in just a few short years, he turned the Egyptian world on its ear.

The first noticeable change that occurred after the succession came in the form of art. Depictions of the royal family at this time have a surprisingly realistic look. The pharaoh and his wife, Nefertiti, were shown with full, shapely bellies and thin torsos. They were also seen playing with the royal children and kissing them. In every way, she was shown to be his equal. Compared to modern times when members of royal households have their own talk shows and presidents spend nights on late-night talk-show circuits, this seems rather minuscule. But in ancient Egypt, this was sheer vulgarity.

This was only the beginning. Next, the pharaoh changed his name from Amunhotep, meaning "Amun is satisfied," to Akhenaten, meaning "one who is beneficial to Aten." This slap in the face to the priests of Amun-Ra was a direct challenge. Akhenaten began closing the temples to Amun and redistributing funds given to them by the government. Like the priests who said only they could communicate to Amun-Ra, the pharaoh said he was the son of Aten and had a direct line of communication with him. He went one step further by abandoning the old gods and declaring that Aten was the only god. The plural form of the word "god" was no longer used. Put in perspective, this would be like today's Congress passing a law forbidding people to watch television.

These drastic changes were still not enough for the new pharaoh to ensure power over the people. The priests of Amun retained significant influence in the capital city of Thebes, so Akhenaten undermined them even more by moving the capital to a more remote location in the desert. He called his new capital Akhetaten, meaning "the horizon of the sun." Tens of thousands of people were expected to make the move to what must have seemed like a wasteland. Mass building projects began almost immediately. The new

city would have all the amenities: palaces, lakes, and, most important, the temple to Aten. Much of the country's resources were tied
up in new building projects. In fact, so much of Akhenaten's efforts
went into building his new city that he forgot the importance of
maintaining the good relations that his father established with the
neighboring countries. Lines of communications and diplomacy
were all but broken.

In the twelfth year of Akhenaten's reign, tragedy struck. His
beloved Nefertiti suddenly disappeared from all records. The reason for this is a bit of a mystery, but what is known is that Akhenaten
launched a full-scale war against Amun-Ra and his priests. He
tried to eradicate all traces of the name Amun. He even went so
far as to defile his father's name by scratching out the "Amun"
from Amunhotep. All his energies turned toward the destruction
of Amun. Akhenaten began to neglect the needs and will of his
own people. The country slowly began to spiral downward. Blame
for this was laid on Akhenaten for angering Amun-Ra, but the
jilted god soon had his revenge. In 1336 BCE, Akhenaten died,
leaving his nine-year-old son, Tutenaten, as his successor. People
began to flee back to Thebes in droves, and all construction at the
new capital city stopped.

Immediately after Akhenaten's death, the priests of Amun-Ra
reestablished their dominance in the community. Then they went
to work on the young pharaoh. Gaining control over the naive
leader proved to be an easy task. They pressed him into changing
his name to Tutankamun, meaning "the image of Amun." Tutankamun then issued a statement, under the "guidance" of the
priests, faulting his father for Egypt's decline. Akhenaten was declared a heretic. All images of him and his queen were defaced or
destroyed, and the capital city was knocked down stone by stone.
The name of Akhenaten was erased from Egyptian history and his
father's god, Aten, was reduced to a minor status.

Akhenaten's dream of monotheism through the god Aten
never came to fruition. By pushing his new religion too strongly,
Akhenaten guaranteed its failure. Had he been a better and wiser
pharaoh, this might not have been the case. Certainly a thousand
years later another monotheistic religion that was introduced

from the bottom up and against great resistance, Christianity, joined Judaism as a monotheistic faith.

Of course, this is not the end of the story. How, you ask, do we know anything about Akhenaten? The answer lies in the very stones used to build the city of Akhetaten. These small stones, called *talatat*, were much smaller than the ones used to build the pyramids. They could be easily transported, allowing building projects to progress at a faster rate than before. Unfortunately, they could also be destroyed with the same swiftness. After dismantling the abandoned city, workers used these same talatat as filler for buildings in Thebes. As a result of being able to study the stones and even reconstruct sections of the original walls they came from, we now know more about Akhenaten's dynasty than perhaps any other Egyptian dynasty. But the stones were not the only thing uncovered by modern archaeologists. In 1922, Howard Carter made the discovery that has yet to be matched, the tomb of the boy king, Tutankamun. Hidden in the glory of the magnificent riches hung a depiction of King Tutankamun and his wife. Etched in pure gold, the king and his wife stand basking in the rays of the sun god, Aten.

3

||||||||||||||||||||||||||||||||||||||||||||||||||||||||||||||||||||

SHORTSIGHTED

Divided We Fall

1020 BCE

||||||||||||||||||||||||||||||||||||||||||||||||||||||||||||||||||||

The Jewish kingdom began its rise to being a regional power under King Saul in 1020 BCE. His successor, David, raised the status of Israel to that of a major local power using a combination of diplomacy and military successes. It was David who truly united the twelve Israeli tribes into a single kingdom, with its capital city at Jerusalem, when he defeated Ishbaal in 993 BCE. David was followed by Solomon, who ruled—well, okay, I have to say it—wisely until 931 BCE. At that point, Israel was a rich and fairly powerful state tied by treaty with all its neighbors, and it was more than capable of defending itself. Israel under Solomon was a rich trading crossroads; it had developed its copper and other metal industries, and many new cities and towns were founded and old ones fortified. It was under Solomon that the Temple in Jerusalem was built.

The problem arose after Solomon died. To begin with, Israel was prospering, but the Jewish people under Solomon had been subjected to an ever-increasing burden of taxation to pay for defense (including a strong army) and the Temple. So when Solomon died in 931, there was an open rebellion by the ten smaller northern tribes. Under the leadership of Jeroboam, a former court official, they split with the tribes of Judah and Benjamin and founded a kingdom in the northern half of the formerly united Jewish land and established the new capital at Samaria. The two remaining tribes formed the new nation we call Judah, which was ruled by David's son Rehoboam and whose capital remained Jerusalem; Judah continued to be ruled by the descendants of David.

Somehow during the split, the Jewish people lost the size and prestige needed to stay an important regional power. Less than 200 years later, the Kingdom of Israel was defeated by the Assyrians, and its people were scattered throughout the Assyrian empire, where they soon lost their identity. These are the ten lost tribes. Judah managed to hang on for more than another century before it was overwhelmed by the Babylonians, in 586 BCE. By deciding to split apart, the Jewish tribes may have dealt with immediate problems, but they forever lost the opportunity to become a realm strong enough to survive. Had the kingdom not split, the Jews would likely have been able to maintain themselves as a nation and a people. After all, Judah was able to survive its fall to the Assyrians, and a united Jewish kingdom might have done so as well. Who knows what such a state might have achieved?

4

||||||||||||||||||||||||||||||||||||||||||||||||||||||||||||||||||||||

MISPLACED TRUST

A Slave Changes History

480 BCE

||||||||||||||||||||||||||||||||||||||||||||||||||||||||||||||||||||||

t was a time when civilization in the West was divided between two cultures. The largest was the Persian centralized empire, which was based on having an all-powerful ruler with little regard for the individual. The other culture was much more dynamic, but smaller and poorer; it was the emerging democracy of Greece. In spite of the fact that there were places in ancient Greece with dictatorial and oppressive city-states, such as Sparta, individual heroism was honored. It is a divide we still see today in the different values found in Iran, Iraq, and the other nations that are descended from ancient despots, and Western cultures that are descended from the Greek traditions.

In 480 BCE, things had not gone all that well for Xerxes, ruler of the Persian empire, particularly in regard to his invasion of Greece. His object was to revenge his father's loss at Marathon and to incorporate the impudent and pugnacious Greek city-states into the Persian empire. The free city-states were both a direct threat and a threatening example to the many diverse peoples in his empire, especially those of Greek descent.

The war had started well, with the construction of a remarkable bridge across the Hellespont (the Dardanelles now dividing modern-day Istanbul). This bridge still is considered one of the great engineering achievements of ancient times. The crossing was followed by the rapid conquest of Macedonia and a number of smaller Greek cities. Then Xerxes' army marched south along the coast of Greece to Athens. Numbers in ancient battles are often exaggerated, but it is likely the Persian emperor had as many soldiers in his army as there were residents of the city itself. The people of Athens had fled to the safety of the Aegean islands, many to the nearby island of Salamis. The resistance of the few Athenians who had instead retreated to the city's citadel was easily squashed. Then the most important and richest city in Greece was burned to the ground. This may well have been in belated revenge for the burning of the Lydian capital (see page 4) twenty years earlier. But Xerxes' destruction of Athens had come only after his army took painfully high losses while forcing the pass at Thermopylae against the 300 Spartans and 6,700 other Greek warriors, mostly from Thespiae. These losses led to extremely low morale among the men of the Persian army, including the generals.

The Persian army continued to march southward, easily conquering smaller cities along the coast, while being well supplied by a steady stream of ships sailing from many of the empire's ports, just across the Aegean Sea. Control of the seacoast was important because cargo ships were the only way Xerxes could supply his massive army. There simply was not enough food and fodder in all of northern Greece to keep his army fed. The need for the Persians to maintain this naval supply line was perhaps the only vulnerability the greatly outnumbered and often argumentative Greeks could exploit.

Since the time when Xerxes broke through at Thermopylae, there had been a series of violent storms on the Aegean Sea. Because there had to be a steady stream of supply ships and triremes to guard them, there was always a good part of the Persian navy at sea. The result was that more than a third of the navy had been lost in the storms. This, however, still left Xerxes with four times as many warships as those of all the Greek cities combined.

Things seemed to be looking up for the Persian emperor. It was the era of oared galleys, triremes, and larger vessels, and men rowed into battle and sunk their opponents using massive bronze rams. The Greek city-states had gathered all of their ships into one fleet, totaling about 370 triremes, under the command of Themistocles. Being so outnumbered meant that a battle in open waters just guaranteed they would be flanked, surrounded, and sunk. All of the Greek ships had fled into the narrow waters between the island of Salamis and the shore near Piraeus. There, in true Greek fashion, the captains vehemently debated whether to fight or flee in the hope of a decisive land victory that might come when the Persians fought an even more badly outnumbered Greek army led by Sparta. This army was preparing a defense at the narrow entrance to the southern peninsula of Greece, the Peloponnesus.

The remaining Persian fleet still consisted of over 1,200 triremes, all manned by Phoenician, Greek, and Egyptian sailors who were experienced in battles fought on the open sea. Many of the Persian ships were also much larger, if less maneuverable, than the Greek ships, and they often held more than twice as many warriors. Those extra soldiers on the larger Persian ships were a significant factor at a time when the only two naval tactics were ramming and boarding. So Xerxes had every reason for confidence. His fleet was much larger than that of the Greeks, who were understandably reluctant to sail out into battle. They seemed to be cowering in the narrow passage even as the Persian emperor watched from the heights above. Xerxes was so confident that he had a throne built and scribes ready to record the names of his captains who distinguished themselves in the upcoming victory.

Understandably, Xerxes was more worried about the Greek triremes slipping out the other side of the straits than of losing the sea battle. He anticipated a retreat by the Spartan captains by sending a large contingent of Egyptian triremes around Salamis to close the "back door." Even with them gone, Xerxes had a three-to-one advantage in number and larger ships; plus time was on his side. As long as the Greek fleet was penned up, his army could be supplied without interference as it moved down the Greek coast. If it broke through to the Peloponnesian peninsula, there would not even have to be a naval battle. And with the Greek fleet trapped between his ships, there was nothing to stop that march, and the Greeks knew this. All Xerxes had to do was wait for the Greeks to come out and watch the slaughter.

It was at this point that a slave named Sicinnus appeared. He had been Themistocles' personal servant. When he swam ashore, he demanded to see Xerxes. The emperor met and questioned the escaped slave, who informed him the Greek fleet was in disarray. Disagreements were so intense that there was a good chance that the largest contingent, the Athenians, would side with the Persians in hopes of mercy and future prominence in a Persian-controlled Greek satrapy.

There is no way to understand why Xerxes chose to change his strategy of waiting for the Greeks to emerge based on the words of one escaped slave. Perhaps it was a case of overconfidence. Certainly Sicinnus was telling the emperor what he wanted and expected to hear. It would not be the first time that the fractious Greeks were arguing with one another, and they were easy prey. Xerxes' decision to believe Sicinnus was a mistake that changed history forever. It was time, Xerxes thought, to end the standoff and complete his conquest while the enemy was divided and unready. Preparations were made for the Persian ships to enter the straits the next morning.

The problem for the Persians was that it was all a lie. Sicinnus

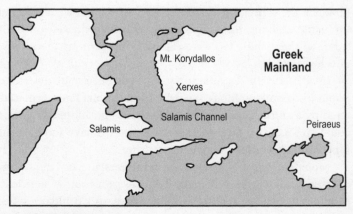

The Battle of Salamis

was devoted to Themistocles and was soon both rewarded and freed by the Athenians. Later, he set up his own successful business in Thespiae, where he became a full citizen. Xerxes really should have gotten the hint and called the attack off when Sicinnus disappeared that night. But he didn't.

So the next morning, based on no more than the word of an escaped slave of the enemy admiral who was nowhere to be found just hours after speaking with him, Xerxes ordered the Persian navy to enter narrow waters between Salamis and the Greek mainland. Rather than being in conflict, every Greek ship was prepared and ready to follow Themistocles' battle plan.

Rowing with the oars of one ship almost touching those of the trireme on either side, in a solid line formation 100 galleys wide, the Persians entered the Straits of Salamis. It certainly was a slaughter, but not the one the Persian emperor expected. In the tight waters, the larger Persian ships could not maneuver as well as the smaller Greek triremes. Persian ship after Persian ship was rammed and sunk. Except when ramming, the nimble Greek ships easily stayed away from the Persian vessels, meaning the extra crew and soldiers on them were of no use. When another line of large Persian ships poured into the straits, they met the same fate. The larger size of the empire triremes, which would have been a great advantage in open water, had proven to be a terrible disadvantage. Persian morale plunged, and fleeing ships broke up the formation of the reinforcements that were entering the battle, making them vulnerable to being attacked on both sides. So these ships too were rammed and sunk by the nimble Greek vessels.

Incidentally, the Egyptian ships that had been sent around the island of Salamis to block the back of the straits had been scattered by a storm before they could get into position. All Xerxes could do was sit on his throne and watch as his navy and his plan for conquering Greece were both destroyed.

More than 200 of the best ships in the Persian navy, thousands of veteran sailors and soldiers, and even Xerxes' brother were lost. Most of the Persian sailors whose ships were sunk could not swim and drowned. Those who made it to the shores of Salamis were killed on the beach by Greek warriors. The Persian ships that managed to withdraw from the straits were not in any shape to continue the battle or the war.

Without the fleet, the large Persian army could not be supplied. Worse yet, with the Greeks dominant in the Aegean Sea, they could sail north and destroy the bridge across the Hellespont—the bridge that was Xerxes' and his entire army's only line of retreat. Leaving a large force in northern Greece, Xerxes led most of his army out of Greece before it starved in place. The remaining army, however, was defeated the next year at Platea.

Because the emperor of Persia acted on the word of a slave, he sent his entire fleet into the Straits of Salamis, virtually guaranteeing Greece would remain independent. If he had not listened to Sicinnus, Persia might well have triumphed, and the cradle of Western culture would instead have become a relatively poor, backwater province of Eastern culture. The world as it is today—including the historic predominance of democracy, our Roman culture, and Christianity—simply would have never been. But they all do exist because Xerxes made the fatal mistake of believing exactly the wrong man at the wrong time.

5 and 6

|||||||||||||||||||||||||||||||||||||||||||||||||||||||||||||||||||

AMBITION
AND SUPERSTITION

Risking It All

415 BCE

|||||||||||||||||||||||||||||||||||||||||||||||||||||||||||||||||||

It took two very different mistakes to destroy the power of Athens, but with great effort the leaders of that city made them both. There are few wars that contain as many military and political mistakes as the Peloponnesian War fought between Sparta and Athens. From the very beginning of the war, when Sparta completely misjudged Athens' response to their invasion, until the whimpering end of Athenian power, the entire conflict was a tragedy of errors. This war, due to a nearly unending series of mistakes, misjudgments, and just plain egotism, lasted twenty-seven years and ended only when Athens found a way to lose. But even among so rich a selection of errors, two stand out that changed everything and took Athens, in one year, from the edge of victory to total defeat.

Until the Battle of Mantinea, in 418 BCE, Athens had been winning its long war with Sparta, who was being financed by Persia. After the Spartan victory at Mantinea, several cities had been forced by Sparta to quit the Delian League (an alliance of city-states dominated by Athens), cutting back on the manpower and taxes available to Athens. By 415 BCE, the city's leadership had devised a plan that they hoped would give them back the edge.

One of the Greek cities supporting Sparta was Syracuse, located not in Greece, but on Sicily. This island just south of Italy contained a number of cities that had grown from Greek colonies. As large and nearly as prosperous as Athens, the distant city was a tempting prize. Syracuse had occasionally supported Sparta in the war, and it was a source for selling supplies and ships to the primarily land-based military power. The Athenians decided that knocking out Syracuse would restore momentum to their side. Not to mention that looting the rich city would pad their flagging treasury.

Another Athenian hope was that while most of the cities in Sicily maintained a cautiously neutral stance, if the largest city on the island fell to Athens, the others would have to join the Delian League. This would greatly increase the resources Athens would have to finance future battles. The risk involved by invading was that Athens would force those cities into the Spartan camp until Syracuse fell. They had to win fast and they had to defeat a powerful city far from their own bases. A few leaders maintained that the whole venture seemed like a serious mistake. The skeptics thought there was no reason to extend the war to somewhere so far from Greece, fighting against a powerful city that would add to but was not really vital to Sparta's power. Furthermore, the naysayers argued that Syracuse was the other leading democracy among Greek city-states, making the moral justification of the attack very tenuous. They maintained that there was very much to lose and not much to gain in attacking Syracuse. And they were, history shows, painfully correct.

So why did the expedition to Syracuse happen at all? Part of the reason has to be desperation by the Athenians to find some strategy that could end a war that had already gone on for sixteen years and seemed destined to continue forever. That is twice as long as the United States fought in Vietnam or has been in Iraq. Another reason was that old inspiration for disaster: ego. Alcibiades, a notoriously self-serving politician, had managed to become a major influence in the Athenian Senate. To further aggrandize his position he needed to lead a successful military expedition. Many argued against attacking Syracuse, but in the end, Alcibiades

persuaded enough citizens to support the attack for it to happen
and for him to be in charge of it.

A fleet carrying just under 9,000 veteran soldiers landed on
Sicily in 415 BCE. They approached several of the smaller cities
near Syracuse, requesting that they be allowed to base there, but
all of them refused. Still, Syracuse was unprepared, and when the
Athenian fleet was able to sail right into the city's harbor, the populace was thrown into a panic. But for some reason, perhaps simply because there wasn't enough glory yet, Alcibiades did not
attack immediately. The Athenians instead sailed off and managed
to capture Catana, a small city located a half day's rowing from
Syracuse.

At about this same time, politics intervened, and Alcibiades
was recalled to Athens to stand trial for sacrilege. The trial never
occurred because Alcibiades fled to Sparta. Command passed to
a notoriously cautious commander, Nicias, who had opposed the
entire Syracuse venture. He did not attack Syracuse. Instead he
sent the bulk of the fleet and army off to rampage and threaten
along Sicily's northern coast, but the cities there were not intimidated, and none joined Athens. After they returned to their original camp, the Athenian forces managed to lure Syracuse's army to
move near the base at Catana, but even after defeating them, the
Athenians were unable to pursue the fleeing enemy soldiers due
to a lack of cavalry. They could not win even by winning. Soon
winter came, with the invading Athenians no closer to conquering
a quickly arming Syracuse, and the other cities of Sicily avoided
involvement.

The next year, Nicias attempted to surround Syracuse with a
wall that would have cut the city off from supplies of food and
wood. The long siege and the reputation of the Athenians sapped
the will of the citizens of Syracuse. Before the Syracusans could act,
a Spartan commander, Gylippus, arrived, and his leadership restored Syracusan morale. Nicias knew only of the falling faith of
the Syracusans and failed to realize the situation had changed.
Within a few months, the Athenian efforts to build the wall were
stopped, and forts were erected to ensure the city's supplies. But

even though Nicias' strategy had been prevented, the Athenians held on. By 413 BCE the Syracusans had hired 7,000 mercenary soldiers. Then the Athenian commander discovered that the Sicilian city was in the process of building and manning a substantial navy.

Nicias asked to be relieved of command due to illness and strongly suggested the whole invasion be withdrawn. Instead, the Athenians decided to double their bet by sending a second fleet and 5,000 more hoplites (citizen-soldiers) to Sicily. Yet even the new troops failed to force Syracuse into surrendering.

Finally seeing that there was no hope of success, Nicias announced the entire expedition would return to Athens. This meant failure, but he prevented the failure from being a total disaster. That was a good decision, but a subsequent mistake nullified it and changed history.

Before the Athenians could return to their ships, there was an eclipse of the sun. Nicias was superstitious, as most Greeks were, and he saw this as a sign and ordered the retreat to be halted. Fear of the anger of the gods, often in the form of storms that could sink entire fleets, was great. So when a soothsayer advised that the Athenians wait "thrice nine days" before departing, they did.

The Syracusans did not simply wait for the invaders to leave, though. They fought a sea battle and managed to destroy a number of Athenian triremes. By this time, the Athenian fleet was anchored near Syracuse on the far side of the city's harbor. With morale soaring after defeating what was a portion of the best navy in the world, the Syracusans used ships chained together to block the exit from the harbor, trapping all of the Athenian ships. With their ships trapped, the Athenian army was trapped as well.

An attempt to break the blockade failed. With supplies running low and morale running lower, Nicias ordered a retreat to Catana, which Athens still controlled. He split the army into two columns, made up of about 20,000 men each, and they marched toward the small city. By now the bulk of Athens' army was in the two columns. Sicilian troops blocked every road, bridge, and pass, slowing the retreat to a crawl. Each column was pressed from behind by the main Syracusan army and harassed from all sides.

With only 6,000 men still alive, Demosthenes surrendered his column. Nicias had less than a thousand soldiers left when he too surrendered. After four years of bitter siege, the leaders of Syracuse were not feeling benevolent. Of the 7,000 survivors only a few hundred ever saw Athens again. Most were worked to death in Syracusan stone quarries. Athens paid a high price that it never recovered from by invading Sicily. It was a totally unnecessary mistake that was done for all the wrong reasons, to the wrong people, and carried out in the wrong way.

That delay of twenty-seven days to retreat, for no other reason than superstition, changed the entire Peloponnesian War. Athens never recovered from the loss of more than 12,000 hoplites and twice as many rowers and light infantry. Sparta proved unable to replace Athens as the politically dominant city in Greece. The military dictatorship had lost too many of its highly trained hoplites in the war as well. Rather than a strong central leadership, such as Athens had provided for Greece before the war with the Delian League, the Greek world was once more split owing to jealousy and constant bickering among the city-states. This left the area vulnerable to the eventual conquest of one Philip of Macedonia.

Athens might have survived Alcibiades' mistake in starting the invasion if it had not been for Nicias' miscalculation. Without the first mistake caused by the ego of Alcibiades, Athens likely would have continued to win the Peloponnesian War and maintained its dominance of Greece. Without Nicias superstitiously forcing that last-minute, highly risky delay, the army and fleet would not have been lost and the mistake of attacking Syracuse would have embarrassed, but not crippled, the city-state. Had Athens not been drastically weakened on Sicily the world of the ancient Mediterranean and our world today would have been totally different.

If Athens had stayed strong, there would have been no Macedonian domination under Philip and so no Alexander the Great. Persia, playing a key role in Greek politics, might well have remained an intact Eastern empire for centuries longer. Instead of becoming the dominant culture in all the lands from Egypt to Babylon, Greek culture and democracy might well be a footnote rather than a force in history. That their city's defeat and collapse led to the ideals of democracy and Greek values later being spread to all of Europe and Asia would likely be of little consolation to the people of Athens, who paid a very high price for both Alcibiades' and Nicias' mistakes.

7

||||||||||||||||||||||||||||||||||||||||||||||||||||||||||||

COWARDICE

How to Lose an Empire

331 BCE

||||||||||||||||||||||||||||||||||||||||||||||||||||||||||||

I n 331 BCE, Emperor Darius III made a decision during the Battle of Gaugamela (fought near present-day Irbīl in northern Iraq). His army greatly outnumbered his opponent's, and he was fighting where and almost when he wanted. At the point Darius lost it all with one bad decision, the Persian emperor still had plenty of uncommitted troops and the other side was on their last reserves. Almost everything still favored Darius, except that he had an immediate and personal problem. The opposing commander was leading a charge directly at the king of kings, and that commander was Alexander of Macedon.

Alexander's charge was a grave threat to Darius, but at that point, the rest of the fighting was actually going well for the Persians. On the Persian right, they were pressing back the Greeks, who were commanded by Alexander's top general, Parmenion. The Persian center was only lightly engaged except directly in front of the throne from which Darius was commanding the battle. There the elite companion cavalry, and a number of the best Macedonian phalanxes, had reversed a march across the Persian front and were cutting their way toward the emperor. Virtually no Greek forces faced the much larger Persian army's left.

A few years earlier, in the Battle of Issus, Darius had fled when the battle seemed lost. He had hurried back to Babylon with no ill effect on his control of the heart of his empire. There he raised a newer and much larger army. He intended to use that superior army to defeat Alexander in the current fight. Darius' survival was politically important. Being a Persian emperor was a highly personal position; for Alexander to claim the throne and be recognized by the rest of the empire, he had to capture or kill Darius III. Perhaps the fact that he fled at Issus with no problems encouraged the emperor to think he could flee again without it being a disaster. Or maybe, although he was a most capable leader and politician, Darius III was just a coward when physically threatened. Whatever the logic or reason, before the Macedonians even got close to his throne, the Persian emperor got into a chariot and fled the battle.

There were more Persian infantry covering Darius' retreat than there were phalangists, the heavy infantry who carried the thirteen-plus-foot-long metal-tipped pikes known as *sarissas* and who endured the burden of the "push" that was the basis of the fighting in Alexander's Macedonian army. And Parmenion was in the process

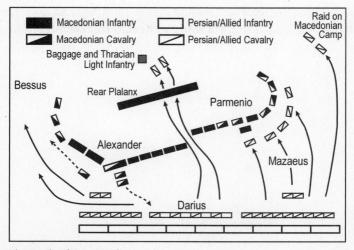

The Battle of Gaugamela

of being mauled by far-superior Persian infantry and horsemen, and almost half the Macedonian army was in danger of being destroyed. So decimated were Parmenion's troops that Alexander had to use his entire attack force to assist the hard-pressed left side of his army. This command decision was made all the more difficult because Alexander knew that all he had to do was eliminate the king of kings to win a clear victory. Fortunately, since the leadership of Persia was a very personal thing, when word got out that Darius III had run away, the rest of his army either backed off or fled outright.

By almost any standard, Darius was not losing the battle when he hurried away. He still had plenty of uncommitted forces that could have been called on, including a large number of cavalry. If he simply moved to another location and had his army continue to fight, he might even have won. Certainly he would have punished the Macedonian army, which was already at the end of a very long supply line with few reinforcements expected, and at the point where it could not effectively occupy the capital. Alexander the Great might today instead be known as the Alexander who overreached himself and failed. But for whatever reason or personal flaw, Darius did run and run hard. He was still fleeing when he died weeks later at the hands of his own generals. Because he abandoned the Battle of Gaugamela, the Persian threat to Greek culture was ended, and the world as we know it, democracy, heroes, and all, came to be.

|||||||||||||||||||||||||||||||||||||||||||||||||||||||||||||||||||||||||||||

8

LACK OF PLANNING

The Death of
Alexander the Great

323 BCE

|||||||||||||||||||||||||||||||||||||||||||||||||||||||||||||||||||||||||||||

Of all the historical figures to have the identifier "the Great" tagged onto their names, Alexander the Great is one who really lived up to the title. No other leader has been able to cross cultural boundaries or capture the imaginations of world leaders like he has done. He has stood the test of time. His tactics are still taught in military academies all over the world. He has become the measuring stick by which all others have compared themselves. When Julius Caesar came across a statue of Alexander, he fell at its feet and wept, marking how the great conqueror had accomplished more by his death at the age of thirty-two than Caesar himself had at the time of viewing the statue. Why does Alexander still have this immortal grip on us? If he was so great, why did his empire collapse? For one simple reason . . . Alexander did not name a successor. The vast empire that he created fell apart because he was unwilling to pass on the gauntlet.

Philip II of Macedonia had his hands full when his wife Olympias gave birth to a son in 356 BCE. The overzealous mother named her son Alexander, meaning "the lion." Most mothers believe their firstborn sons will rise to greatness, but Olympias believed her son was the son of a god. Philip himself doubted the child's lineage when he supposedly spied his wife in the embrace of a serpent, a creature of which Zeus often took the form. Philip had to be sure. He sent an emissary to the Oracle of Apollo at Delphi. The oracle answered that Zeus should be revered above all other gods. She also said that Philip would lose the eye through which he saw his wife with the serpent. Two years later, Philip lost his eye.

Stories such as these are probably legends created long after Alexander's death, but they do lend merit to Alexander's belief that he was the son of Zeus: a seed no doubt planted by his mother, who wanted more than anything to secure her son's place on the throne. Philip had many wives, and Olympias was a foreigner. If Philip married a Macedonian woman and the union produced a son, that son would become the rightful heir. Olympias knew that if her son was believed to be a god, then no one would dare challenge him.

Alexander grew up in the capital of Pella and attended a prestigious school. He trained in athletics and learned how to fight and be a leader. He also studied academics as well as philosophy and ethics. Philip provided only the best for Alexander. He even supplied the greatest philosopher of the day, Aristotle, to tutor him. Alexander relished all that Aristotle taught him. He once said, "My father gave me the gift of life, but Aristotle taught me to live well."

He also learned to love well. In his youth, Alexander befriended a young man named Hephaestion, whom many believed was also his lover. For the rugged King Philip, the idea of having an effeminate son as an heir was an embarrassment. So he had prostitutes brought in for Alexander to "sample." Although Alexander later became involved with several women and eventually married, he still remained close friends with Hephaestion for most of his life.

Philip may have had doubts about his son's sexuality, but he had no doubts in his son's ability as a leader. In 338 BCE, Philip put the eighteen-year-old Alexander in command of the 2,000-man Companion Cavalry. It might have been a risky move, but in the end it paid off. Philip found himself facing the Athenians as well as their Theban allies in a place called Chaeronea in central Greece. When the Athenians moved toward Philip's forces, they left a gap between their army and that of the Thebans, who stood their ground. Alexander wasted no time. He charged his cavalry in between the two armies, encircled the Thebans, and wiped them out. Not one was left standing. The Athenians in the meantime were outmanned by Philip's Macedonians and surrendered. The victory at Chaeronea gave Philip control of all of Greece. It should have been the beginning of a great father-son alliance, but Philip did something that threatened Alexander's succession. He got married . . . again.

This time, Philip married a twenty-year-old Macedonian woman named Cleopatra. (Not to be confused with the famous Egyptian queen of the same name.) If Cleopatra produced a male heir, this Macedonian prince would rule after Philip's death, while Alexander would be reduced to the rank of general and would have to take orders from his younger brother, the king. Alexander was not about to see that happen, and neither was his power-driven mother, Olympias. Tensions in the family grew high.

On the night of the wedding feast, when all the men were full of spirits, Attalus, the uncle of the bride, proposed a toast that the union would result in a legitimate heir to the Macedonian kingdom. To which Alexander replied, "What do you take me for, a bastard?" He then threw his wine in Attalus' face. Philip started toward Alexander, tripped, and fell down. Alexander scoffed, "This is the man that wishes to cross from Europe into Asia, yet he cannot even pass from one couch to another." These words, spoken in anger, severed the father-son relationship. Alexander did not have the chance to reconcile with his father. In 334 BCE, just after the birth of his son to Cleopatra, Philip died, killed by one of his own bodyguards. At the tender age of twenty, Alexander became ruler of a vast Greek empire.

Alexander had one goal upon rising to the throne—and that was to fulfill his father's dream of conquering Asia and the Persian king Darius. He massed 40,000 troops and transported them across the Dardanelles (the Hellespont), a feat unheard of in his day. Darius did not encounter Alexander at sea. Had he done so, events might have taken a different turn. Darius' navy was three times as large as Alexander's. In the end, Darius refused to fight the "Greek boy" head-to-head. Instead he sent his Greek mercenary general, Memnon, to face the young upstart.

Memnon chose the Granicus River as his battleground. When Alexander crossed the Granicus and defeated Memnon's forces, Darius realized he was facing a man, a man who believed himself to be invincible. Alexander led his armies from the front, wearing plumes in his helm. There was no mistaking his identity. He made himself the target of all who would dare to fight him. Darius would not make the same mistake again. He gathered an army of 600,000 men and made his way toward Issus. Although modern historians believe the number of troops to be closer to 100,000, Alexander's forces of 30,000 to 40,000 men were still greatly outnumbered. Having far fewer troops, and his supplies cut off in the midst of the engagement, seemed to matter very little to Alexander, who managed to crush Darius' army. Upon which Darius fled for his life.

Alexander didn't wish to be seen as a tyrant. He thought he was the son of Zeus, and gods flourish in praise. He allowed Darius' family to keep their status and live as they had always done. They kept their servants and were under his protection. Darius wrote Alexander a letter offering friendship, his daughter's hand in marriage, and all the land west of the Euphrates. He also offered to pay ransom for the Persian prisoners. Alexander responded by telling Darius he should not address him as an equal, but as the king of all Asia. His first move as the new ruler of Asia was to try to conquer the island fortress of Tyre. The Babylonian king, Nebuchadnezzar, tried for thirteen years to break through the walled defenses and failed. Alexander did it in seven months. He built a half-mile-long causeway across the water leading to the fortress. His troops penetrated the wall and killed 8,000 people. The rest were sold into slavery—so much for not looking like a tyrant.

After crossing into Egypt and officially being pronounced a god, Alexander once again came head-to-head with Darius. In what is now known as the Battle of Gaugamela, Alexander defeated the forces of the Persian emperor because Darius III had a flaw that cost him everything (see pages 24–26). After which, the Persian empire really did belong to Alexander. He took over the palace at Persepolis and captured 180,000 talents of gold. Considering that one talent was 57.5 pounds of gold, the amount was almost obscene. It was the greatest treasure ever captured. Alexander was easily the richest man in all of the known world. He celebrated with a night of drunken revelry, during which the palace was burned down and men wreaked havoc inside the city. Many of the soldiers felt like they had achieved their ultimate goal, but Alexander's lust for conquest was not yet satisfied. He decided to turn his troops toward India.

Alexander had a fascination for unknown lands. These exotic places had a lot to offer a man with a great many lusts. The women were strange, mysterious, and excitingly beautiful. Alexander fell passionately in love with one in particular, Roxanne, the daughter of a Sogdian baron whom he had captured. No doubt it came as a great surprise to Hephaestion and the other men when he decided to marry her. Alexander became completely engulfed in the culture. He donned white robes, and gave the order that his men should kiss his hands and prostrate themselves or kneel before him, for the sake of "appearances." In Greece, this was an act reserved only for the gods. When Alexander's historian refused, Alexander had him executed.

Alexander's lust for battle was challenged to the extreme when he encountered a most formidable foe: elephants. King Porus used the creatures to great advantage and nearly defeated Alexander and his troops. In the end, Alexander managed to overcome Porus, but at enormous cost. His advisers agreed that the best move would be to return to Greece. It was not the advice Alexander had hoped for. He did, however, turn his army back, but not without taking every city in his path. It was during one of these encounters that Alexander received a near-fatal wound. He was shot through the lung with an arrow. He eventually recovered and left India.

Back in Greece, Alexander received an even worse blow than that of the arrow. In July 324 BCE, his beloved companion Hephaestion died from a fever. Alexander threw himself into grief. Many felt this was ultimately the cause of Alexander's untimely demise. He was never the same. Two years later, Alexander also succumbed to fever. He lingered in his sickness for eleven days. His men worried. Who would take his place? Could anyone take his place? Would any one man be able to hold the vast empire together? At his sickbed, the men leaned over and asked the all-important question, "To whom do you leave your empire?" With his last breath, Alexander uttered words that have since become famous: "To the strongest."

The empire did not go to the strongest. In just twelve years, it was divided between twenty different rulers, each with his own agenda. If Alexander had only known what those words would cost the empire he fought so hard to establish, the world might have been a different place indeed. Assuming he had named an heir and the Greek empire had survived under one government, then much of the conflict over the next thousand years would have been unnecessary. A strong, unified empire, stretching across Europe and Asia, would have existed 500 years before the establishment of the Roman empire. Had Alexander's multicultural views become the norm, the world could have avoided much darkness.

9

||||||||||||||||||||||||||||||||||||||||||||||||||||||||||||||||||||||||

SPLIT COMMAND

Tradition
Destroys an Army

216 BCE

||||||||||||||||||||||||||||||||||||||||||||||||||||||||||||||||||||||||

One of the worst defeats in Roman military history was due not to just bad generalship but rather to an antiquated command system that begged for disaster and got it. The mistake that lost Rome 50,000 legionnaires in 216 BCE, and almost cost the city of seven hills control of Italy, had its basis in a problem that had occurred ever since there were Greek city-states. In times of war it is necessary to put a great deal of power, such as command of an army, in the hands of one man. This man was known to the Greeks as a "dictator," a word that has come down in time with amazingly little shift in meaning.

The problem that the Greeks found with dictators was that if you put control of the army, the navy, the administrators, and the treasury in the hands of one man, he may be reluctant to let go of all that power. What do you do with a man who has all the power and won't let go? The answer was often that there was nothing anyone could do, and trying to get rid of a dictator could have fatal consequences.

So to avoid this trap, the Roman Senate created two equal consuls, who were effectively co-dictators, in the theory that they would counterbalance each other. When not together, the two consuls would separately command the legions with them. The problem and mistake was what happened when you united the entire Roman army into one force, such as was the case at Cannae.

You cannot have two commanders giving orders. But the Senate did not want one commander to become superior because he alone would control all of the legions. Then there was nothing to stop a victorious consul from marching on Rome at the head of his army and taking over. So the solution Rome used was to have the two consuls take turns being in command. One consul would be in charge, and then he turned over control of the entire army to the other consul the next day.

At Cannae, the two consuls were very different men with opposing attitudes and motives. Aemilius Paullus was an experienced soldier, and he was a survivor of the trouncing Hannibal had given the Romans two years earlier in the Battle of Trebia. He was a cautious leader who understood that most of his soldiers were inexperienced and much of Hannibal's smaller army were blooded veterans. He took a very conservative approach and avoided battle except on terms that greatly favored his army. One of those terms was mandated by the fact the Roman army had plenty of infantry but very little cavalry. Hannibal had four times as many horsemen as the Romans. Most of his cavalry men were both more heavily armored and more experienced than Roman horsemen, and all of them were much better trained and disciplined. In response to this weakness, Paullus kept the Roman army camped in the hills near Hannibal so that if the Carthaginians attacked, his superior cavalry would be of little use.

The other consul was Terentius Varro. He was a member of the Roman Senate and not a soldier. Though shown later to be brave, even resourceful, Varro had an agenda beyond just keeping Hannibal at bay. He was part of a Senate faction that had for two years been frustrated by the tactics used by Fabius, appropriately called "the Delayer," after the defeat at Trebia. For two years as consul, Fabius had avoided major battles with Hannibal while the Roman army was being rebuilt. But this meant Hannibal had been free to wreak a lot of destruction and destroy a lot of estates all over Italy. His tactics frustrated a good many Senators who constantly demanded more direct action. Varro also needed a victory while he was in command to enhance his prestige in the Senate. So where Paullus wanted to play it safe and fight in the hills, Varro wanted to force a battle where he was sure the superior Roman army (50,000 soldiers versus 40,000 for Carthage) would prevail.

For a few weeks, the two armies camped only a few miles apart. Hannibal was anxious to do something before his supply situation in hostile territory got worse, and Paullus was willing to wait until Hannibal came to him. But here is the rub: Paullus was in command only every other day. For a while he convinced Varro to go along with the waiting. But pressure from Varro's allies in the Senate and his own ambition made the inexperienced and over-confident consul anxious to have at it.

Finally, on a day he was in command and Paullus could do nothing, Varro moved the entire Roman army out of its strong position in the hills and onto the level ground near what is now called the Ofanto River. When Paullus took over command the next day, the deed was done. They could not retreat without being attacked in the rear by Hannibal's horsemen. Because of Varro's impatience, the Romans would be forced to fight where Hannibal's cavalry had all the advantages. So, being Romans, they attacked.

The Romans moved against Hannibal in a massive column that slammed into the Carthaginian center. Their plan was to break through the center and then turn on both flanks. With superior numbers, the Romans were confident of success and would pit their numbers against the Carthaginians' best troops. This simple plan and large formation also was easily within the capabilities of an army made up of mostly inexperienced legionnaires and commanders. It was almost a return to the days of the phalanx. The problem was that Hannibal had not, as was normally the case, put his best troops in his center. In fact he put his worst infantry, the brave but undisciplined Gauls, there. This meant that at first the Roman juggernaut pushed forward over the bodies of dead Gauls, but, at the same time, it left the real strength of the Carthaginians untouched.

The massive column rolled forward and began to push the Gauls back as expected. But elsewhere the plan fell apart. Instead of holding the flanks long enough for the infantry to smash through the enemy center, the Roman horsemen, protecting the troops from the sides, fled almost without a fight. In fact, most ran right past the fortified camp and some didn't stop until they were back in Rome. This left the light infantry that remained on the flanks exposed and almost defenseless before Hannibal's horsemen. They too were driven off, exposing both flanks. Still the Romans pushed forward, and the Gauls were close to breaking. Only then, with nothing to slow them, did the Carthaginian commander order his best unit, his Spanish Infantry, to curl around and attack both flanks of the thickly massed Roman infantry.

This was long before the time when the Roman legion was a highly trained and incredibly flexible military machine. The massive Roman column could do nothing but push harder, hoping to literally fight their way out by breaking through the Gauls. But at just the wrong time for it to happen, the Carthaginian armored horsemen returned from chasing off the Roman cavalry and slammed into the back of the thickly packed Romans.

The most experienced Roman soldiers made up the last lines of the attacking column, and they turned about, met the Carthaginian charge, and held it. But to do this they had to stop moving and plant their pikes facing the rear, away from where the Romans were attacking. This brought the entire Roman army to a dead stop, and the operative word there is *dead*. Packed fifty men deep to ensure they broke the center, this awkward Roman formation, which resembled a phalanx without the spears, meant that most of the Roman soldiers could not fight until the men in front of them had been killed. Since most of the men were now totally surrounded by the Carthaginian army, all they could do was wait to die. And 40,000 did, though Varro, who had caused the battle to be fought, escaped and even distinguished himself when he reorganized the survivors. The Carthaginian losses were in the hundreds, mostly expendable Gauls.

Cannae is often considered one of the most one-sided victories in history. All the more amazing as it came against a Roman army that would go on in the next four centuries to conquer the

Mediterranean world. But the battle was really lost because of where it was fought, which gave every advantage to the brilliant Hannibal. A mistake that was forced on Paullus by a system that put an inexperienced politician in command of the entire Roman army at just the wrong time.

10

PRIDE

An Offer They Should
Not Have Refused

204 BCE

I n 204 BCE, the war with Rome was not going well for Carthage. The city had lost its final holdings on Sicily and other islands. Spain, the merchant city's main source of mercenary armies, had fallen. Now Gnaeus Cornelius Scipio, the same Roman commander who had defeated their armies in Spain, had landed a large Roman army near the city itself. Making things worse was that one of the Carthaginians' closest allies in Africa, Massinissa, had changed sides and had led his experienced cavalry to join the Romans. He brought with him several thousand horsemen, nicely rounding out the Roman order of battle.

Carthage gathered an army and called on its remaining major ally, Syphax, and his army and moved to defeat Scipio. But in a night attack, the smaller Roman army and its ally routed and then slaughtered the camped Carthaginians. There was only one response left for the great merchant city that had been fighting Rome for more than a decade. They recalled Hannibal and the last army they had left from Italy.

Hannibal Barca and about 15,000 of his veterans slipped past the Roman fleet and soon were in Carthage. At this point, Scipio made the city a proposal. He was under pressure from an untrusting and jealous Senate and wanted the war over before they could recall him to Rome. So Scipio made the city a very generous offer that would not only have allowed Carthage to keep its merchant fleet, a major source of the city's wealth, but would also have left it a large degree of independence and even a small fleet of warships. Carthage would not again be a military threat to Rome, but it could remain an economic powerhouse, wealthy from trade and manufacturing.

The city of Carthage was now at war with a Rome that controlled the entire western Mediterranean. They no longer had their main source of soldiers, their manpower was limited, and one of their key allies had changed sides. Even if they defeated Scipio, they would not, and probably could not, win the war. Rome, which had proven amazingly resilient, would simply send another army and then another until they finally won. But the return of Hannibal and his veterans gave the people of Carthage hope. The city's leaders flatly refused the Roman commander's offer.

A few days later Hannibal and Scipio's armies faced each other near Carthage. Hannibal's army had elephants and his core of veterans. The Roman army had its flexible and well-trained smaller units and superior cavalry.

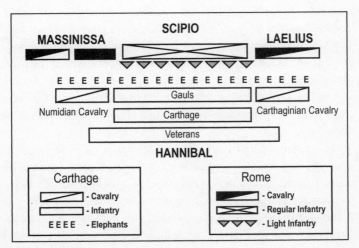

The Battle of Zama

Hannibal's Carthaginians were formed into three lines each behind the other. The legions were in long columns made up of maniples, numbering between 100 to 180 men. They lined up not shoulder to shoulder but behind one another in long columns. This was unusual because the legion normally deployed in a checkerboard formation that allowed for maximum maneuverability or in a line to allow the most soldiers to fight for the frontage.

The battle began when Hannibal ordered a charge by the war elephants that were spread all across the Carthaginian front. It was hoped the large beasts would disrupt the Roman formations and scatter its cavalry. But like most animals, these elephants ran along the line of least resistance. Those that were not frightened or driven away by javelins simply hurried down the open spaces between the columns while their riders were fired at from both sides. Worse for the Carthaginians was that the elephants, charging the Roman right, were actually turned around by the noise and pain. Instead of disrupting the Roman cavalry, they slammed into their own Numidian horsemen, who were protecting the Carthaginian left flank. Observing this happen, Massinissa charged his larger cavalry force and infantry against the disorganized Numidian horsemen. The Numidians broke and ran almost immediately. Seeing this, the Roman horsemen on the other side of the battle charged as well. There was a violent melee and then the Carthaginian cavalry abandoned Hannibal's right flank as well. The Carthaginian flanks were open to attack, but since both Roman forces followed the enemy horses off the field in pursuit, these flank victories did not determine the battle. For a while, the Roman successes simply left the field to the infantry. This was good news for Carthage because they had 45,000 soldiers to Rome's 34,000.

Hannibal ordered his front line to charge Scipio's Romans, who, with the threat of elephants gone, had re-formed into a solid front. That first line consisted of mostly Gauls: individually brave but not skilled at fighting in a unit. They smashed into the Romans, and the fighting degenerated into man-to-man combat. They were doing what Hannibal hoped, breaking up the solid Roman front.

For some reason Hannibal's second line, made up of newly trained Carthaginians, failed to advance and take advantage of the Gauls' attack. Seeing they were not being supported but were left to die in front of the Romans, the Gauls turned and fled. But the unmoving line of Carthaginians refused to open to let them pass. Needless to say, the Gauls now were sure they had been betrayed and began attacking Hannibal's second line. The two Carthaginian formations were still fighting when the front of the Roman army, Scipio's *hastati* (a class of infantry), slammed into them both. When the second line of Romans, the *principes*, joined in the fighting, the surviving Gauls and Carthaginians of the second line were both routed.

The retreating Carthaginian second line then ran directly toward the last of Hannibal's formations. This was a line formed by the veterans who had come back from Italy with him. They knew that if they broke formation to let the fleeing Carthaginians through, the Romans advancing just behind the fugitives would tear their line apart. So, they too held solid against their own retreating soldiers. For a second time, one of Hannibal's lines fought against the other as the Romans advanced behind it.

By the time Scipio had re-formed and moved his maniples to attack Hannibal's veterans, the fugitives who had survived from the broken two-thirds of the Carthaginian army had either died or escaped around the edges of the final line. From having a numerical advantage in infantry of four to three, the odds against Hannibal had now changed to a disadvantage of two to one as his 15,000 veterans attempted to defeat more than 30,000 legionnaires. And for a time they held, fighting off twice their number and not even being pushed back. But then the Romans' two victorious cavalry forces returned to the battlefield. Both slammed into the back of those Carthaginian veterans. Surrounded and outnumbered, the last and best of Hannibal's army died. Hannibal himself fled into Carthage and then into permanent exile.

Scipio, soon to be known as Africanus in honor of his victory, approached the walls of Carthage, but lacked siege artillery. He could besiege the city, but that would take months and the Senate was likely to call him back anytime. So again he offered terms, though not as generous as those he had been willing to give a few days before. Now Carthage did not have a single army left. The oligarchy that ruled Carthage had no real choice but to accept. Among these terms was the provision that Carthage could never again wage war without the Roman Senate's permission. The peace agreement guaranteed that the city survived but also ensured Carthage could not rise again to greatness or be a threat to Rome. They ignored a basic rule of diplomacy that is all too often ignored: If you have everything to lose and winning will not win the war, accept any peace you can get.

Having lost two wars to Rome, the merchant princes of Carthage should have known better. But less than fifty years later, the city hired another army of mercenaries and attacked a Roman ally in Africa—an ally that they felt had betrayed the city. Rome's reaction was not only to conquer the city but effectively to eliminate it. Although it was one of the most successful merchant cities in history, Carthage never seemed to realize that it had a good deal when it really mattered.

Had Carthage survived as a major economic presence in the Mediterranean, the city might well have slowed or changed the expansion of Rome. Certainly its mercantile philosophy and family-centered social structure would have been more present in today's Western culture as opposed to the patriotic and state-centered ideal that we have all inherited from Rome.

||||||||||||||||||||||||||||||||||||||||||||||||||||||||||||||||||||||||||||||||

11

PERSONAL AMBITION

Political Suicide

133 BCE

||||||||||||||||||||||||||||||||||||||||||||||||||||||||||||||||||||||||||||||||

Tiberius Gracchus was born with just about as noble a pedigree as a Roman could. The Gracchi were an old and wealthy family. His grandfather was Publius Cornelius Scipio Africanus, the Punic War hero who finally defeated Hannibal Barca. He was married to another blue-blooded noble, Aemilia Pulcher, and the future looked good for young Tiberius Gracchus.

In 137 BCE, the young noble was appointed quaester, chief quartermaster and financial officer, for his brother-in-law, Scipio Aemilianus, in a campaign in Hispania (Spain). The war did not go well, and the entire Roman army was trapped. With his brother-in-law dead, Tiberius took charge and managed to negotiate a peace treaty with the local tribes that saved the lives of thousands of skilled Roman legionnaires. But rather than praising his efforts, many Senators condemned Gracchus, and the body even voted to nullify the treaty. It was the beginning of a battle between Gracchus and the Roman Senate that changed, and damaged, the empire forever.

Feeling alienated from the nobles who controlled Rome's Senate, Tiberius Gracchus turned to the common people. What he saw angered him. For years the noble families had been grabbing up all the small farms. Often these were the farms of soldiers who were serving in the empire's wars of conquest. With no male to work the land, many went into debt or were unable to pay the rising taxes. Then the farms were snatched up by the nobles, many of them Senators, and the people became slave labor to work the estates. This meant that when a soldier returned from the wars he would likely find himself and his family homeless and destitute. These penniless and unemployed former soldiers then flocked into the cities, especially Rome, hoping for work.

So in 133 BCE, a bitter and idealistic Tiberius Gracchus campaigned for and was elected to one of the two positions of tribune of the people. It was his job to represent the needs of the people to the Senate. He immediately began agitating for land reform. He tried to limit the amount of land any one person or family could hold. The attempt failed since there was simply no one to tell the Senators they could not acquire more land for themselves. He then called for all newly captured lands and any confiscated lands to be divided up between the former farmers. This, he explained, would both provide a living for the urban poor and create a pool of landowning farmers who could serve in the legions. It was a good idea, for the farmers and Rome, but not for the rich families controlling the empire.

The Senate refused to act on the proposed laws. On a personal level, the enmity between Gracchus, who constantly harangued for the lower classes in Rome and stirred them up, and the Senators, who benefited from the status quo, became vicious. When the Senators managed to pressure the other people's tribune, Marcus Octavius, into vetoing the land reforms, Gracchus first forced his fellow tribune out of office, illegally, in most scholars' opinions. Then he used his power, as the person who officially opened the temples and markets, to shut down the city. With what was effectively a strike supported by the people, Rome ground to a halt. Vital services were not maintained, and the food supply dwindled. Riots threatened, and the masses were angry.

The Senate reluctantly accepted the changes in the land laws and appointed an Agrarian Reform Commission to implement the new laws. Then they gave that commission a budget so low it could not actually do anything. It seemed a beautifully bureaucratic way to kill changes that would cost the Senator's families a fortune. That ploy worked for a while until one of the client kings, Attalus III of Pergamum, died and left his kingdom and large personal fortune to Rome. Forcing leaders to do this was one of the main ways the empire took direct control of an area without having to conquer it. It was not an unusual bequest, but then Gracchus hijacked it. Against all law and precedent, because he felt the greater good required it, the tribune used Attalus' fortune to implement his land reforms. The real problem for the Senate was not the loss of land or the illegal actions of the remaining tribune. What frightened them was that Gracchus then had a large and fanatic following among the common people. He had enough of a following to gain more control of the city of Rome than the Senators. Furthermore, he continued ranting against the Senate, declaring that it was acting only in self-interest.

There was a very real chance that Tiberius Gracchus could use the mobs of Rome combined with the reluctance of the legions to intervene against their fellow citizens to make himself dictator. Effectively, he already controlled most of the city through the mobs. Soon rumors were heard of Gracchus being seen wearing purple robes, such as the old kings had worn before the Senate replaced them. But the Senate had found a way to deal with the upstart tribune within the system. He had clearly broken the law in driving out Octavius so he could override the veto of the land reforms. As Gracchus' one-year term as tribune (yes, just one year; he had been busy) ended, the young populist announced he planned to run for reelection. This was an unusual but not unprecedented event.

Soon, with the election in full swing and Gracchus appearing before large crowds all over Rome, his trial in the Senate began. The tribune began promising the crowds much more radical changes. These included shortening the time men needed to serve in the legions in order to get the free land; allowing common people, not just the Senators, to serve as jurors in major cases; and opening Roman citizenship to allied peoples who served in the legions or otherwise aided Rome. These ideas may not seem radical today, but when combined with the threat to the power of the Senate he already represented, this was truly radical stuff and a direct threat to their power and wealth.

On the day Rome voted, feelings were at a fever pitch as the trial continued. In the street in front of the Senate, a threatening crowd grew. Soldiers were called in. The trial became more of a series of threats and counterthreats, with tempers running high. Finally, dozens of Senators came off their benches and literally beat Tiberius Gracchus to death with the legs of their chairs. The Roman Senate was made up of some very tough men, and you can see they were willing to kill to protect themselves and their power. This was something Julius Caesar should have been aware of a century later when he usurped their power, but that was another mistake and not just his. The tribune's body was thrown into the Tiber to prevent any embarrassing funeral, and the crowd in front of the Senate Building was violently dispersed by the army.

When word of Gracchus' murder spread through Rome, many parts of the city rioted. In an ironic attempt to protect themselves, the Senate quickly approved almost all of Gracchus' reforms. This helped to quell the riots and restore their support among the population. The mistake of murdering the populist leader effectively forced the Roman Senate to concede to everything the tribune had demanded. Because of these changes, power in Rome gradually shifted from the noble families to the masses and the army. The people who lived in Rome began to learn that they were more powerful than the Senators who ran their government, and the army learned that they could control who among different factions controlled the Senate. Because of Gracchus' willingness to ignore the laws, combined with the Senator's greed and then fear, Rome did not have a truly stable government for almost a century. And that century ended in the civil wars. In 49 BCE, Gaius Julius Caesar used the support of the mobs and his legions to take complete control of all of Rome, and the power of the Senate was lost forever.

12

PLAYING TO THE ENEMY'S STRENGTHS

Trapped in Alesia

52 BCE

|||||||||||||||||||||||||||||||||||||||||||||||||||||||||||||||||||||||||||||||

The Battle of Alesia in 52 BCE was the final conflict that determined whether the Roman or the Celtic way of life would dominate northern Europe. It was the culmination of the five-year conquest of Gaul (France, Belgium, Denmark, and Luxembourg) by Gaius Julius Caesar. The entire war and Julius Caesar's intelligence and courage were made famous even as it was fought by that brilliant bit of self-serving propaganda, Caesar's Gallic Wars.

In 60 BCE, three men agreed to share control of Rome. These were Crassus, Pompey, and Julius Caesar. While theoretically equals, each strove to be the first among equals. Crassus was very rich. Yes, the old phrase "rich as Crassus" refers to him. Crassus had also proven himself a competent general by defeating Spartacus and his slave rebellion. Pompey also was a proven general, having won a number of victories in the name of Rome. The younger Julius Caesar had the greatest need to prove himself and the most to gain.

So Crassus went off to Syria, where he managed to get himself killed while losing two entire legions to the Parthians. Pompey mostly stayed in Rome. He was already rich with the spoils of his earlier victories and had a great reputation. Caesar saw where the greatest opportunity was and chose to take over the province known as Transalpine Gaul. This was really the most northern parts of Italy and much of the south coast of France. This province gave him a base from which he could conquer the rich lands of the Gallic tribes.

From 58 BCE until Alesia, Julius Caesar defeated one Gallic tribe after another. While not happy about the situation, no one tribe or local alliance could stand against his army of more than 50,000 highly trained legionnaires. It wasn't until Julius Caesar was in northern Italy dealing with Roman politics that all the Gauls found themselves a leader. This was the charismatic and often brilliant Vercingetorix.

Through strong oratory and good politics, Vercingetorix managed to get almost all the tribes in Gaul to swear to follow him into rebellion. That summer, the Gallic leader put tens of thousands of his warriors through a regimen of training. Then in the late fall, he led his army against the Roman garrison at Orleans (then called Cenabum). The city fell, thousands of Romans were killed, and Caesar suddenly had a major problem. His political strength came from being the conqueror of Gaul, and Gaul was looking very unconquered. To make things worse, Vercingetorix was a very good general, and he had chosen Orleans because the city was the main Roman grain storehouse. His army was now living off the Roman army's supplies, and Caesar's legions could expect short rations without them. In fact, Vercingetorix used food as a weapon throughout his rebellion, often effectively using scorched earth tactics against Caesar. Ironically, starvation would ultimately cause his surrender.

Caesar rushed back to Gaul and united the legions that had been spread out in winter quarters. For the rest of the winter, Caesar either chased Vercingetorix or captured the cities that were in rebellion. After capturing Loire, today's Paris, the Roman army turned toward the richest city still controlled by the rebelling tribes, Provence. Vercingetorix correctly guessed Caesar's intentions, but the mistake he made was in how he reacted, and that reaction was what lost the war.

To understand the mistake Vercingetorix made, you need to look at the strengths of the two sides. You have the Romans, who were technological, highly organized, and efficient at fortification and siege weapons. The Roman soldier was not individually a great warrior. He was smaller and shorter than most Gauls and carried a far shorter sword. One-on-one, the Gauls often won any fight. But the Romans never fought in a "heroic" manner involving individual duels. Fighting as part of the Roman legion, they could take on twice their number or more and be assured of victory.

The Gallic warriors were a different breed. They were warriors and not soldiers. While Vercingetorix's training had helped make them more effective as an army, personal heroics were still highly valued. They were not experienced at siege warfare, and while quite capable of building fortifications, they were not as adept in attacking or holding them. This is demonstrated by the number of Gallic cities that had fallen to Caesar that decade. The Gauls were masters at moving quickly and hitting hard.

Knowing where Caesar was going and that he had an army about twice as large as the Romans', Vercingetorix moved his army to a strategic point along the route to Provence. Then he made a move that almost ensured defeat.

The city of Alesia had great natural defenses. It was set on steep cliffs with rivers on two sides. Vercingetorix knew that the Romans could not just bypass his army or it would attack them from the rear while they besieged Provence. So if they could not go past, he assumed they would have to stop and lay siege to his army, held up in what was perhaps the best defensive position in Gaul. What he did not realize was that by doing this, he was in a situation that played into just about every strength of the Romans, while neutralizing the personal courage and endurance that set apart his own forces.

Julius Caesar did arrive at Alesia and found more than 100,000 Gauls entrenched in the city and ready to resist any attack by his 60,000 Romans, auxiliary, and German cavalry. He could not leave that large an army in his rear. Vercingetorix was right; Caesar could not continue to Provence. It was also obvious that attacking the high walls of Alesia with almost double their number in defenders behind them would have been suicidal for the Romans.

So Caesar did not attack.

Instead he ordered his army to begin building a wall around the entire city. Crossing two rivers and fronted by a twenty-foot-deep trench, Caesar's inner wall ran for ten miles and completely cut off Alesia. There was a tower every 120 feet and all sorts of traps and sharp objects scattered in front of the wall that served to break up any Gallic attack. And the Roman legionnaires could dig. Every night they fortified their camps within walls made from stakes they carried on the march. The walls around Alesia soon proved as immune to attack as the walls of that city itself.

So the Gauls waited vainly for a Roman attack that never came. By locking himself up in a city, Vercingetorix had managed to take a great field army and trap it inside Roman walls. He had turned it from a battle of swords and spears to one of shovels and picks. He had managed to put his larger army in a position in which they had to fight on Roman terms, and no one could dig, build, or defend any wall better than the Roman legionnaires.

When it became obvious he was under siege and unable to break out, the Gallic leader sent out riders to summon all the warriors not trapped in Alesia to come to his relief. They got out just before the first wall was completed, but not without the Romans learning of their mission. Knowing that someday another army would most likely appear to relieve the siege of Alesia, Caesar ordered yet another wall built. This wall faced outward and ran for fourteen miles. By the time the relief army arrived, the second wall was finished. It all came down to a climactic battle fought among the Roman walls.

Vercingetorix also now had a serious problem: Inside Alesia they had run out of food. He had already driven out the women and children, whom Caesar refused to let pass out through his walls. So they starved, exposed just below the city's walls and in sight of their husbands and fathers. The Gauls had to break through both walls and free Vercingetorix's army or starvation alone would force it to surrender.

Over 200,000 more Gauls, less well organized but ready to fight, appeared outside one section of the walls. The Romans were facing perhaps nearly 300,000 Gallic warriors inside and out with 40,000 legionnaires and 15,000 other auxiliaries, including 5,000 Germanic horsemen. They were outnumbered six to one, but they were fighting their kind of battle. The battle was fought on Roman terms and amid the Roman fortifications. Even so, the final confrontation at Alesia was a close thing and only a last-minute charge by the Germanic cavalry saved the day.

The relief army was stopped, broken, and scattered. The men in Alesia remained trapped and starving. A few days later, Vercingetorix personally rode into the Roman camp and surrendered his army. His 90,000 warriors became slaves and never again did the Celts of Gaul resist rule by Rome.

Vercingetorix made one mistake in an otherwise brilliant revolt. He voluntarily trapped his army inside Alesia in a position that played to the Romans' strengths and nullified his own. Had Caesar attacked, the Romans would have suffered terrible casualties, but in war you should never assume the enemy will do what you want. Had the Gallic army of 300,000 warriors met Caesar in an open field, they might well have triumphed. If Vercingetorix had not made the mistake of locking his army inside Alesia, France, then the world today would have a lot more Gaul and a lot less Roman in it.

13

||||||||||||||||||||||||||||||||||||||||||||||||||||||||||||||||||

NO GOING BACK

Most Useless Cut of All

44 BCE

||||||||||||||||||||||||||||||||||||||||||||||||||||||||||||||||||

In 458 BCE, when the consular army of Rome was besieged by the Aequins, the Senate declared a state of emergency so they might elect a dictator to save them from their peril. They chose Lucius Quinctius Cincinnatus to take up this noble cause. He defeated the Aequins in one day, led a triumph through Rome, and shortly thereafter returned to his quiet, peaceful life as a farmer. Though most people today have not heard of Cincinnatus (aside from the city bearing his name), he had quite an important role to play in history. In the eyes of the Roman republic, he was the ideal citizen. He took command when the country needed him most, and he gave it up just as easily when the danger had passed.

In the glorious days of the republic, citizens recited the accounts of Cincinnatus as a reminder to those seeking absolute authority. Not all who listened heeded the warnings. Gaius Julius Caesar, for example, took far more interest in stories about fighting men like Achilles and Alexander the Great than he did in those about part-time warriors like Cincinnatus. He believed leadership must be determined by might, and in 49 BCE he exercised that might when he crossed the Rubicon with his army and marched on Rome. His army then controlled the city, and the mob adored him. After Caesar's exploits in Egypt, his influence increased again, and he became even more powerful. Certain members of the Senate thought that he meant to take total control, and they came to the conclusion that he had to be stopped at all costs. So, on the Ides of March 44 BCE, these members stabbed Caesar to death on the Senate floor, thus ending the reign of the would-be dictator and stamping out any possibility of empiric rule. With Caesar's threat gone once more, the Senate would rule the empire. Well . . . not exactly. In fact, the death of Julius Caesar had the opposite effect and forever put an end to the great age of the Roman republic.

Rome became a republic in 509 BCE when the people rose up against the last of the Etruscan kings, Tarquin the Proud, and deposed him. Although they rebelled against their king, the people still saw the need for supreme authority. So, they gave this power to two consuls who served one-year terms of office. Each had the power to veto the other, and neither could change the laws without the other's permission. The government also included a Senate made up of the fathers of the community, or *patricians*. In the fifth century BCE, the government created the Tribunate of the Plebes in response to outcries by the *plebeian* class. Similar to the House of Commons, this branch consisted of a plebeian assembly and a *tribune*. The plebeian assembly included all the plebes of Rome, and they elected the tribune, who served one-year terms and had the power of veto, which by the way means, "I forbid." The system seemed flawless, but it did not take into account humankind's hunger for power.

Rivalries grew rampant in the government with each man vying for his own political gain. These rivalries came to a head in 91 BCE after the assassination of the newly elected tribune, Marcus Livius Drusus, who had some radical ideas like extending citizenship to all cities on the Italian peninsula. Needless to say, "Power to the people" was not in vogue at that time. Ten years later, antagonisms flared up again because of contention between two men, Lucius Cornelius Sulla and Gaius Marius. Sulla wanted to strengthen the power of the Senate, but Marius resisted him. Upon being elected consul in 88 BCE, Sulla had his authority undermined when Marius tried to take command of the army from him. Although Sulla was in Naples preparing to go to war against the king of Pontus, whose forces were encroaching on Rome, he elected instead to turn back to Rome and lead his forces into the city to face Marius once and for all. It was the first time in history that a Roman commander led troops against the city.

Sulla proclaimed himself dictator and remained in the role even after the death of Marius years later. He retired from politics in 79 BCE, but not before he had packed the Senate full of his friends, giving them more authority, while decreasing the power of the tribunes. Sulla's rise to power put a sour taste in the mouths of the government officials, and they vowed to prevent any future recurrences. So, to curb the enthusiasm of overzealous generals, new laws were put into place. In spite of these laws, a new golden boy rose up through the ranks and won favor with the Senate.

Gnaeus Pompeius, better known as Pompey the Great, became consul despite being underage and having never before held office. He immediately rescinded one of Sulla's laws, thereby restoring authority to the tribunes. Pompey seemed to be paving the road to his own dictatorship. However, after defeating the Mithridates of Pontus, Pompey disbanded his army and waited for an official invitation to enter the city in triumph. Although the Senate granted him a triumph, they refused to honor the agreements Pompey had made with foreign monarchs, and they did not approve the land grants for his veterans. Pompey formed a secret alliance with two other men who had been slighted by the Senate—Marcus Licinius Crassus and Gaius Julius Caesar.

Crassus is perhaps best known for his part in squelching the slave rebellion led by Spartacus. Caesar, of course, needs no introduction. In what became known as the First Triumvirate, the three members sought to use their influence to control choice offices and military commands. They did not seek total control. But, as is often the case, the appetites grew with the taking. Each man gained his own victories and jealousy soon began to rear its ugly head. After the death of Crassus in 53 BCE, Pompey and Caesar launched campaigns to destroy each other. While Caesar gained status from his military victories in Gaul, Pompey consolidated his power in Rome. Through their persuasion, the two men used the Senate as pawns to gain the upper hand in their personal feud. Pompey convinced the Senate to order Caesar to disband his army. It was the final straw.

Caesar's famous march across the Rubicon was in direct response to Pompey's vie for power. With the exploits of Sulla still fresh in their minds, most of the Senate fled, along with their ill-prepared leader. Caesar pursued Pompey through Spain, Greece, and finally Egypt, where his old rival and in-law was promptly stabbed to death as soon as his feet hit the dry Egyptian land. The assassin worked for the boy-king Ptolemy, who feared befriending Pompey on account of Caesar and also feared letting him escape. Ptolemy ruled Egypt alongside his alluring sister, Cleopatra, and we all know the scandal she caused. So Caesar became involved with the beautiful, exotic woman from a far-off land; he wanted to be worshiped as a god and wanted absolute power.

When Caesar returned to Rome, his authority far surpassed that of the Senate. With this power, he accomplished a great many deeds. He pardoned many of his old rivals, including Cicero, and had them reinstated into office. He created jobs for the poor and put a tighter leash on crime, and he corrected many problems in the empire's administrative system. He planned roads, and he even gave us the Julian calendar. Many Roman nobles concerned themselves less with Caesar's accomplishments and more with his motives. They suspected that, like Sulla, Caesar sought to make himself dictator. In fact, his unlimited power coupled with the fact that Caesar believed himself to be a god, left very little doubt in the minds of the people as to his plans. He would not be willing to simply step down from such a powerful position. This is what convinced certain members of the Senate in 44 BCE that the only way to put an end to Caesar's reign would be to put an end to Caesar.

The conspirators should have taken a page from their own history, because looking back from the time of Drusus it becomes evident that the death of a dictator did not always guarantee the fall of the dictatorship. There would always be someone waiting for his chance to rise up and seize power. In the case of Caesar, three men rose up to take his place. This Second Triumvirate was made up of Caesar's friend Marc Antony, who ruled in the east; Caesar's great-nephew and heir, Gaius Octavius, who ruled in the west; and one of Caesar's lieutenants, Marcus Aemilius Lepidus, who ruled in Africa. As with the First Triumvirate, each one of these leaders had his own personal agenda, and each wanted absolute authority.

The only deed they accomplished together was punishing the conspirators in Caesar's assassination. After that, it was every man for himself. Octavius seized power from Lepidus in Africa, and he took over total control of the Italian homeland, which the three had originally ruled together. He then set his sights on Antony and produced a document that was allegedly Antony's will and read it aloud before the Senate. The will bequeathed all of Rome's interests in the east to Cleopatra. The enraged Senate gave Octavius permission to revoke Antony's power and wage war on Cleopatra. Octavius crushed the infamous duo, after which the two lovers reportedly committed suicide. The Battle of Actium finally put an end to the constant civil wars that beleaguered Rome. Unfortunately, it also put an end to the Republic. For the next 500 years, Rome would be ruled by one supreme authority, known as "the Caesar."

What Gaius Julius Caesar's assassins failed to realize was that the power of Rome lay in her army. Control the army, and you control Rome. Numerous great generals who rose up through the ranks, many of them not even Italians, were able to become emperor of Rome just because they had an army behind them.

When Julius Caesar died, he was at the peak of his popularity with both the army and the people of Rome. But, as modern-day polls have shown, popularity waxes and wanes. Today's star is tomorrow's has-been. Before his murder, Caesar's health was already failing him. Eventually, his funds would have run low. And, it is likely that the people's esteem for him would have run out when he failed to solve all the problems his predecessors had wrestled with. From this position, the Senate could have then undermined their dictator's authority and regained control of the army. With the Senate as the head of government, Rome might have avoided the rise of despotism altogether, and the names of insane radicals such as Caligula and Nero would have faded into oblivion.

14

||||||||||||||||||||||||||||||||||||||||||||||||||||||||||||||||||

GOTTA KNOW THE TERRITORY

Varus' Lost Legions

9 CE

||||||||||||||||||||||||||||||||||||||||||||||||||||||||||||||||||

The worst loss of Roman legions in the history of the empire came about because just one man had poor judgment. That man was Quinctilius Varus. In 9 CE, the Roman empire was still expanding. Julius Caesar had conquered Gaul up the Rhine, and other Roman commanders had later expanded the conquest under Augustus until they nominally controlled much of today's Germany. Yes, at the high point of Roman expansion the empire did rule Germany . . . just not for long.

Quinctilius Varus had been a very competent governor of Syria. He had even led some small, but very successful, military actions there. Mostly, he was an administrator. Governors in the Roman empire were expected to enrich themselves with a piece of the tax revenue along with delivering large amounts of gold and silver to Caesar Augustus in Rome. Most of the ways they did this would get you arrested today, and Varus had proven he was very good at squeezing taxes out of the rich merchants and large estates of Syria. His reward for success, when his term as governor ended, was to be given another province to govern. Unfortunately for Rome, this one was Germany.

The basis of the mistake that cost Rome their legions was really the differences between the two provinces. Syria was a settled, highly civilized, and wealthy province. Germany was none of those things. Where Syria had great cities, some a thousand years old already, the German tribes were mostly seminomadic. Even their villages tended to be temporary. While Syria had been ruled by distant empires for most of its 2,000 years, the German tribes were fiercely independent and resented the new intrusion of Roman rule. Finally, Syria was a land with plenty of gold and silver, whereas Germany was metal poor and wealth was often measured in cattle, not coins.

The basic mistake that Quinctilius Varus made was to take the way he had successfully governed in Syria and try to apply it to the very different German province. Soon he was pressing very proud and independent German chiefs to send him taxes they did not have the coinage to pay. Augustus really didn't have an interest in Varus sending him his cut of swine and cattle—a mistake, but one that could be corrected. Varus' real error was not to realize how badly he was governing and what the reaction to that would inevitably be. To give the governor some excuse, he was encouraged to think all was well by a German noble, named Arminius, who worked in Varus' provincial court. Arminius had been trained by the Roman army and commanded auxiliaries so well that he was even made a member of the Equestrian order: a Roman noble. In reality, Arminius hated Roman rule, and while making every effort to show Varus how popular a governor he was, the German commander was organizing a revolt.

The Roman governors of Germany tended to spend their summers in the center of the province near the Weser River and in the fall move to a more civilized location on the Rhine for the cold months. It was in the fall of 9 CE, and the oblivious Varus and his three veteran legions prepared to make their march back to the Rhine camp. Just before they started, Arminius suggested to Varus that they change their route so they could march through a few areas that had been threatening revolt or were refusing to pay taxes. Varus agreed, and the column of 15,000 legionnaires and perhaps 10,000 followers set out on the last-minute route.

The history-changing difference was that the new path went

through the densest part of the Teutoburg Forest. This was important because the Roman army's strength was fighting in formation with coordination between units. The German warrior was unskilled at fighting in any formation, but he was brave and very effective among the thick trees and broken terrain.

As soon as the march started, Arminius rode ahead to scout the way. In reality, the deceptive German went out to command an ambush by more than 25,000 German warriors. They were swarming toward the narrow paths the Romans would have to take and waited ready to pounce. When they did, the legionnaires were unable to move into their familiar, cohesive formations. Also burdened with defending the thousands of civilians cluttering their column, the three veteran legions were torn apart in hundreds of small ambushes and attacks. Even their cavalry was unable to fight its way clear of the woods, and they were eventually surrounded by an ever-increasing number of German fighters. Varus was wounded and committed suicide, almost every man in three legions was lost, and never again did a Roman army try to occupy any land beyond the Rhine River.

The disaster of Teutoburg Forest marked the end of Roman expansion. Augustus was said to have panicked. He forced conscription of enough men to form legions to meet a German invasion that never came. Arminius was unable to get the extremely independent and proud Germans to cooperate, unless a Roman army actually invaded Germany itself. Eventually, Arminius was assassinated by other Germans in 21 CE. But Augustus did not know this and spent months fearing the barbarians were coming. He is said to have not cut his hair or shaved, often calling out in frustration for Quinctilius Varus to give him back his legions.

Rome never returned to Germany. Germania remained unique, and German culture was never Romanized like those of France and Britain. Would the steppe barbarians have been able to sweep through a Germany that combined German courage with Roman military skill? If Varus had not lost the province, would Rome still stand today? Certainly the entire history of Europe would be totally different if Quinctilius Varus had ruled Germany well. But he did not, and Caesar Augustus lost a province and his legions.

15

||||||||||||||||||||||||||||||||||||||||||||||||||||||||||||||||||||||

THE HIGH COST OF
THE EASIEST WAY

Leaded

30

||||||||||||||||||||||||||||||||||||||||||||||||||||||||||||||||||||||

S ometimes, a mistake, even one that changes history, comes from ignorance, not stupidity or bad judgment. But even with that said, in this case, the difference between intent and ignorance does not make the consequences less disastrous.

A simple and economical decision made by the city planners of Rome may well be the most important cause for the fall of the Roman empire. The mistake happened because the magistrates who ruled the city of Rome found what appeared to be the ideal solution to a problem. That problem was how to supply water to all the buildings and fountains in the city.

As the city of Rome grew, eventually surpassing a million residents, the water problem grew acute. The majestic aqueducts, which still thrill twentieth-century tourists, could carry plenty of water from the mountains to the city. The problem was how to spread that water out among its users. A solution was found: an ideal metal that was malleable and easily made into pipes. These pipes could be made cheaply enough to allow their use all through the seven hills.

The problem was that this metal was lead. Yes, it's the same material that requires tearing down walls in houses or apartments if a few flakes of lead-tainted paint are found there. But back then, lead looked like the perfect choice. It was relatively inexpensive (always a bureaucrat's concern), could be easily rolled flat and then curled into pipes of all sizes, and its low melting point meant that the joints could be welded shut with nothing more than a good campfire. Lead pipes seemed the ideal solution to getting the water from the aqueducts to the people. The problem was that these same pipes were effectively poisoning the entire population of Rome. More important, they were extensively used in the palaces of the major Roman families and the emperor. The Centers for Disease Control and Prevention's (CDC's) description of the symptoms of lead poisoning pretty much says it all:

HOW CAN LEAD AFFECT MY HEALTH?

The effects of lead are the same whether it enters the body through breathing or swallowing. Lead can affect almost every organ and system in your body. The main target for lead toxicity is the nervous system, both in adults and children. Long-term exposure of adults can result in decreased performance in some tests that measure functions of the nervous system. It may also cause weakness in fingers, wrists, or ankles. Lead exposure also causes small increases in blood pressure, particularly in middle-aged and older people and can cause anemia. Exposure to high lead levels can severely damage the brain and kidneys in adults or children and ultimately cause death. In pregnant women, high levels of exposure to lead may cause miscarriage. High-level exposure in men can damage the organs responsible for sperm production.

Organ failure, brain damage, a lower birth rate, anemia, and weakness—quite a list. Now, when a good portion of the population of the capital of an empire suffers from mild to severe symptoms, you have a crippled population. Remember all those mad emperors from Caligula on? Drinking lead-contaminated water has to have contributed to their cognitive problems. So what appeared to be the ideal solution to a practical problem most assuredly weakened Rome and the other major Roman cities.

16

||||||||||||||||||||||||||||||||||||||||||||||||||||||||||||||||||||||||||||||

. . . AND DENARII
FOOLISH

Destroying Your Economy

55

||||||||||||||||||||||||||||||||||||||||||||||||||||||||||||||||||||||||||||||

This mistake is one made over and over by great nations and empires. It is hoped that our current leaders have learned from history. The mistake here is using inflation to pay the bills. Now, before the use of paper money, which was introduced hundreds of years ago by Muslim rulers to great success, all money was in coins. Today when we work with coins, the pureness is guaranteed and enforced, but it is easy to forget that this was not always the case. This is a mistake that history has seen time and time again. Perhaps the temptation is just too great. Recently Zimbabwe printed itself into a situation in which there were days when the value of its currency would halve every hour. The Weimar Republic, in post–World War I Germany, created hyperinflation by just printing all the money they needed and hence decreasing the deutschemark until it was effectively valueless. Weimar's government was voted out of office, and the Nazis were voted in on the promise to fix the economy. We all paid a high price for that inflationary spiral. The caliphs made this same error, and it crippled Islam, ending its most vibrant and expansive period. But if you go even further back, you will find that this mistake was yet another factor that brought down both the original and later the Eastern Roman empires.

The original economic strength of Rome was built on land. As the empire conquered more countries, more land was available to produce more goods, and the economy grew in proportion. Adding to the empire's coffers was the sale by the state of captured soldiers or even families from newly conquered areas as slaves. Then the empire stopped expanding, and most of the land was already owned by the major families. With no more slaves or land to sell or grant, the wealth of the government had to come from taxes. Initially, being able to tax the rich families suited most emperors well. Those rich and influential noble families were the only real counterbalance to his power as emperor. So being able to tax them into poverty reinforced his own position by eliminating any competition. It was not too subtle economic warfare. And, of course, as always, the poorer classes much preferred the rich and noble families carry all of the tax burden.

But by the time of Emperor Nero, the well was running dry. The rich weren't very rich anymore, and without them to create new income, by hiring the workers and buying from artisans, the entire Roman economy was slowing down. So to raise the money needed for the army and his court, Nero had to start taxing the poor and middle classes. This action slowed the economy even more, and it did not make the leader very popular with the masses, and that was even before the fire.

Nero, though, had grand plans for rebuilding the city of Rome in marble and erecting a palace for himself that would embarrass a modern Dubai emir. But with tax income down, there just weren't enough coins—or silver to make new coins—to pay for all of his plans. Nero's solution was to mint silver coins that weren't all silver. This practice is called "debasing the currency." This policy caused some inflation and unrest during his reign. Soon the older, undebased coins were being treated as more valuable, and they were. Nero's debasing of the Roman currency set a precedent that many future emperors were happy to follow. By the reign of Claudius II Gothicus in 268 CE, the actual silver content of a "silver" denarius was less than 1 percent. There was not enough silver in a Roman silver coin to mine it if it had been ore. In value, the debased coins were the same as that of paper money today. They were a promise and symbol of wealth, but they had no intrinsic value. And the emperor found himself in a never-ending loop. With the coins worth less, the emperor needed more to pay for his army and bureaucrats. But if he minted more debased coins, the value of each coin was less. So he had to create even more coins with even less silver, and so it goes. The ever-creative Romans had managed to find a way to have both useless coins and runaway inflation.

The long-term effect on Rome of three centuries of gradual, and occasionally not so gradual, inflation was that the empire could afford to support fewer soldiers who were less well trained. It meant that governors had to press their provinces even harder to produce ever-increasing demands for more of ever-less-valuable coins to fill their treasury. The collapses of the Western Roman empire and, a thousand years later, of the Eastern or Byzantine Roman empire were not caused directly by debased coinage, but the practice certainly contributed.

It would be nice to think that knowing all of this might mean that modern governments would not make the same mistakes. Here is some food for thought: Seventy years ago the U.S. dollar was first devalued when the Federal Reserve Bank decided to raise the cost of an ounce of gold from $20.67 to $35 per ounce. Then thirty-five years ago, the value of gold or silver was totally detached from the U.S. dollar. That was called "going off the gold," and later the United States went off the silver standard. It was then that the bills marked as silver certificates were withdrawn from circulation. That was because technically they could be turned in at a Federal Reserve Bank for silver coins or bars. Since then, nothing has actually supported the U.S. dollar, or most other currencies, beyond the faith and promise of each government.

Just like the Roman denarius, the gradual debasing of the value of the U.S. dollar has continued without slowing. With inflation and the growing price of gold, the dollar can buy only 10 percent as much gold as it could have in 1971. That means in terms of hard exchange, the United States has debased its currency 90 percent in the last forty years. With the deficit increasing, the spiral of inflation threatens. It seems we may have learned the wrong lesson from Nero.

17

||||||||||||||||||||||||||||||||||||||||||||||||||||||||||||||||||||||||||||||

OVERCONFIDENCE

Destroyed by a Victory

70

||||||||||||||||||||||||||||||||||||||||||||||||||||||||||||||||||||||||||||||

What have the Romans ever done for us? The Jews of the first century CE asked themselves that very question. Despite the obvious benefits so aptly pointed out in the opening scenes of Monty Python's *The Life of Brian*, the Jews were not willing to give up all they held sacred for the sake of progress and profit. All the roads, running water, education, and medical attention in the world could not take the place of their religion. But for a time, it seemed that even a 3,000-year-old religion might not be able to withstand the might of the Roman empire.

Judea during the time of the early Roman empire was a volatile place. In addition to being inhabited by a people dead set on removing the Roman occupants, it was also filled with opposing factions within the Jewish community. One of these factions in particular used radical and violent means to try to push out the occupying forces. These Zealots grew tired of the religious leaders like the Pharisees and the Sadducees playing puppet to the Roman rulers. They also resented the corrupt reigns of incompetent political hacks who were the procurators that Rome had chosen to rule over Judea. Tensions came to a head around 66 CE, when the procurator, Gessius Florus, took seventeen talents of gold from the Temple treasury. That was a massive amount of wealth. Public outcry from both within the walls of Jerusalem and outside spread like wildfire. Florus answered this outcry by allowing his soldiers to pillage part of the city. In response, the city's masses rose up against their Roman leaders and drove them out of Judea. Gessius Florus fled to the protection of another Roman garrison on the coast in Caesarea.

The people of Judea had more to contend with than corrupt government officials. Herod Agrippa the younger, who was king of Judea, had the right to nominate the high priest in Jerusalem. The Herod dynasty is sometimes a confusing one to follow, as they weren't very innovative in naming their heirs. So, just to clear things up, this particular Herod was the nephew of Herod of Chalcis, the one mentioned in the Bible in Acts 25 and 30. Although he claimed to live by the laws of the Jews, Herod Agrippa lived with his uncle's widow, and he spent most of his time in Rome, relishing the pagan lifestyle within the capital city.

The Zealots despised Agrippa and believed the only way to counter his oppressive regime was to start an open revolt. The Zealots demanded three things. All sacrifices to appease the emperor had to stop because they were in direct conflict with God's law, the sanctity of the temple had to be preserved, and—most important—Judea had to have its independence. These were the only acceptable terms, and to show they were serious, the Zealots took control of the Temple in Jerusalem, while the less fanatical Jews held the rest of the city. The rebels immediately refused and forbade others to make the sacrifices required by Rome. Agrippa attempted to put the revolt down with the forces he had on hand. The Zealots led a Jewish army that first defeated Agrippa's force of 3,000 horsemen and then later took the fortress of Masada.

Rome could not let any revolt go unpunished lest other provinces follow suit. They sent in the governor of Syria, Cestius Gallus. He tried and failed to quell the rebellion. When Gallus saw how heavily defended Jerusalem was, he hurried back to Antioch. On the way, rebel forces ambushed the unsuspecting governor and his escort. The last part of Gallus' return to his capital was more in the form of a panicky rout.

With each Roman defeat, the rebels grew in strength and number. The Zealots, under command of John of Gischala, soon controlled most of Jerusalem. Josephus commanded the forces of Galilee. This is the same Josephus who would later write *Bellum Judaicum* (The Jewish War), giving us our main source of information about the revolt. Josephus gathered and trained troops, fortified cities, and set up an administrative body in Galilee, which was able to operate separately from Jerusalem.

The previous failure of Agrippa and then Cestius Gallus embarrassed Rome, so Flavius Vespasian was sent in to squash the rebellion once and for all. Vespasian was an experienced field commander who had been ousted from Rome for falling asleep during one of Nero's infamous poetry readings. Apparently the general's lack of couth in court did not carry over into his military career. He massed troops in Antioch while his son, Titus, brought in more troops from Alexandria. The two forces met and merged on the way to Judea in Ptolemais. The news of the approach of a large force of Romans reached Josephus, and he fled to the fortified city of Jotapata with his followers. The unprotected land outside of the cities fell into Roman hands without a single blow being dealt.

Vespasian focused his attention on Jotapata. The siege lasted forty-seven days. Josephus, along with forty of his men, took refuge in a cave. When their position was revealed to the Romans, Josephus decided to surrender; however, his companions did not allow it. So, Josephus had another idea. Every third man would kill his closest neighbor. When the last two men were left standing, they would draw lots to decide which man would kill the other. The last man would kill himself. This meant that only one man would break Jewish law by committing suicide. Of course, Josephus was one of the last of two men left alive. He stated in his writing that it was God's will, but it could have simply been the result of someone who could perform simple mathematics. Josephus was taken prisoner but was later released. He lived out the rest of his life in Rome.

After taking the city of Jotapata, Titus also captured the cities of Tiberius, Taricheae, Gamala, and the Zealot base of Gischala. John of Gischala fled, and by 67 CE all of Galilee was back in the hands of the Romans. Most of Judea was also now under Roman control, leaving the holy city of Jerusalem as the final key to crushing the rebellion. But Jerusalem would not be an easy nut to crack. The fall of Galilee gave the Zealots a stronger position within the Jewish community. They assumed control of all of the city as well as the Temple. That wasn't the only obstacle the Roman general faced. Troubles in Rome and infighting among the would-be emperors meant Vespasian would delay attacking Jerusalem for the better part of a year. Only after he had secured his place in the Roman hierarchy was he free to deal with Jerusalem.

Vespasian had to stay in Rome, so he sent his son, Titus, to retake Jerusalem and so finish what he had started. In April 70, Titus began his direct assault on Jerusalem. He stunned the Zealots by breaking through the first wall in a mere fifteen days and the second after only eight days. The third wall was quite another matter. Fifteen feet of stone separated the Roman troops from the inhabitants on the other side. Titus built massive siege towers, seventy-five feet tall, in an attempt to send his men over the top. Each tower could carry dozens of troops. The Jews answered this new threat by tunneling under the walls of the city to attack the troops inside the great towers.

They managed to cripple or destroy them all. So Titus came up with his most ruthless plan. Taking a note from Julius Caesar, he had a 4.5-mile-long wall built completely around the city. If the Jews wouldn't surrender, he would starve them into submission. Just like at Alesia a century earlier, the Roman wall meant no supplies could reach the inhabitants within. All Titus had to do was to wait.

Then an unexpected disaster happened. The tunnel that the Jews built to try to infiltrate the siege towers collapsed. In doing so, it undermined a section of the third wall. Several meters of wall collapsed into rubble. The city was now vulnerable. Roman legionnaires stormed through the city, taking out years of frustration on the inhabitants. In the end, the Temple was destroyed and hundreds of thousands of Jews were killed. The rest were sold into slavery.

Some Jews saw this as divine punishment for those who had practiced the Roman ways. Others became even more bitter. With its main population center gone, the Jewish state became a province. Whatever the case, the destruction of the Temple of Solomon devastated the Jewish community. The rebellion that sought to empower the Jewish people instead resulted in their near destruction. They fought for their beliefs and the things they felt were theirs by right as God's people. They wished to honor their God by refusing to make sacrifices to other gods, they wanted independence, and, most of all, they wanted to preserve the most sacred of God's holy places, the Temple in Jerusalem. Instead, thousands were enslaved, many more were killed, and the Temple was destroyed. The heart of the Jewish people was no more. A once-strong and -vigorous people were broken and scattered. Their history changed forever because the Jewish people thought that a little bit of military success meant they could take on, most literally, the rest of the known world.

And what happened to all the gold and other artifacts that were stolen from the Temple? Vespasian used it to finance one of Rome's most powerful symbols, the Coliseum.

18

||||||||||||||||||||||||||||||||||||||||||||||||||||||||||||||||||||||||

TAKING THE EASY WAY

The Great Divide

324

||||||||||||||||||||||||||||||||||||||||||||||||||||||||||||||||||||||||

When the Roman emperor Diocletian decided to divide his realm into an eastern empire and a western empire, he did so in order that his forty-four provinces might be more easily governed. He obviously had never read anything on Roman history; otherwise he would have known that every time the empire had been divided to make it more manageable, it resulted only in civil war or invasion. But it is unlikely that Diocletian knew his history, because he was illiterate. The requirements for being emperor had vastly deteriorated since the time of Marcus Aurelius. Diocletian proved his ability as a military commander, but his inability to learn from the errors of his predecessors would cost his citizens greatly, eventually lead to civil war, and hasten the collapse of Roman rule in the western half of the empire.

Diocletian had grown anxious about the growing number of barbarian invasions in Gaul. He had already created a mobile army to deal with the situation, but he decided that the best way to handle it would be to have a stronger power base in the west. He appointed his close friend Maximian as his co-emperor to rule from Gaul while Diocletian would rule from Nicomedia in Asia

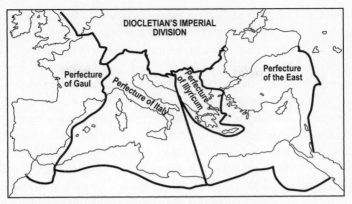

Emperor Diocletian's plan to partition the Roman empire

Minor. In doing this, he set up a structure that was supposed to ensure peaceful succession to each office. The two emperors would be called Augustus, and they were to pick a successor who was not a son, no matter how competent the son might be. Diocletian then chose two co-regents, who would be called Caesar. Galarius became the Caesar in the east and heir to Diocletian, while Constantius ruled with Maximian as the Caesar in the west. With separate leaders, separate armies, and even separate tax collectors, the Roman empire became in effect two empires.

There was still the risk that family ties would interfere with his plans to ensure that the Caesar would become the Augustus. To keep the family ambitions of each man in the tetrarchy at bay, Diocletian "requested" that their sons live in his court. One of these sons was Constantine, the son of Constantius. Although the sons were virtually hostages, Diocletian treated them well. Despite being illiterate, he gave the boys the best education and even made sure they learned Greek. Constantine eventually became one of Diocletian's most trusted soldiers, but the Augustus grew uneasy. The emperor had issued the Great Persecution against the Christians and, although Constantine himself did not fall into the sect, his mother did. As one of the emperor's top men, he had witnessed many atrocities under the new edict. When the aging emperor fell ill, he failed to include Constantine in the exchange of power. Constantine realized for the first time what his position had been. He was a mere hostage and was also expendable.

Constantine fled to Boulogne in Gaul to meet his father. His arrival could not have been better timed. Constantius then ruled over Spain, Gaul, and Britain. In Britain, his father faced an uprising of the always unruly Picts. So father and son went to Britain together. Constantine soon won the favor of his father's army by leading them in defeating the Picts. When his father died in 306, the army recognized Constantine as their new leader. They chose wisely. Not long after, when the Barbarian Franks invaded Gaul, Constantine led the cavalry charge against them and defeated them. Constantine celebrated this victory with a triumph that marched through the streets of Trier. The citizens loved him.

While Constantine was gaining support in Gaul and Britain, a usurper rose to power in Italy and North Africa. Maxentius had taken over by promising lower taxes and free grain. (He is not to be confused with Maximian, who was one of the original tetrarchy.) When the people realized the promises he made would be delivered only to the wealthy, they began to revolt. Riots broke out all over Rome. Constantine saw it as his duty to overthrow the upstart and restore order. He formed an alliance with Licinius, who now controlled the eastern half of the empire. Together they rallied their troops to fight their fellow Romans just outside Rome. This was exactly what Diocletian had sought to avoid, civil war.

On the eve of battle, Constantine is said to have seen the Greek letters chi and rho appear in the sky (the first two letters of the word *Christ*). He heard a voice say, "Under this, you will conquer." Constantine had witnessed the resilience of the Christians when they were undergoing persecution by Diocletian. Rather than discouraging the faith, the number of Christians had grown at an enormous rate. It is possible that Constantine saw a people whom he could use to help win the empire. Whether it was motivated by politics or a spiritual awakening, Constantine ordered his men to paint the Christian symbol on their shields. Together the forces of Constantine defeated Maxentius at the Milvian Bridge. Constantine had the head of his enemy paraded around the empire. With this single victory, Constantine became the sole ruler of the western empire.

Despite Constantine's victory, there was no peace. The alliance Constantine formed with Licinius broke down. As the conflict between the two rulers grew more tense, Licinius found a way to strike out against his nemesis in the west. Like Diocletian before him, he persecuted the very sect of people whom Constantine had claimed as own: the Christians. The persecutions were not founded on religious divergence; they were purely political. Licinius saw the Christians as Constantine's people. For nine more years, tensions between the east and west worsened until the antagonism came to a head. Once again the country was on the verge of civil war.

The battle that would decide who would take possession of all the vast expanses of the Roman Empire took place at Chrysopolis in 324. Constantine defeated Licinius' army and became the sole emperor. Because Constantine's sister, who was married to Licinius through the previous alliance, had begged for mercy for her husband, Constantine spared him, at least for a while. But he later had his enemy killed while imprisoned.

With his enemies annihilated, Constantine could focus on what meant the most to him: his new Christian empire. Because the brunt of economic and military activity in the empire took place in the northeast, he decided to establish a new capital on the site of the former Greek city of Byzantion. He chose the location because of its great strategic advantage. It lay near the Mediterranean Sea and the Black Sea and allowed access to Anatolia and the Danube. He changed the city's name to Constantinople. The city became his obsession. He focused all of his resources on building roads, elaborate cathedrals, schools, and more secure walls. He transformed the city into the jewel of the east. It became a center of knowledge, wealth, and prosperity. It was cosmopolitan. It was Christian. But, most of all, it was Greek. The split Diocletian began was complete.

After Constantine's death, his capital city continued to flourish. But the Latin-speaking west did not. The empire was politically and culturally split due to language differences, philosophical differences, and eventually religious differences. Power struggles developed between the pope in Rome and the patriarch in Constantinople. These would eventually lead to the Great Schism in the Church. By 395, the empire was officially split yet again. Without the support of the east, the west fell prey to barbarian invasions and was lost in the sixth century. This is often seen as the end of the Roman empire. But it was not until 1453, when the Turks took Constantinople, that the last and long separate eastern half of the empire truly ceased to exist.

Once Diocletian split the Roman empire, it changed everything. The rich east even diverted barbarian invasions toward the west. Diocletian's dream of an efficient and divided but cooperative empire was a nightmare that doomed the western half of the Roman empire. Had the empire stayed united, Rome might have had the resources and strength to survive for centuries more, like Byzantium did. At first it was more efficient for Diocletian to divide up the empire. But for millions, the split was a mistake that doomed them to a millennium of darkness.

19

‖‖‖

FIGHT YOUR OWN WARS

Who Will Watch the Watchers?

375

‖‖‖

By the late fourth century, the Roman empire stretched across Europe and Asia and contained many diverse cultures and races. Despite that, officials still had reservations about embracing the barbarian people of Germany and inducting them into the army. Those who revered the illusion of a classic Rome resented that the world was changing rapidly. It would yet again change for the worse with the invasion of the Huns and a few benchmark decisions that, now looking back, were probably not in the best interest of the empire.

It all started in 375 when the Huns attacked the Ostrogoths in the Black Sea region. The Visigoth king Fritigern believed his people would be targeted next, and he appealed to Emperor Valens for help. He asked the emperor to allow his people to settle in Roman territory just south of the Danube. Valens resisted at first, but then he relented on the condition that the Visigoths would disarm. In exchange, Rome would provide food for the new refugees. It seemed a mutually beneficial solution. But Valens had not counted on the hatred of his own people, especially the hatred veteran Roman soldiers held toward the Germanic people. Once the Visigoths had settled, they had to endure mistreatment by their Greek neighbors and the Roman soldiers. They also had to endure hunger. Valens had known there was not enough extra food, but had made the deal despite this.

The following year, Fritigern and his Visigoths revolted. The culturally linked Ostrogoths joined them in their struggle. Valens was killed. Later, Emperor Theodosius persuaded the Ostrogoths to leave Roman territory as the Huns moved eastward. He provided settlements for the Visigoths in what is today Bulgaria. Theodosius also offered them new lives as soldiers in the Roman army. Being a Roman soldier paid enough to feed their families, and many Goths accepted. With the increasing pressure on the borders generated by the Huns, the integration of the Germanic people into the eastern and the western armies took place at a rapid rate. The Latin and Greek soldiers resented the new arrivals. The empire had been fighting the barbarians for more than 400 years. This longtime hatred of Germanic and Steppe peoples would not simply vanish because they were suddenly allowed to serve in the army.

In 395, the Visigoths elected Alaric as their king. Many considered Alaric an activist for his people. When supplies once again ran low, he led them farther into Europe in search of food and grazing land. At the same time, another disgruntled barbarian decided to rise up against Rome. Radagaisus marched his Vandal-Burgundian army across the Danube and into the Alps. They had to be stopped. Stilicho, the Frankish-Roman military commander, set out to subdue them. He did so without a battle. Rather than stamping these people out, he incorporated many of them into the army.

Alaric and his Visigoths took advantage of the distraction caused by Radagaisus and moved into northern Italy. Stilicho turned his sights on the Visigoths. Radagaisus saw his chance to make a nuisance of himself once again. In 405, while Stilicho busied himself against Alaric, Radagaisus and his Vandals made way for Hispania and settled on Roman lands. Alaric did not want to be left out in the cold, so he and his people followed the Vandals onto the Iberian peninsula in hopes of gaining new lands and better opportunities.

Rome was outraged. Someone needed to take the fall for this massive blunder. The emperor in the west, Honorus, decided that Stilicho was the cause of all of Rome's problems with the barbarians and ordered his assassination. Tensions grew within the army until it finally split between the two rival factions. The split was along ethnic lines between the long-term Roman citizens and the new Germanic recruits. Roman soldiers began murdering the families of their German counterparts. The Germans left to join Alaric. Without the Germans to fill the ranks, Italy was without an active army.

The situation was less than agreeable. For the next four years, Alaric and the barbarian tribes continued to settle in Hispania and even northern Italy. Without an active army, the emperor resorted to bribery to keep Alaric from sacking Rome itself. But Alaric didn't necessarily want to destroy Rome. What he really wanted was to be a part of the empire. He wanted his men to be reintegrated into the army, he wanted provisions, land his people could live peacefully on, and he wanted all the benefits of being a citizen of Rome. Honorus refused. It turned out to be a poor choice. Honorus fled to Ravenna.

Rome elected a new emperor for the west. Attalus proved to be far more accepting of the barbarians. He believed that the integration was inevitable and would benefit Rome. He agreed to Alaric's demands of reintegration and food. There was just one problem. Rome had no extra provisions. When Attalus failed to meet Alaric's demands, the Visigoths led an attack on Rome. By this time, the Roman army was totally dependent on Germanic troops. There were simply not enough Romans left who would or could fight to protect the city. In 475, the barbarian chief Odoacer replaced the Roman emperor with himself. By filling their army with Germanic recruits, the western Romans forgot the hard-learned lesson that the army controls who is emperor. Had they not depended on the often troublesome barbarian tribes for defense against effectively more barbarian tribes, perhaps Rome and the Western Roman empire might have survived. But instead, the citizens of Rome let others become their defenders and soon found that those defenders became their masters.

20

||||||||||||||||||||||||||||||||||||||||||||||||||||||||||||||||||||

NOT-SO-FREE-
FIRE ZONE

One Arrow

378

||||||||||||||||||||||||||||||||||||||||||||||||||||||||||||||||||||

I n 378, a single soldier, not even an officer, made a mistake that greatly hastened, and perhaps even led directly to, the final destruction of the Western Roman empire. It all started far away in the steppes of Asia. This is the traditional home of most tribes of horse barbarians, and among others, the Goths had started there before moving into eastern Europe. The Goths were tough, but they migrated toward the borders of both Roman empires (Byzantine and western) because a much nastier bunch of barbarians were pushing them. These were the Huns, as in Atilla the Hun, who were destined to wreak havoc across most of Europe a generation later. But at this time, the Huns were still a distant threat, and the Goths were on Rome's border asking to cross and settle into territories then controlled by the western empire. They were split into two groups: the eastern Ostrogoths and the western Visigoths. As described in Mistake 19 (see pages 77–79), Visigoth leaders met with Roman officials and asked permission for their people to enter Roman territory. It was agreed that if the men left their weapons behind, the Goths would be welcome. It was also agreed, since there would be no chance for the Visigoths to raise crops, that Rome would provide them food to get by until the next harvest.

The entire population migrated; hundreds of thousands of men, women, and children, with tens of thousands of warriors among them, crossed into the Roman empire. Even though they had not agreed to the deal, the other large group, the Ostrogoths, under pressure from Hun allies and caught amid the confusion, also crossed over the river that marked Rome's boundary. It became obvious fairly quickly that there simply was not enough food available for the Romans to keep the Goths supplied. Starving, the Visigoth tribes began taking what food they could find, often pillaging the villages while doing so. A near-constant fight between small groups of Goths and small Roman units erupted. To try to deal with the problem the two Roman governors requested a meeting with all of the Visigoth leaders. The meeting was a ruse with the intention of assassinating all of the Visigoth leadership, likely as a prelude to enslaving the hungry and (they hoped) leaderless Goths.

The assassination attempt failed, miserably. The Visigoth leaders escaped, their army was soon reinforced by the Ostrogoths, and open warfare resulted. For months, both sides sparred, small bunches of horsemen raiding and then ambushing one another, as infantry units defended the larger Roman towns and cities. Finally, Emperor Valens arrived to take control of the war. He hoped to win a decisive battle that would crush or drive the Goths away. The Visigoth king Fritigern offered peace if the Romans would allow his people to virtually take over the province of Thrace. This was rejected by Valens, who collected a large army made up of both cavalry and infantry. Fritigern also gathered the Goths, but once more offered to negotiate.

At this point in history, the Goths as a people were almost as civilized as the Romans and were actually more literate than the Roman citizens of Gaul. Their leaders were angry, but they also saw that both sides had more to lose than win. They did not really want a war or a battle whose loss would destroy them as a people. Even if they won, they were just weakening a potential future ally against the Huns. What the Goths really wanted was a safe place to settle. This is later shown by the fact that the Goths did unite with what was the last real Roman army to face down and defeat

Atilla and the Huns eighty years later. The Visigoths may not have liked Rome, but they feared the Huns more.

The two armies met near Adrianople and camped in sight of each other. It was agreed that Valens would send a delegation into the ring of wagons that formed the Visigoths' camp. Remember, this was a movement of the entire Visigoth people, and in that camp were not only warriors but also families. Each side, not without cause, watched for betrayal and formed up their horsemen, ready to attack as needed. But Fritigern seems to have been more than ready to talk peace. Then a small mistake doomed Rome.

As the Roman delegation rode toward the Visigoth camp, they had to be nervous. Their side had just used a similar maneuver in an attempt to assassinate the very leaders they were riding to meet. Around them, thousands of horsemen armed with bow and lance stood poised to attack one another. For months, both sides had been fighting small, bitter battles and rarely taking prisoners.

Maybe it was in response to some sort of unusual movement on the wall of wagons as the Romans approached. Or maybe he saw an old enemy. One of the soldiers, who was acting as the bodyguard for the Roman delegates, fired an arrow, one arrow only, toward the disturbance. The other guards may have fired then as well. None survived to say if they did or did not. The Visigoths reacted with a shower of arrows. Most of the Roman delegation fell, and the survivors fled.

Seeing this, the Roman cavalry charged the Goths' camp from their position on both flanks of the infantry. The horsemen were unable to break into the Visigoth camp they surrounded. The bulk of the Visigoth and Ostrogoth heavy cavalry, well-armored men on fresh horses, had returned late. They had been waiting out of sight, behind a small wood, to one side of the battlefield. These armored horsemen charged first one, then the other force of Roman cavalry. Assailed by arrows from the wagons and attacked from behind by thousands of armored warriors, both groups of Roman horsemen fled. This left the still-unformed and badly trained Roman infantry at the mercy of the entire Gothic army. About 40,000 men died, and the power of the Western Roman empire was broken forever. Roman armies became less and less Roman and more and more barbarian. The vaunted infantry of the legions was shown to be gone. Rome never again ruled more than parts of Italy, and within a century, the city of Rome itself had fallen twice and the barbarian Odoacer held the meaningless title of emperor.

If that one arrow had not been fired, there was a very good chance that peace could have been achieved. It was the Visigoths, who had valid claims and concerns, who had asked to talk, and it was very much in Valens' interest to have them as allies and not enemies. Without the disaster at Adrianople, Rome would have remained stronger and much more capable of defending itself. A Rome that still had a real army with Gothic allies might have maintained the high level of culture and literacy the Romans and Goths shared. The centuries that followed the Battle of Adrianople are described as the Age of Barbarians and the Dark Ages. Except for one arrow fired by an anonymous bodyguard, those times might have been much less barbarous and far less dark.

21

||||||||||||||||||||||||||||||||||||||||||||||||||||||||||||||||

HIRING OUT HOME DEFENSE

We Are Here to Help You . . .

425

||||||||||||||||||||||||||||||||||||||||||||||||||||||||||||||||

Sometimes the enemy of your enemy is just your enemy too. In the early part of the fifth century, Roman occupants withdrew from Britain to defend Gaul and Italy from the invading barbarian tribes. They left behind a defenseless land with an uncertain future. The lack of a strong government and military presence sent the country spiraling into chaos. Bands of Picts, who dwelled on the north side of Hadrian's Wall, began raiding villages on the south side. They took food, slaughtered countless Britons, and robbed the local homes and churches. Without the support of the Roman legions, British chieftains felt they could not stop the plundering and raids. So, they hired Saxon mercenaries to come over and quell the troublesome people of the north. They soon learned to regret their decision.

Not much is known about the details concerning the events, but according to tradition and the Venerable Bede, the story goes something like this . . .

In about 425 there lived a king named Constans, who had as his most trusted adviser the lord Vortigern. The king had lived his life in a monastery and therefore knew nothing of the affairs of state. So Vortigern managed the country on his behalf. It didn't take long for Vortigern to figure out that if he ran the country, he might as well be king. He concocted a plan to usurp the throne from the pious King Constans.

Vortigern first persuaded the king to put the treasury in his care and then asked for control of the cities and their garrisons. He convinced the king that the Picts planned to invade and would be aided by the Norwegians and the Danes. Vortigern told Constans that the best way to avoid this would be to fill the court with Picts who could act as spies against their own people. The real reason Vortigern wanted to pack the court with Pictish nobles was that he knew they could be easily bought. When they arrived, Vortigern treated them with favoritism. Once he had their loyalty, he told them that he planned on leaving to seek his fortune, as he could not live off of the measly allowance the king provided him. The outraged Picts decided to take action against the king. They broke into his bedchamber and cut off his head. Vortigern played the part of the grieving friend well. He ordered the execution of all involved in the crime. This played well with the Brits, but when word got north to the Picts, they wanted revenge.

Vortigern not only had to contend with the fact that he had made an enemy of the Picts, but he also had made an enemy of Constans' two brothers, Aurelius Ambrosius and Uther Pendragon. (They both had fled to Brittany, but returned to play a part in the story later.) Hengist and Horsa, two Saxon leaders, appeared off the coast of England in what likely was supposed to be a raid. The Saxons landed in Kent with a band of fully armed warriors. Rather than gathering men to repel their invasion, Vortigern saw this as an opportunity. He invited the two Saxon bands to fight for him in exchange for land and money. It seemed like the perfect match.

Together, the trio won many victories over the Picts, and in return Vortigern granted Hengist land in Lincolnshire. Hengist told Vortigern that to keep the enemy at bay he must send for more men from Germany. He was given permission to do so. As if that were not stupid enough, the king also made Hengist an earl and allowed him to build a castle stronghold. The newly appointed earl named his castle Thongceaster.

If you think Vortigern acted foolishly so far, just wait. It gets worse. Vortigern fell in love with Rowena, the beautiful daughter of Hengist, and asked for her hand in marriage. Hengist agreed, but only if the king would give him the county of Kent to compensate for his loss. All involved totally ignored the fact that Kent already belonged to Earl Gorangon, who was also sworn to Vortigern's service and must have been furious. Vortigern then appointed his newly acquired father-in-law as his chief adviser. He also gave Hengist's sons land between Hadrian's Wall and the southern part of Britain as a buffer between the raiders and his own people. While all this was happening, the number of Saxons settling in Britain increased daily. They owed loyalty only to Hengist. It became clear to every Briton except Vortigern that Hengist planned to take over.

When the British nobles voiced their concerns to Vortigern he ignored them. But if things continued, the nobles realized they would lose all of their lands to the Saxons. So, they declared Vortigern's son Vortimer their king. Vortimer immediately set about driving the Saxons away. He fought and won many battles. In one of those battles, Horsa, the other leader who had arrived with Hengist, was slain. Many Saxon warriors had to flee back to Germany, often leaving their women and children behind. The family members left behind were usually enslaved. Soon all of the Saxon warriors and leaders were back across the Channel. Upon hearing of all this, Rowena decided to take revenge on Vortimer and had him poisoned. When news of Vortimer's death reached Hengist, he raised an army and set sail back to Briton. When he arrived, he sent a message to Vortigern, who was king again. Hengist told him that the army had been brought over to deal with Vortimer, and he claimed he was unaware of Vortimer's death. The two leaders arranged to meet with their top barons at Amesbury Abbey to negotiate terms. Tradition was that no one brought weapons to a negotiation. The British nobles obeyed the tradition, but the Saxons did not. Once the meeting had begun, Hengist and his men pulled out their daggers and cut the throats of the unarmed Britons.

At this point, the story slips into legend, with tales of Merlin the wizard woven throughout. Vortigern did not die in the massacre, but was killed later by Ambrosius, the exiled son of Constans. The legend does have a ring of truth to it, if only a literary one. It conveys the feelings of betrayal that the Britons felt toward the Saxon invaders, and it provides archaeologists and historians with a possible explanation for the sudden shift of power and the mass migration of the Saxons. The tale also offers a moral. So for all you men and women out there with plans of world domination, take a lesson from Vortigern, not to mention Rome: Never hire someone to fight your enemies. And if you do so, don't allow them to achieve greater strength in numbers. The leader with the biggest army almost always ends up as king.

22

BLIND OBEDIENCE

Another Time

In many ways the European Union is an attempt to set the clock for Europe back just over a thousand years. In 771, Charles became the sole king of a relatively small German kingdom whose capital was Aachen. In fifty-three military campaigns, and by having the distinction of being one of the most competent administrators in history, he was able to carve out an empire that was larger than anything Europe had seen since Rome. He worked hard all his life to create a prosperous and united kingdom, generally succeeding. Literacy grew, and the economy of central Europe, including today's Germany and France, surged. But law and tradition waited to doom the first united Europe.

The law that put an end to one of the brightest periods in the Dark Ages was a long tradition that attempted to deal with the often murderous rivalry between the heirs of a king or other noble. This law decreed that any kingdom or noble's holding was to be divided between all of the sons of a king. This may help minimize the rivalry between siblings, but it also meant that large viable kingdoms and fiefdoms were split and split again.

This was going to happen to Charlemagne's empire on his death, but all the possible heirs except one, Louis, died before

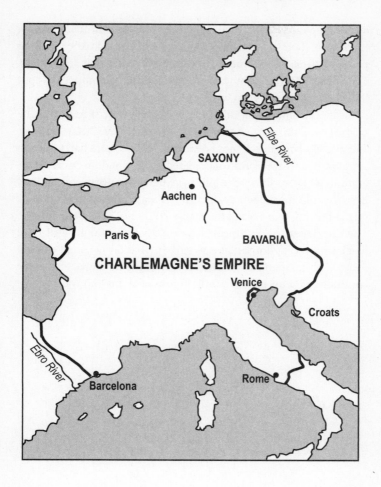

their father. So Louis became the sole ruler of the empire and also did a good job of ruling. Unfortunately, he also did an equally good job of begetting sons. His three, Pepin, Lothair, and Louis, all proved ready and anxious to inherit their third of the kingdom. They even accepted that they would have to share with their two brothers. But in 823 Emperor Louis' second wife had a fourth son, Charles. When Louis tried to change his will so that the new son got a fourth part of the empire, the older sons organized a revolt within the palace. The conflict simmered and likely threatened to become open civil war. Louis tried to meet with Lothair, hoping to restore their relationship. When he arrived at the meeting place, all three of the older sons were there with their supporters. They forced Louis to abdicate. At this point, the empire was split into three parts, never to be united again.

Had the law been different, with one son inheriting, the history of Charlemagne's family might well have been bloodier and all of Europe much more peaceful. If his empire had not been split apart by a tradition that created rival kingdoms every generation, a united Europe might have been the norm. Millions of deaths could have been avoided if the wars between the nations formed from the pieces of his realm would not have been fought. The unity that the European Union strives for might well have been achieved a thousand years earlier. That law, created to keep peace within a family, was a terrible mistake for Europe, and the continent paid for it with a millennium of chaos and war.

BAD PRIORITY

Family over Future

1001

There are many descriptions of Vikings written around the year 1000. Perhaps the mildest of them described the fearsome Norsemen as violent and impulsive. Most use very graphic and negative terms, which are used today to describe psychopaths and worse. Basically, the Vikings' main pursuit for over two centuries was raiding, plundering, and taking over other people's lands. The land stealing becomes more understandable if you consider the poor, rocky soil and frigid weather that dominates Scandinavia. So it took a real effort to stand out among the Vikings as being the most violent of them all. But one Viking was just that, and he was banished twice, until he ended up living at the far western edge of the entire European world. This Viking was called Eric the Bloody. Eric the Red is the more tempered translation, which is suitable for consumption by schoolchildren. Eric the Bloody managed to get himself banned to remote Iceland and then from all but a corner of that small island. But even after killing several neighbors in what should have been easily settled disputes over boundaries, the man had enough charisma to gather a group of followers and lead them even farther west. They settled on an island he called, more for good PR than reality, Greenland. The name stuck.

The settlement had Eric the Bloody as the acknowledged leader so at least there, no one could banish him again. The settlement thrived for a while, and Eric raised two children. These were Leif, called for obvious reasons Ericson, and Freydis Eiriksdottir (Eric's daughter). Leif too was a leader and explorer. When old enough, he gathered a crew and sailed west again. It is likely Leif had heard accounts of a rich land to the west from native traders and fishermen. And after a surprisingly short sail, the Viking party landed on what must have seemed a verdant landscape after frozen Greenland. Leif named it Vinland, the fertile land.

As was the Viking habit, they decided to take the land where they had arrived as their own. Leif's followers showed this by laying out a town and building stone houses. This upset the local peoples, who eventually attacked the settlement. They drove the small party back to their ships. The season was late so they returned to Greenland. This is when we first hear about Freydis, whose rage changed history. At this point she is a hero—well, heroine—fighting in the rear guard and helping hold back the far more numerous Native Americans until the boats could be launched. Women, particularly the daughters of higher-class Vikings were trained to use weapons. Since the men of a village might be away for weeks at a time raiding, this was almost a necessity.

Not long after his two children returned from Vinland, Eric the Bloody died. Leif took over as ruler of Greenland. He no longer could take the time to go exploring. But Vinland was not forgotten and another, stronger expedition formed to return there. There were more ships sailing west this time, and the way was known. They may have started together, but the ships sailed at different speeds, and some arrived sooner than others. Unfortunately for two families, their ship arrived earlier than the one Freydis was on. There was another Viking tradition. In abandoned lands, the first to arrive got to take their pick of the houses. Normally, those would be Saxon or British homes from which the owners fled, but the rule was applied to Vinland as well.

So when Freydis arrived at the site where she had been a hero, there was a problem. She was the daughter and sister of the king and hero of the retreat. Evidently, Freydis had her heart set on taking the largest and, most likely, best-made of the stone houses. But the two families who had arrived earlier had already moved into the one she had chosen. So Freydis ordered them out. They said no. The law was on their side. There was likely a real confrontation and many unfortunate things were said. It ended with Freydis, and possibly her personal guards, killing the two men who had moved in first.

This was not good, but seemingly within acceptable limits for the daughter of Eric the Bloody in 1001. Remember, this was a violent culture and her brother was king. But then Freydis didn't stop. She ordered those with her to also slaughter the wives and children of the two men. When they refused to do this, she grabbed an ax and did the deed herself. It was a rage truly in the tradition of her father. The murder of women and children was also highly unlawful, even among the Vikings.

The colony was not off to a good start. By fall, perhaps by plan, everyone returned to Greenland. This put Freydis' brother, who was also her king, in a bad position. By law, she was a murderer. Like most highly armed cultures, the Vikings took the law very seriously. Killing men was one thing, but killing the rest of their families was too much. There were never enough Vikings, and mothers and children were highly valued. He should have executed her, but if he did, there was another complication. To avoid a serious shortage of siblings in such an ambitious and violent culture, there were strict laws about killing off anyone in your own family as well. Whatever Leif did, he was going to break a law. If he broke the law, there was a good chance he would be ousted as king. So he chose instead a compromise. Freydis was banned from Greenland. Then he ordered that the colony was never to be returned to or even spoken of. The entire incident was hushed up.

The Vikings never did return to Vinland. It was five centuries later when Europe again "discovered" the Americas. How different this world would have been if the Norsemen had settled and stayed. The Native Americans most likely would have absorbed European technology and culture in smaller doses. Without rifles and cannons, there was no way for just a few Europeans to be able to come to dominate or destroy the native cultures on two continents. At the very least, northern Europe, not Spain, would have benefited from the wealth of the new continent. The world of today became a far different place, all because a thousand years ago Freydis flew into a rage.

24

FOOLISH PROMISE

Godwinson's Offer

When William the Conqueror came over from Normandy in 1066 and defeated the English forces, it came as a great surprise to many, especially his adversary, Harold Godwinson, whose father had sought the appointment of Edward the Confessor as king. However, the greater shock came after the battle when William launched a campaign to wipe out the Anglo-Saxon and Anglo-Danish culture that had been established in England and replace it with that of the Normans.

The lead-up to this battle, which took place in Hastings, began years before, after the death of King Canute in 1035. Canute came to England as a conqueror but embraced the Anglo-Saxon culture and way of life. His death marked the beginning of the end of the Anglo-Saxon empire. The hopes of the people lay in Canute's three sons, but they proved to be ignorant and boorish. Many eyes turned toward the sons of the dead king's widow, Emma, and the previous king, Ethelred. The two princes descended from the line of Alfred the Great. The elder son, Alfred (named for his famous ancestor), possessed many fine qualities. He was brave, charismatic, and well liked. Edward, on the other hand was monkish, pious, and had no aptitude for administrative duties. And, because of his family's exile in Normandy, he had been raised as a Norman.

At this time, another man began his rise to power. He was Godwin, earl of Wessex and leader of the Danish party. He wanted total control over the English people and he wanted it under the Anglo-Danish system. When it came to pursuing these goals, his treachery knew no bounds. When the exiled prince Alfred came to England under the guise of visiting his newly widowed mother, Godwin had him arrested. Then he had Alfred's attendants slaughtered and the prince blinded. It is certain that the prince's brother, Edward, would not have forgotten the incident, and it is even possible that he could have been planning his revenge from the moment he found out about it.

Although Canute's sons succeeded him, their reign was short-lived. They died within six years, and once again England had no king. In this vacancy of power, Godwin stepped up to the plate. He had great political influence, but he lacked the support of many of the Saxons. So, he came up with what he thought would be the perfect solution. He decided that the best way to unite the Saxons and Danes, and consolidate his power, would be to make Edward king. A monarch from the line of Alfred the Great would rally the people, but Godwin would be pulling the strings. He believed Edward would be easily manipulated, and through Edward he could spread his sphere of influence.

When Edward appointed his Norman friends to high positions, Godwin allowed it only to a point. To prove his allegiances lay with the English and not the Normans, Edward begrudgingly married Godwin's beautiful daughter Edith. It is likely this was what Godwin had in mind all along. With his daughter as queen, his descendants would inherit the kingdom. The bitterness of his brother's plight must have raced through his mind when Edward decided to defy his overbearing father-in-law. He would destroy any chance Godwin had at being the sire of kings. He refused to consummate his marriage to Edith. Edward lived a pious, monkish life, which earned him the name "The Confessor." His favor increased in the court, especially among the Normans. He gained allies and in 1051 was able to oppose Godwin and send him and his family into exile. He also dismissed his own queen.

During the time of the Godwins' exile, it is believed that William, duke of Normandy, paid Edward a visit. It was during this visit that Edward supposedly offered the succession to William. Considering Edward's history with Godwin it seems more than possible. When word got out about the crown being offered to a Norman, Edward lost favor with the English lords. Godwin managed to win back some of the support he had lost and even mustered troops in Flanders. He then strong-armed the king into letting him return. The king took Godwin and his sons back and gave them their old rank and titles. It didn't take long for Godwin to exercise his authority. Upon his return, many of the Normans lost their titles and land. When Godwin finally died in 1051, those dispossessed lords nourished hopes of regaining their former status. These hopes never saw fruition.

Godwin's eldest son, Harold, stepped forward to fill in the gap. Like his father before him, Harold ruled England from behind the scenes. Harold held his authority with virtually no opposition, despite the unrest that plagued the court between the Normans, Saxons, and Danes. The only direct resistance came from his own brother, Tostig, who quickly won favor with the king. Tostig befriended many of the Norman lords, which endeared him to Edward. He received the earldom of Northumbria, which invoked the jealousy of Harold. The two brothers were at odds, which may have been the king's intention all along. Perhaps Edward had been far underestimated by the Godwinsons. Whatever his intention, Edward managed to drive a wedge between Harold and Tostig.

Although Harold's relationship with his brother had been severed, Harold would find new friendship in an unlikely source. In 1064, Harold's ship ran aground off the French coast. The count of Ponthieu took Harold prisoner and held him for ransom. William sent a request to the count asking for the release of the English king's thane. Harold soon found himself in the court of Duke William. The two had a genuine liking for each other and quickly became friends. Through this friendship, certain alliances formed. According to the chronicle depicted in the Bayeux Tapestry, William proposed that Harold support his claim as the heir to the English throne. In exchange, Harold would be made earl of Wessex and be given William's daughter in marriage. According to tradition, Harold took an oath of fealty to William and promised not to make any attempt to claim the crown. The oath was taken on an altar that hid the bones of St. Edmund within it. Oaths taken on sacred relics were considered unbreakable, no matter what the circumstance.

Toward the end of Edward's reign, the country began a downward spiral as the different factions fought among themselves. The Anglo-Danish council, who believed they spoke for the entire populace, weakened the power of the monarchy without strengthening their own administrative body. Local chieftains began intriguing and pursuing their own interests, and feuds broke out all over the country. In this chaos and uncertainty, Edward took to his deathbed. With his last breath, he allegedly named Harold as his successor, despite having already promised it to William, the duke of Normandy. Conveniently, Archbishop Stigand, a staunch supporter of Earl Godwin, had been present to confirm the announcement. Edward the Confessor died in January 1066. (The Church later canonized him and he became England's foremost saint until replaced by St. George.) Disregarding the oath he took at William's court and the fact that he had no hereditary claim, Harold took over as king. Things quickly got complicated. Much of England accepted Harold as their king, but the royal houses of Europe and the Church in Rome did not. In William's eyes, it became his duty to overthrow the usurper. So, he crossed the Channel and with a little help from Harold defeated the Saxons.

||||||||||||||||||||||||||||||||||||||||||||||||||||||||||||||||||||||

25

RUSH INTO BATTLE

In a Hurry to Lose

1066

||||||||||||||||||||||||||||||||||||||||||||||||||||||||||||||||||||||

Harold Godwinson, king of England, had something to prove. Edward the Confessor had died without having an heir. So the Witan, a council of nobles, named Harold king. He was not a unanimous choice and could not claim that he had a divine right to the throne. The closest he got to royal blood was that Edward had been his brother-in-law. To many, this meant that the rule of England was theirs and was available for the taking. Two men decided to do just that.

Harold's brother, Tostig, also claimed the throne. If Harold's blood was good enough to be that of a king, so was his brother's. To support his claim, Tostig turned to an old enemy of England, Harald Hardrada, the Viking king of Norway. In Normandy, another man had reason to claim the throne of England as well. This was William, duke of Normandy. William, through persuasion and politics, managed to get Pope Alexander II to support his claim. In a religious age, this made recruiting knights and soldiers easier and guaranteed support of the clergy. Both were needed to invade the island and enforce one's claim.

Tostig and Harald landed first near modern-day York. The new English king hurried north accompanied by his *huscarls*—

ax- and shield-wielding warriors sworn to his service—the only professional soldiers he commanded. The king gathered further fighters from the local militia, the *fyrd*, until his army matched that of the Vikings in size if not quality. After marching 200 miles in five days, Harold was able to surprise the normally canny Norwegian king and Tostig at the Battle of Stamford Bridge. It was September 25, and the battle was a tough and costly fight, with Harold Godwinson losing nearly 1,000 dead or wounded huscarls, cutting his personal guard and the island's only full-time military force by a third.

Just a few days later, on October 1, Harold got word that William of Normandy had landed his army near Hastings. The southern fyrd had already been called up, so it was ready to join up with him and his huscarls. But Hastings was more than 300 miles away from York. Having exhausted his army in the march north, the English leader now had to make a decision. If he did not react quickly, William the Norman would be able to establish a strong position. This would be particularly true if William captured a few cities. But perhaps another thought lay behind the new king's mistake, one that may have cost him and the Saxons England. Elected without royal blood, Harold had to show everyone that he was capable of defending England and worthy of being the first of a new line of Saxon kings. To do that, he may have felt it necessary to act before William could do much damage to what was one of the richest parts of his kingdom.

For whatever reason, Harold not only began moving south but hurried toward Hastings in an even greater rush than he had gone north a week before. This had two negative effects. The speed of the march meant that many of his lightly wounded, or just plain exhausted, huscarls could not keep up. Even riding at that speed was punishing. The hurried march also meant that hundreds of fyrd and local nobles who might have joined the Saxon army were unable to do so.

When Harold arrived near Hastings he again did not pause. The Saxon king formed his army on Senlac Ridge and prepared to battle William. Even though he fought on home ground and in

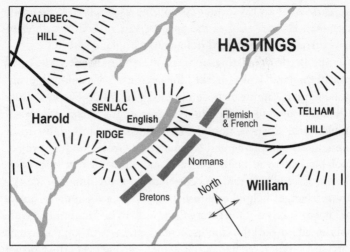

The Battle of Hastings

defense of the land, the new king's haste meant that the two armies were of about the same size.

Harold and his warriors at first stood and beat back the Norman attacks. But the fyrd who were fighting on the right of the Saxon position attempted to pursue a feigned retreat, and they were ridden down by William's mounted knights. Eventually, more than anything else, the Normans wore down and then broke the Saxons. Exhausted and outnumbered, the huscarls died fighting. Harold was hit by an arrow in one eye, and with his death, the Saxon defense collapsed. He had hurried to his death. Had Harold hesitated until he could gather a much larger army, he might have held England. William of Normandy had no reinforcements to match those Harold could have called from all over England. Harold risked everything in the hope of a quick victory that would ensure his position on England's throne forever. But in his haste he, and the Saxons, lost everything. It is impossible to determine how much the exhaustion of his best troops, the huscarls, affected the battle. But William was able to finally break the Saxon formation and went on to become known as William the Conqueror (an improvement on his former commonly used name, William the Bastard). Harold, king of the Saxons, had rushed to defend his new throne and, in the effort, lost all of England.

The Battle of Hastings marked the end of the Saxon-Danish rule in England. It also marked the beginning of a cultural revolution. Unlike Canute, who embraced the Anglo-Saxon culture, William sought to wipe it out. He replaced the Saxon and Danish nobles with Norman nobility, he handed out land grants to his men, and he implemented Norman law. Great building projects took place all over the British Isles, and the crude dwellings of the Saxons gave way to magnificent Norman Cathedrals and castles. These changes helped establish England as a formidable power, but it was surely not the future Earl Godwin had in mind when he appointed Edward the Confessor as king. Godwin sought to make England a nation of Saxons and Danes, getting rid of the Norman influence altogether. Instead, his underhanded tactics and treatment of Edward ended up paving the road to destruction of the very culture he fought so hard to preserve and ensured that the Norman kings and not the Saxons would go down in history as the great kings of England.

||||||||||||||||||||||||||||||||||||||||||||||||||||||||||||||||||||||||||||||||||

26

SELF-INTEREST

King, Not Country

1086

||||||||||||||||||||||||||||||||||||||||||||||||||||||||||||||||||||||||||||||||||

n 1186, the land of Outremer was thriving. *Outremer* in French translates basically to "across the seas." The kingdom had been founded by Christian crusaders in 1098. Its income from trade was substantial. This provided the money needed to construct a strong line of castles and fortified cities that protected the kingdom of the Holy Land from the constant threat posed by Islam. In the age of great castles, those of Outremer were among the most powerful and imposing.

The former king, a leper, had just died, and Guy of Lusignan was elected king by nobles and military orders. He was not a generally popular choice and was painfully aware of his lack of support among those who controlled the bulk of the Christian knights. Unfortunately, some of those knights were also his biggest problem. Even before Guy had taken the throne, some of the nobles had begun raiding the trade caravans of the Islamic merchants. Along with being bad for business, this broke the treaty between the Christian and Islamic kingdoms. The attacks were most definitely a cause for war and also a demonstration that Guy of Lusignan did not really rule most of his new kingdom.

Threatening the Christian kingdom and its new king was

Salah ad-Din Al-Ayyubi, who ruled the Islamic world from Damascus to Cairo. He is known as Saladin in Western history. He had risen to power mostly because of his military skills and charisma. Saladin had won his way to general and had become the most important military leader of the Fatimid caliphs. Eventually, he was so well-thought-of that he was elevated to the throne left vacant when the last caliph in Damascus died without an heir. Even as caliph, Saladin remained a relentless warrior with notorious cunning; he was also known for his strong sense of honor and for protecting the common people. His reputation for chivalry was famous even in Europe. Although the leader of the largest Islamic empire of his time, he is remembered even today as being the fair and just protector of several nearby Christian lands that had also suffered at the hands of the crusaders.

Saladin could not allow the attacks on his merchants to continue. The raids were both an act of war and a challenge. When Guy proved unable to restrain his subjects, war was inevitable. But it was not the decision to go to war that put Guy of Lusignan on the list of people who made the greatest mistakes in history, but it was how he fought that war. Once more we have a case in which a leader takes an army that has tremendous strengths and puts it in a position where those strengths are unusable and the enemy's strengths are emphasized instead. And once more we see this happen because of a king who put his own interests before those of his nation.

The castles of Outremer, and her walled cities, were thick, strong, and almost impregnable to any weapon Saladin could command. This was before the use of gunpowder and a fifteen-foot-thick, forty-foot-high wall enabled even a few dozen men to hold off hundreds. The main field strength of the Christian army was their heavily armored knights. The chain mail and metal armor of the Christian knight meant that on a similarly armored horse, he was nearly invulnerable to the arrows that were the primary weapon of most of Saladin's horsemen. The armor also served the knights well in resisting all but the most skilled thrusts and slashes of the familiar curved cavalry sword that was used in close combat by Saladin's light cavalry. The disadvantage of the armor was that Outremer is located in one of the hottest climates in the world. Being in the armor too long made a knight vulnerable to dehydration and heat stroke, both of which could be fatal.

Most of Saladin's Islamic army was made up of unarmored horsemen who shot bows from the saddle. Backing up these horse archers were more heavily armed and armored nobles and their followers. Even these wealthy horsemen wore only relatively thin and light armor. Although less protected, they were also less vulnerable to the heat. Perhaps the most important difference was that Saladin's army was at least five times the size of the largest force Outremer could gather.

In his castles, Guy of Lusignan and his kingdom could easily repel any attack by any number of Islamic horse archers and nobles. But he was new and not established on the throne. Guy needed not only to repel any attacks but also to demonstrate he was a strong leader. By doing this, he would have rallied the support he needed to maintain his throne and gain the upper hand on Outremer's highly independent nobles. So instead of waiting for Saladin to throw himself against stone walls, Guy decided to gather an army, the largest he could, and go out and defeat Saladin in battle. But to gather enough trained soldiers and knights, the Christian king had to strip all of the garrisons from the castles. This meant that if he lost, there would not be enough men to defend the massive and expensive fortifications. It would be an all-or-none risk, not for the good of Outremer, but for the benefit of King Guy.

On July 2, 1186, the largest army Outremer had ever seen marched out with King Guy at its head. To ensure the righteousness of their cause, monks carried a piece of the True Cross in front of the army. That relic was considered the greatest treasure in the kingdom. Behind them, they left castles, often garrisoned by less than a dozen men, and cities with just enough men-at-arms to maintain order.

Between the Christians and Saladin was a stretch of brutally dry desert. Almost as soon as the Outremer army entered the dry wasteland, they came under continuous attack by Muslim horse archers. Each attack forced the column to slow or stop until knights could gather and drive the light horsemen off. By evening, the Christian army had traveled less than half as far as planned. They were still several hours short of any wells. But marching in the dark left the column even more vulnerable, so it was decided to make a dry camp. This is significant because it meant their horses also went thirsty or drank up much of the water that was on hand.

By the second day, the lack of water was becoming a real concern. What few wells the army could use were unable to supply enough water for such a large number of men and horses. Saladin's horse archers caused few casualties, but the constant threat of arrow fire meant that everyone had to stay in their armor, metal or padded. The hot sun and a lack of water soon caused men to collapse and horses to flounder. Anyone left behind was killed. By the end of the second day of marching in armor in the desert heat, the forces of Outremer were reeling with exhaustion and thirst.

As the sun set, the army staggered up two hills, the largest of which was said to have a good well at its top. These hills were named the Horns of Hattin. There was no relief. Saladin had collapsed the stone walls surrounding the well into it, making the water below impossible to reach. In the distance, the Christian army could see two lakes that were less than two hours' march away. They contained more than enough water to relieve any thirst and replenish their supply. The problem was that Saladin's entire force waited between the knights and the lakes. But the position on the Horns of Hattin was strong because the steep hills were easy to defend and slowed any mounted attacks. So Guy ordered yet another dry camp.

By morning, the Islamic army had completely surrounded the two hills and the army on them. Trapped with no water, the knights and men-at-arms endured hours of a near-constant rain of arrows. They could barely move within the camp, much less organize to fight a major battle. Horses began to die from heat and thirst. Men soon followed. A few of the nobles gathered their followers and tried to break out. Balian of Ibelin and a few hundred knights actually cut their way through the surrounding horsemen and managed to escape the trap. He turned to see if he could help relieve those still inside and was confronted by ten times his number of Islamic riders charging toward his small force. He wisely turned and fled, eventually becoming one of the few survivors. Reginald of Sidon led another breakout and also escaped. He was the last to do so.

After hours, a good number of the Outremer infantry had endured enough. They formed themselves into a solid mass of men and tried to push their way through to the lakes and the precious water. Every one of the hundreds of men were slaughtered before they even got close to the water.

Saladin then ordered his horsemen to attack the hills. One attack was beaten back, then another, and another. But the waterless defenders lost more men with each charge. By the end, only a few hundred knights remained able to fight when yet another charge overwhelmed them at the top of the hill. Many of the fallen Christians were found to be only lightly wounded and many had passed out from dehydration and heat stroke. Most of these were revived and spent the rest of their lives as slaves building stone walls around Cairo, Egypt. In the weeks that followed, with too few defenders, most of Outremer's castles and cities had no choice but to surrender when Saladin approached.

Guy of Lusignan had fought the war in the way that he needed, but he risked losing all the kingdom to Saladin. And lose it he did. It was almost 200 years before the last Outremer holdings on Cyprus were captured, but after Guy put his army in a position that played to the enemy's strengths, the end was inevitable. The original goal of so many crusades, Jerusalem, was lost forever, and the history of the Middle East became a tale of only Islam.

27

|||||||||||||||||||||||||||||||||||||||||||||||||||||||||||||||||||

SHORTSIGHTED

Constantinople and Bust:
The Fourth Crusade

1204

|||||||||||||||||||||||||||||||||||||||||||||||||||||||||||||||||||

Venice in the late twelfth century was a unique place. Although it had originally been a Byzantium port, it grew to be a world power through commerce and trade. In a time when feudalism was at its peak, this mercantile city ran much more like a modern business than a medieval city. Rather than being ruled over by a king, Venice had a ruling council of nine men, who behaved more like a board of directors than royal advisers. At the head of the council sat the CEO, the doge. Most of us have heard the title of Venice's elected ruler, but few grasp the importance the doges played in the history of the Western world. One doge in particular, Enrico Dandolo, instigated an act that had resounding repercussions throughout the medieval world as well as our world today—the sacking of Constantinople.

What did the doge have against Constantinople? Quite a bit as it turns out. In addition to holding a monopoly on the markets in Germany and northern Italy, the Venetians also set up trade with eastern Europe and the Muslim world. They traded for silk and spices. In exchange, they manufactured ships and became the world's leading exporter of glass and ironworks. Their focus on a maritime economy ensured Venice's rise in status over Genoa and Pisa. The

Achilles' heel in their great enterprise was the Byzantine empire. To trade with the East, merchants in Venice had to pass through Constantinople. In 1183, Andronicus Comnenus seized power as emperor in Byzantium and revoked all permits for Venetian merchants. This put Venice's status as the leader in world trade in jeopardy. Just when the city started to feel the pinch of economic pressure due to its limited commerce, an opportunity presented itself.

In 1201, Pope Innocent asked for the doge's help in transporting men and supplies for another expedition to the Holy Land. He intended to send his crusading armies into Alexandria in Egypt. The pope wanted to avoid asking for too much help from the European princes because it might call into question his authority. And, he did not wish to upset the Holy Roman empire. The doge was more than willing to help with the expedition . . . for a price. After all, business is business. He asked for half of everything captured in the expedition, and he wanted money up front. In exchange, he would provide transport and fifty Venetian galleys to escort the crusaders on their venture. The following year, 11,000 crusaders made their way to Venice under the leadership of Boniface de Montferrat. However, Montferrat put the expedition on hold because the crusaders could not pay the huge sum the doge asked for. The doge was first and last a businessman. He knew that having 11,000 men camped within the city would not be good for business. So, he offered an alternative.

Hungary had recently captured the Venetian city of Zara off the Adriatic coast. Lacking the military strength to recapture it, the doge saw the chance to use the crusaders for his own interests. He offered to postpone the initial payment in exchange for the crusader's help in taking back Zara. Many of the crusaders were outraged at the concept of fighting their fellow Christians, and the king of Hungary had fought in previous expeditions to the Holy Land. The doge took up the Cross, not because of a strong religious conviction, but because he saw a chance to manipulate the crusaders into thinking he was a man for their cause. In the end, they relented. Thousands of Venetians also joined the expedition. This was not a holy expedition led by the pope. It was a business venture led by the doge of Venice.

In October 1202, 200 Venetian ships made way for Zara. They arrived in November and laid siege to the city. After only two weeks, the people of Zara surrendered. This was not the expedition that Rome had in mind—Christian fighting against Christian. The pope excommunicated all involved. The crusaders did not wish to lose their souls in an endeavor to appease the doge, so they petitioned Rome, saying that they had no choice in the matter. The pope lifted the excommunication for all except Doge Dandolo and his men.

Meanwhile, a situation arose in Constantinople that would work in favor of the doge. The emperor, Isaac, had been blinded and imprisoned by his brother, Alexius, who took the throne as Alexius III. Isaac's son, also called Alexius, went to Zara to solicit help from the Venetian and crusader forces. What he offered in return was too irresistible to refuse. The Byzantine Church would be placed under the authority in Rome, huge financial incentives were offered to all who helped, and 10,000 soldiers would accompany the crusaders to Alexandria in Egypt, which was the original destination, after all. The doge could not have been happier.

The Venetian and crusader forces arrived off the coast of Constantinople on June 24, 1203. They soon captured the suburb of Galata, which lies just north of the city across the Bosphorus. Then they launched a simultaneous land and sea attack on Constantinople, which failed. Despite the failure, Alexius III became frightened and fled the city. Advocates for Isaac freed him and returned him to the throne. Isaac and his son ruled together. They recognized immediately that they had a serious problem. They would have to abide by the terms agreed to in the treaty. Alexius went throughout the city raising funds to pay the crusaders. In the meantime, anticrusader sentiment raged throughout the city. The citizens revolted. Isaac and Alexius were killed and the anti-Western figurehead Ducus Murzuphlus took over as Alexius V. He immediately made it clear that he had no intention of paying the crusading forces anything.

Doge Dandolo took full advantage of the situation to persuade the crusaders to attack the city. On April 12, 1204, the Venetians penetrated the walls of the city. What they and the crusaders did to their fellow Christians was unconscionable. They looted homes and churches, murdered and raped the citizens, and held a thanksgiving service after all was said and done. The clerics who were involved in the expedition justified the action by saying it was done to reunite the Church. Although Pope Innocent did not authorize the action, he did not condemn it either. No doubt he saw the act as beneficial to the Western Church.

The act would not be beneficial to the Church in the long run. The Byzantine empire disintegrated and was replaced by small, autonomous Greek and Latin provinces. Without the strong presence of the Byzantines, the Turks were able to easily take Constantinople, giving them a gateway into Europe.

28

||||||||||||||||||||||||||||||||||||||||||||||||||||||||||||||||||||

PRIDE

Baiting the Barbarians

1300

||||||||||||||||||||||||||||||||||||||||||||||||||||||||||||||||||||

This mistake involves two great rulers whose lands and ways were very different. It is a story of how one insulting mistake changed the lives of every person in Europe and Asia. It begins with a cruel show of power and ends in millions of deaths.

The first of these rulers was Ala' ad-Din Muhammad, the emperor of the Khwarezm empire. In the thirteenth century the Khwarezm empire controlled all of central Asia, including today's Iran, Iraq, Pakistan, and Afghanistan. This was a rich kingdom for it controlled the Silk Road on which all of the trade from China flowed. The taxes paid by the merchants supported palaces and gardens that were the wonders of their time. Khwarezm was also a powerful empire with as many as half a million men, mostly well-equipped and thickly armored horsemen, in a full-time army. Its capital at Samarkand was a center of learning and wealth, featuring many acres of magnificent gardens. It was unquestionably the wealthiest and likely best-armed nation in the world. But having the best-armored and largest army does not always mean you will win every battle.

The second leader was a very different man, though he too commanded a magnificent army. At this time, his highly organized and mobile army was in the process of conquering northern China. This was the man known to his people as "the Perfect War Leader," or Genghis Khan. Genghis Khan had spent most of his life uniting the Mongols and other steppe tribes into a single force. At this point in history, the Mongols also controlled a stretch of the incredibly profitable Silk Road. This was the section that ran between China and Khwarezm across the Mongolian steppes. With his armies busy in wealthy and populous China, Genghis went to great efforts to ensure all of the caravans that ran on this route traveled safely—and paid substantial taxes for the privilege. For some time, this courtesy was returned by the Khwarezm as it seemed to be in everyone's self-interest. Genghis Khan showed how pleased he was with the arrangement by sending gifts and messages of friendship to Ala' ad-Din Muhammad.

Then the Khwarezm got nervous. The Mongols were being too successful in conquering areas of China. They feared they would be next. A friendly barbarian was one thing, but one who was successful in battle could be a threat. Suddenly, and likely accurately, it was decided that the growing number of Mongols who accompanied the caravans from China were spies. The result was a series of attacks on suspected caravans not by bandits, but Khwarezm soldiers.

Genghis Khan was not happy. He had gone to great lengths to protect the Khwarezm merchants and their caravans in his lands, but suddenly Khwarezm was slaughtering his merchants. He sent a caravan with an ambassador and other important Mongol nobles to Samarkand to protest. When it arrived, the Mongol ambassador demanded not only that the attacks stop but that Ala' ad-Din pay restitution for the goods and lives already lost.

For weeks, the Khwarezm emperor did not formally respond. The details of this time have been lost, but we can surmise. Perhaps the Mongol ambassador became strident or maybe the Khwarezm just felt secure with a half-million-man army, a border protected by high mountains, and the bulk of the Mongol army still busy in

China. Or maybe Ala' ad-Din just had a sadistic sense of humor. Whatever the reason, his response was clear not only in its meaning but also in the total disdain it demonstrated.

The emperor gathered up everyone from the Mongol party, and in front of his court lit their beards on fire. Since the men had full beards, it seems likely every face was horribly scarred and many of the Mongols were blinded. Then, to make sure the message was clear, the Khwarezm emperor also beheaded the ambassador before sending the survivors back to Genghis Khan. It was an insult, a direct and unequivocal insult. It was also one of the ways you declared war. This was also perhaps the greatest mistake any ruler has made in history.

Genghis Khan moved as quickly as possible, avoiding the normal passes between the two lands and taking a different route. In 1219, almost 100,000 horsemen were suddenly within Khwarezm while that empire's army was still waiting to stop Genghis in the wrong place. Within a matter of months, those 100,000 Mongols had completely obliterated five times their number of Khwarezm soldiers. In retaliation, every city in the empire was not just conquered but destroyed, and its population killed or enslaved. Mostly the people were mercilessly slaughtered. Glorious, rich, sophisticated Samarkand was turned into rubble, and every man, woman, and child inside the city slain. By the end of Genghis Khan's attack, there simply was no more Khwarezm. As much as three-quarters of the population were dead. Not a single city remained in the heart of the empire; there was no army, and its ruler had fled. Ala' ad-Din Muhammad is said to have died of fright 2,000 miles from Samarkand, still hounded by 20,000 Mongol riders led by their most brilliant commander, Subotai.

So great was the destruction caused by this burning of the beards that even today lands that were fertile centers of civilization 700 years ago are still impoverished tribal areas. If Ala' ad-Din had instead placated Genghis Khan, the Mongols might well have not felt the need to turn west. Poland and Hungary would have been spared a crippling invasion, Russia would not have suffered from centuries of debilitating occupation, and NATO would not now be fighting in the wastes of Afghanistan.

29

SUPERSTITION

The Black Death and the Revenge of the Cats

1348

The Black Death was one of the worst pandemics in human history. It led to one of the most self-defeating slaughters in history. Cats were rumored to be the source of the plague. In those panicky times, no more than a rumor was needed. All over Europe the house cats were slain. Cat lovers today can take consolation in the slaughter along with the ghosts of murdered cats. They had their revenge in the form of millions of additional Europeans succumbing to a horrific death.

The killing of tens of thousands of cats during this time, encouraged primarily by the Catholic Church, caused the flea-infested rodent population in Europe to soar. Those rats most likely carried the bubonic plague, passing it on to humans through fleas that had been on the host rat, become infected, and then bitten humans. There were no insect sprays and no protection. Fleas and other pests were everywhere in the newly growing cities all over the continent. It is estimated that perhaps half of the population in Europe succumbed to this horrendous death from 1348 to 1352.

The bubonic plague was the most common type of infection seen during the Black Death. It was characterized by black spots on the chest and black swelling under the armpits and at the tops of the legs. The buboes, or swollen lymph nodes, turned black, oozed pus, and bled. Of those contracting the disease, four out of five died within eight days. The second most common type of infection seen at this time was the pneumonic plague, which affected the lungs, causing the victims to choke to death on their own blood. This type of plague had about a 95 percent mortality rate. The plague struck and then killed so quickly that the Italian writer Boccaccio said its victims often "ate lunch with their friends and dinner with their ancestors in paradise." It is no wonder that even the hint of the plague caused a panic. Not only did cats suffer, but often Jews and other minorities were blamed and murdered.

Now, cats were not always considered the "diabolical creatures" that Pope Gregory IX declared them to be in a papal letter in 1232. The ancient Egyptians had developed elaborate ways to store large amounts of grain and other food. Rats and mice were attracted and could damage much of the crop. The Egyptians found that cats were natural predators of the rats and could be used to protect the stores of food. Cats eventually moved into Egyptian households, and they became thought of as godlike and were revered and worshiped. Eventually in Egypt killing a cat was considered an extremely serious offense, punishable by death. The Romans were introduced to cats by the Egyptians, and they were the first European group to keep cats primarily as pets. But the animals were still valued for their ability to keep rodent populations down.

The Black Plague first surfaced in Mongolia, spread to China, and was brought over to Europe on merchant ships. During the early thirteenth century, cats began to be looked at with suspicion. The pagan Egyptians had venerated them and the pagan Romans valued cats. The Catholic Church was determined to root out heretics and eliminate paganism in Europe. In medieval society, cats were already somewhat misunderstood for their aloofness and independent nature. If you do not handle kittens, they become quite feral as adults. That makes them good hunters, but wary of humans. Pope Gregory IX first made an association between cats and the devil. The Church focused on the Albigensians, a group the Church leadership suspected of worshiping the devil. During

Satanic masses, it was alleged that the devil took the form of a black cat. It was said that the Albigensians were required by Satan to kiss the back side of the black cat during the mass. The concept of "a familiar" also coincided with the persecution of the Albigensians and other heretical groups during this time. A familiar was a supernatural being who could take many shapes, and it was believed to be something Satan gave to witches and other devil worshipers to facilitate evil acts. Cats were thought of as a common familiar. In fact, manuals that were developed to help authorities hunt witches often cited that ownership of a cat was compelling evidence that the cat's owner was actually a witch.

During this time, if a person was declared a witch, he or she was condemned to burn at the stake. If this happened, the cat was burned along with its owner. Many commoners became afraid of being accused of witchcraft, so they killed or got rid of their own cats. Cats were slaughtered by the tens of thousands in cities and villages across Europe, and the domestic cat population came close to being eliminated.

Some in the aristocratic class were less vulnerable to the superstitions wracking Christianity. They kept their cats exactly because of the animals' ability to reduce or eliminate the rat population in and around their homes. Of course, they had no idea that the rats actually carried disease, but having some of those cats in the homes of the aristocracy certainly helped keep the plague from wiping out many in the upper classes. The mass killing of cats preceded the arrival of the infected rodents, greatly compromising the barrier between humans and the rats.

Many people during that time believed that the devil granted to witches the power to exact revenge for any slight or threat. This made them, and their familiars, a source of fear. It was thought that a witch's revenge could devastate large portions of a country. So when things went wrong, the witches and their cats took the blame. Between 1300 and 1700, persecution of witches was at its peak in Europe. It is not surprising that this persecution coincided with successive waves of plague, which wracked the continent.

The Black Death was certainly the most devastating of all of these plagues. Not only did it decimate the population, but it also was the catalyst for profound social and economic changes. In western Europe, landlords had to compete for peasant labor, providing increased wages or even freedom for the peasants. When peasants demanded higher wages, and the landlords refused, revolts broke out in England, Italy, Belgium, and France. Many historians have suggested that the roots of capitalism took hold at that time. The disease also had a profound effect on the Catholic Church. So many believers had prayed for deliverance from the plague and killed their cats. When those prayers weren't answered, the power of the Church and its numbers declined, and a new period of philosophical questioning emerged. The resulting social upheaval started an era of contemplation and concentration on the arts, music, and literature. The Renaissance had begun.

If it weren't for the domestic cat's existence in Europe and the sheltering of those cats by the aristocracy there, even more than half of the population could have been wiped out when the Black Death peaked between 1348 and 1350. The disease had enormous social, economic, and religious consequences, including the end of feudalism and the rise of the Renaissance. It took Europe's population several hundred years to recover from the devastating impact of the disease. And the severity of this loss could have been dramatically reduced had it not been for the fear-mongering of religious leadership at the time.

Some superstitions about cats, which started in the panic seven centuries ago, still remain. These include such baseless notions as crossing the path of a black cat bringing you bad luck, cats being a threat to newborns, and cats being familiars to devil worshipers. It is no coincidence that the more cats were demonized and the more their owners were viewed as possible witches and heretics, the more widespread the Black Death became. Cats were the first line of defense against the real carrier of the plague.

30

IIIIIIIIIIIIIIIIIIIIIIIIIIIIIIIIIIIIIIIIIIIIIIIIIIIIIIIIIIIIIIIIII

STUBBORN PRIDE

The Same Old Way

1415

IIIIIIIIIIIIIIIIIIIIIIIIIIIIIIIIIIIIIIIIIIIIIIIIIIIIIIIIIIIIIIIIII

In a show of British understatement, when asked to describe his victory at Waterloo over Napoleon, the duke of Wellington said, "He came at me the same old way and I beat him the same old way." That description only somewhat fits the Battle of Waterloo, but it completely summarized the identical mistake made by two French kings in fighting against the English sixty years apart.

The first time the French made the mistake was at the Battle of Crecy. If being in the right always meant victory, then Edward III, the king of England, should have lost at Crecy—badly. A few years before, in 1327, the last of the Capetian line of French kings died. Edward III had perhaps the best claim to that throne. But the claim was sure to be contested by some of the most powerful French lords, and his success was far from assured. Since he was already king of England and could lose his control of the rich French duchy of Aquitaine, trying for the throne seemed like a bad idea. Edward instead supported Philip Blois, who became Philip VI. A few years later, Edward changed his mind and started what is now known as the Hundred Years' War. (Which actually lasted 116 years.)

In 1346, Edward III landed in northern France. A city he

owned in the south of France was under siege, and he hoped to draw most of the attackers away. The way he chose to attract their attention was to lead a *chevauchée* across France. The chevauchée involves leading your army across an area while burning, pillaging, raping, and torturing as much as possible. Edward's army left devastation from the coast to near the walls of Paris. Another incentive for a chevauchée was that you also pillage anything of value, and the king got a large cut of the loot.

Philip and the rest of France were outraged at Edward's raid. Thousands of knights, and every peasant they could arm, rallied to the king. Edward, with at most 11,000 men left, and fewer than 2,000 knights, found himself in the middle of a hostile France, pursued by perhaps 20,000 knights and 40,000 men-at-arms and armed peasants. He turned and ran for the Channel and safety.

The English backtracked as fast as they could; the French were often only a few miles behind them. Edward and his raiders almost got trapped against the Loire River but slipped over a ford Edward bribed a local peasant to show him. This gave his tired soldiers a short rest near the village of Crecy-en-Ponthieu. It was there, late in the day, that the French army of 60,000 caught up with his 7,000 archers, 2,000 knights, 1,500 skirmishers, and 500 lightly armored horsemen.

Edward formed up his outnumbered army into an arc, with one flank protected by a deep stream and the other by the thick trees of the Crecy Forest. It was only a few hours before sunset when the bulk of the almost formless mass of French knights and soldiers had gathered across a wide field from the English. In their front were about 6,000 Genoese crossbowmen the French king had hired to counter the English archers. Just as the French knights began to form up for an attack, there was a heavy thunderstorm. It drenched both sides and the ground in between them.

Eventually, the crossbowmen moved toward the waiting English. It is surprising that, though they outnumbered the English six to one, the French made no effort to go around the position prepared by the English with pointed stakes; the entire French army just waited to charge in and slaughter the men who had done such terrible things to their land. The Genoese marched slowly toward the English until they stopped to fire their cross-bows. But they stopped too far away for their bolts to do any damage to the English.

The range of the longbow was much farther and the rain of arrows that answered the Genoese's single volley was deadly. Hundreds died, and the remainder turned and fled. After seeing the crossbowmen break through the first line of French knights, the horsemen could be restrained no longer. They charged forward, some riding down the retreating Genoese. But as they churned through the mud, the longbowmen began to fire.

The English archers could fire from six to eight arrows per minute. At that rate of fire, an archer could have another arrow in the air before his first one landed. Firing high, their first arrows fell from the sky almost vertically and easily penetrated the quilted padding protecting the knight's horses. As the riders got closer, the arrows came in at a lower trajectory. Even at more than 200 yards away, a shaft fired from a longbow could penetrate the thickest armor worn by a knight. Several thousand French knights, many having already lost their mounts, were met by thousands of deadly arrows. Hundreds died, and the rest were forced to retreat. The men who were still on horseback joined thousands of fresh knights, just minutes later, in another charge across the muddy, body-strewn field. After they were driven back another charge formed, and then another.

The French made no fewer than a dozen charges. A few reached the barricaded archers, but they were driven back by the dismounted English knights. Charge after charge continued, until the bodies in the mud were so thick they slowed down the later attacks. By the time it was too dark for further fighting, 1,500 French knights were dead along with more than 10,000 of their less well-armored footmen. Fewer than 100 Englishmen were lost.

The English stayed in their position all night, and sure enough, there was another charge the next morning by knights who had arrived after dark. It too failed miserably. Edward was able to retreat with the loot from his chevauchée. It could be said that the tactics used by the French army were deeply flawed and a deadly mistake, but they weren't organized enough to characterize the mistake as a tactical one. French chivalry was out of control. When they saw an enemy, they attacked; no tactical decisions were involved. It was such a colossal mistake that after Crecy the days of the mounted nobility were numbered. But at least it was a new mistake . . .

Sixty-five years later, in 1415, another English king, Henry V, was being pursued across France. He had landed months earlier with more than 10,000 men, but after a tough siege and after a large number of men decided to return to England, he had begun his own chevauchée across France with just under 6,000 soldiers of all types. In Paris, the French king John and his constable had appealed to the chivalry of the French. The army they gathered totaled more than 40,000: a quarter of these were mounted knights. This time, the English were brought to bay near the village of Agincourt.

Once more an English king formed his men into a crescent. Again there were woods on the English right, and this time the town of Agincourt was anchored to their left. The two armies formed up, thousands of French knights anxious to attack, but this time the French king managed to restrain his men. Maybe he had learned enough from history to not make the same mistake that had been made at Crecy.

Henry could not wait for the French. They could easily send a column around to the rear of his position that was larger than his whole army. He had to force a battle then and there. To do this, Henry advanced all 6,000 men toward the 40,000 angry Frenchmen. The French knights must have watched in amazement as the audacious British approached. The English army stopped a mere 200 yards from the unformed mass of French horsemen. They were standing less than a minute's ride away. There was no hope of retreat or escape.

Something needs to be mentioned at this point. There was another deterrent to attacking any set position with cavalry that day. The English on foot recorded sinking up to their boots in the sucking soil even before the battle began. Mud churns, and in the later French charges some of the survivors mention their horses sinking up to bellies and being barely able to move at all: unable to move as arrows rained death upon them.

The small English army then stopped and planted pointed stakes in front of the new position. The French, possibly still wondering what the English were doing, just waited. The stakes were ready very quickly when Henry V signaled for the longbowmen to begin firing. Each of the thousands of arrows fired in the next minutes could hardly avoid hitting someone in the ranks of the closely packed French position. Just sitting and taking the casualties was too much for the proud horsemen. The knight's reaction was to ignore their king and charge the English. The chivalry of France surged forward just as they did at Crecy. Hundreds died as they were met with a cloud of arrows just as the earlier French chivalry had. Again, there was nothing lacking in the courage of the French. They charged and pressed forward under the archer's hail of death. It must have seemed to the French that this time they were winning. Several times groups of armored men actually reached the English position and had to be driven off in hand-to-hand combat. The battle was so undecided that the English at one point had to slaughter noble prisoners worth many fortunes in ransom. This was almost unheard of at the time. After all, you might be the one captured next week.

The French dead were said to be stacked taller than a man stood. In front of some of the stakes and during the lulls in fighting, the English bowmen ran out between the lines to recover arrows as their supplies ran low. Finally, the French could stand no more, and their army retreated. On the ground in front of the 6,000 English lay more than 5,000 knights and nobles. Many of the greatest names in France had been slain. So many knights had died that French chivalry never again was able to dominate that nation's neighbors with their massed, armored charges. At least as many common soldiers died with them.

King John of France likely never ordered that initial charge at Agincourt. Every military man in France was familiar with Crecy. The impetuous knights most likely acted on their own, repeating the disaster from two generations before. That makes the suicidal charge by the French at Agincourt a mistake that they had no excuse for. Many knights and nobles did know better and charged anyhow.

Agincourt effectively ended the Age of Chivalry. Had the French crushed the English and 10,000 mounted men survived it, history might be very different. How it would be different is another question. There was a good chance that King John would have returned the favor with a reprise of William the Conqueror's invasion of England. Certainly, the French had enough to avenge. A French-dominated England would mean a history so different it can only be speculated on. Without the English tradition of the rights of man, would the revolutions of 1776 and 1789, which changed how nations were ruled forever, have even happened? If King John and his knights had not made the same mistake again, would we all be toasting each night to "the king" and perhaps speaking in French?

31

FEAR OF SUCCESS
China Withdraws
1421

China is responsible for many of the world's grand innovations—the Great Wall, the block press, and gunpowder, just to name a few. Although the entire known world has heard of these, the greatest achievement in China's history was without a doubt the development of Zheng He's navy. Years before Magellan and Columbus set sail, the majestic fleet made its way to the east coast of Africa and beyond. Unfortunately, its days of glory came and went, leaving only whispers of its existence.

The navy came about in 1403, a year after Zhu Di came into power. This emperor was different from his predecessor. He wanted to create an empire devoted to invention and exploration. He funded great building projects, such as the extension of the Great Wall, and he encouraged invention. To create an air of change, he moved the capital to Peking and founded the Forbidden City. He wanted to spread the gift of knowledge, so he employed scribes to accumulate all the information they could gather. The resulting data was collected and used to compile an 11,000-volume encyclopedia. In addition to these marvelous achievements, he ordered the construction of a massive navy. It became the greatest construction project since the building of the Great Wall.

At the head of this project he appointed the eunuch, Zheng He. Zheng He was the emperor's confidant and had played a large role in seizing control from the previous leadership. He envisioned a grand navy, the likes of which had never been seen. To see his dream come to fruition, Zheng He hired 20,000 of the finest craftsmen. Not only did they build ships, but they also built the dry docks needed to house the ships. The dry docks were bigger than any used in the past and are still comparable to any in use today. Although Europeans did not use dry docks until around 1495, the Chinese had been using them for 600 years. The craftsmen engineered special features in the dock. When a ship was ready for launch, the bays could be filled with water, allowing the ship to float out into the Yangzi River. And this was just what the craftsmen accomplished in the dry dock area. What they were able to achieve with shipbuilding is nothing short of miraculous.

Upon its completion, the fleet was larger and more powerful than all the combined fleets of Europe during the age of explorers. It consisted of Fuchuan warships, patrol boats, supply ships, troop transporters, water tankers, and, largest of all, the treasure ships. These colossal vessels were a marvel in engineering. They were more than 120 meters long. (That's longer than a football field.) And, in order to ensure that the ships would still be maneuverable, they were built with a shallow hull. This hull was wide and contained sixteen watertight bulkheads. The use of watertight bulkheads was not perfected in Europe until the nineteenth century.

In addition to being large, the treasure ships had a carrying capacity of 3,600 tons. Two anchors were used to weigh the ship in harbor. Each one measured more than two meters long. Rudders, which could be as long as eleven meters, steered the ship on its journey. So the sailors could make the best use of the wind, craftsmen designed triangular-shaped sails that pivoted around the masts. In the case of the treasure ships, there could be as many as nine masts. Unlike later European ships, Zheng He's vessels did not lose proficiency if the wind was not at their backs.

Another unique feature of the Chinese fleet was that it was

completely self-sufficient. Tankers supplied much-needed water, while cattle ships kept the crews in beef. Poor diet often posed problems for crews. Without vitamin C–enriched foods, crew members suffered from scurvy. Zheng He came up with a solution to the problem. Certain supply ships came equipped with growing beds, which the crews used to raise soy. Not only is soy rich in vitamin C; it also yields a big crop in a small amount of space. Because of the constant supply of sprouts, crew members no longer fell prey to the agonizing effects of scurvy. Zheng He managed to solve the age-old affliction of seafarers, which would continue to plague European sailors until the voyages of Captain Cook some three and a half centuries later.

The fleet itself consisted of 300 ships and 28,000 crew members. Although the ships were large enough to house settlers, the emperor had no interest in colonization. He wanted trade. In particular, the Chinese wanted pepper and frankincense. In exchange for these goods, they offered silk and porcelain. The Silk Road had been closed to them by the Mongols, so the Chinese became masters of the waterways. They raised money for their expeditions by intimidating countries into paying tribute. Most did not refuse because of the great size of the navy. When countries did offer objections, they were met with force and easily defeated by the well-equipped Chinese ships, which used cannons, flame throwers, grenade launchers, water mines, and crossbows that could fire twenty arrows every fifteen seconds. This immense strength coupled with Zheng He's own diplomatic skill ensured his place as king of the high seas. Zheng He used his powerful position for other things besides trade. He brought back medical cures from the Arabic world as well as exotic animals; the most important of these being the Arabian horse, which proved more maneuverable than the Chinese horse.

Despite the improvements made to society, conservative followers of the teachings of Confucius felt that the navy was becoming too costly. They also believed that tradition was far more important and better for the country than trying to attain knowledge from the outside world. These beliefs spread throughout court. The imperial court split into two separate factions; the traditionalists who wanted isolation and those who wanted all the world could provide. The matter soon settled itself.

In 1424 Emperor Zhu Di died. Conservatives wasted no time seizing control of the throne. The new emperor immediately implemented changes that would ensure China's centralization. He ordered that all naval voyages to the outside world cease. He also stopped all construction of naval vessels. None were to be built or repaired. Before long, the ships fell into disrepair. By 1503 the navy was one-tenth its former size. Conservatives destroyed the ship logs and any other evidence they could find of the navy's voyages.

Zheng He did not wish for his greatest work to die without recognition. He erected a monument in honor of the goddess who he claimed protected him during his perilous journeys. Along with praises and exaltation, the monument included detailed accounts of where the navy had traveled. According to the writings, the navy sailed to Sumatra, Taiwan, Java, Ceylon, India, Persia, the Persian Gulf, Arabia, the Red Sea, and the African east coast. There is also modern evidence suggesting that the Chinese navy made it all the way to the Americas.

If this is true, then the Chinese could have easily gone on to be the world's first superpower. With a strong naval presence in China, it is doubtful that the Portuguese would have established ports on the Chinese coast. The same is true for the rest of the Europeans. They may never have branched out as far as they did had the Chinese already established themselves firmly in India and the Persian Gulf. Centuries later, Japan would have thought twice before invading such a powerful nation. These are mere speculations and it is difficult to gauge what might have happened had the Chinese maintained a strong naval presence. However, one thing is certain: A country that once looked outward and led the world through technology and exploration turned in on itself, leaving only hints of its former glory.

32

||||||||||||||||||||||||||||||||||||||||||||||||||||||||||||||||||||||||

FALSE SAVINGS

Point-Blank

1452

||||||||||||||||||||||||||||||||||||||||||||||||||||||||||||||||||||||||

n 1452, Constantine XI Palaeologus ruled over a Byzantine empire that consisted of no more than a few small islands and the city of Constantinople itself. The city at that time was no more than a feeble image of the great imperial capital it once had been. The population had dwindled from more than 1 million residents to about 50,000. The army that could once field tens of thousands of fully armored cavalry now consisted of fewer than 7,000 men, including mercenaries.

What did remain unchanged were Constantinople's massive walls. The entire city was surrounded by at least one thick and high wall, even where the city directly adjoined the water. On its more vulnerable eastern side, Constantinople was defended by double walls with a smaller outer wall six feet thick and twenty-five feet high and an inner wall, or great wall, that was more than twenty feet thick and forty feet high. There was a thirty-foot-deep ditch between these walls. A road ran inside each wall to allow quick and sheltered movement, and only small gates allowed access between them. Most of the gates were on the eastern wall and even more formidable than the wall itself.

Mohammed II ruled a Turkish empire that controlled all of

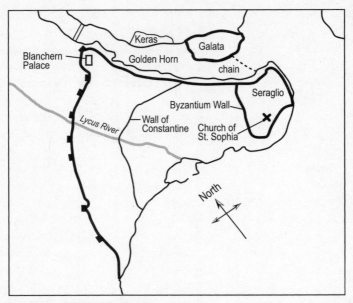

The defenses of Constantinople

the Mideast and parts of Africa. He wanted to expand his control into Europe, but, as it had for more than a thousand years, Constantinople blocked the way. He gathered an army and built a fort to cover his crossing into Europe near the city. There was no question of his intentions and no way for Constantine XI and his city to avoid a siege.

Constantine put out a call for help to all of Christendom. He got very little response. The kings of France and England sent nothing. The pope demanded the Eastern Church recognize his authority. It was a bitter demand for the other center of Christian faith; even so, the Byzantine emperor agreed. When he did, the pope sent only 200 bowmen. The only real reinforcement that arrived in time was a mercenary who was an expert in defending walls. The mercenary brought with him 700 skilled soldiers. But men trickled in until, by the end of the year, the city's garrison had risen to 10,000. Across the straits, Mohammed II waited with almost 100,000 men, and more were being mobilized in various parts of his vast empire.

One other mercenary group answered the Byzantine ruler's call for help. In 1452 gunpowder weapons were just beginning to change warfare forever. Artillery was large, temperamental, and dangerous to fire. Gunners often made their own gunpowder and just as often cast their own cannon as well. The men who operated the cannons were civilian specialists who were paid highly because of the risk and the skills required. Among the greatest of the mercenary cannoneers of this time was Urban of Hungary. Hungary was a Christian kingdom, so before the siege began, Urban offered himself, his cannons, and his men to Constantine XI. Those cannon ranged from small guns that fired a metal or stone ball less than a few pounds, to one named "Bassilica" that could fire only seven times per day but threw a ball that weighed upward of 600 pounds. Now, if the strength of Constantinople was in its wall, you might think that its ruler would understand that the cannons would pose the biggest threat to the walls. But Constantine XI decided the mercenary gunners and their guns were too expensive to hire. Even though there was a good chance that Urban would offer his cannon to Mohammed, for reasons of his own, Constantine turned them away. He passed completely on hiring Urban of Hungary and his troop of mercenary cannoneers. Within a few months, Mohammed II had hired Urban's troops, and Bassilica, to assist him in attacking Constantinople. Having given the Byzantines first chance, the gunner accepted the sultan's offer. Instead of defending the Christian city, his guns would instead batter down its walls.

By the end of the spring of 1452, the Turks had completed the fort that was to cover their army while they crossed the Bosphorus. By spring of 1453, Mohammed II was ready to besiege Constantinople. On April 6, every gun in the Muslim army began pummeling the city's walls. Most of these were those cannons hired from Urban the Hungarian. After twelve days of steady bombardment, there was a narrow breach in one wall. Walls that had held out for a millennium were breached in less than two weeks by the cannon that Constantine XI had turned down. Hundreds of Turks attacked the small breach but were easily beaten off.

On May 6, the cannons created another breach where the Lycus River entered the city through the eastern wall. On the next day, the sultan threw 25,000 men into the attack, which was driven off after only three hours of intense fighting. The garrison did their best to repair the damage, but from this point they were stretched by the need to always keep men near the weakened areas.

Six days later, another breach was opened near the northern end of Constantinople's great wall. The attack on that breach almost broke into the city. Only the timely reinforcement of the defenders by Constantine and his imperial guard saved Constantinople. The siege continued for weeks, with the valiant defenders thwarting an attempt to use a giant siege tower and tunnels to overcome the defenses. All this time, the cannon battered at the walls, attempting to create new breaches and reopen those that had been repaired. Ultimately, even the thick great wall was torn and battered.

After his largest siege tower was lost, some of the sultan's generals began to council him to withdraw. But others encouraged the Turkish leader to give it one more try. If the general assault failed, they would withdraw. The cannon that Constantine XI had previously turned down had seriously weakened the great wall where the Lycus River entered the city. On May 29, Mohammed II threw everything into one final assault. Almost 20,000 Bashi-Bazouks, mercenaries who fought for loot, attacked first. They were driven off, but directly behind them came a second line of Turkish regulars who took up the attack on the weakened wall. They pushed at the partially blocked breaches and were driven off after only two hours of intense fighting. The defenders were exhausted and the great wall provided less and less protection. But before they could recover, a third wave of Turks attacked. Summoning their last reserves, the Christian defenders drove them away as well.

Unfortunately for the city, while almost every soldier was fighting near the Lycus breach in the center of the great wall, a few Turkish soldiers managed to rush through a small gate that had been left open elsewhere. They seized control of a small tower at the far north end of the wall and raised the sultan's banner over it. While this really was just a minor threat, it appeared to be a disaster to the wall's defenders. Their morale and determination plummeted as word spread among the defenders. Then the leader of the largest group of mercenaries was wounded and had to be carried from the wall. Exhausted men who had been fighting on adrenaline lost hope.

The sultan sent in his own elite troops, the Janissaries, who managed to gain control of the section of the eastern great wall from the Lycus to the next gate above it, the Adrianople Gate. Once the Janissaries had that gate open, tens of thousands of Turkish soldiers poured into Constantinople. Constantine XI Palaeologus, the last Byzantine emperor, died fighting in the streets.

The Turkish victory almost didn't occur. Under pressure from his generals, if the last attack had failed, Mohammed II was ready to pack up and leave. Had the Byzantine emperor hired Urban the Hungarian and his cannon, the breaches that weakened the great wall would have never happened. Without those breaches, the sultan's army would have found assaulting the walls of Byzantium an almost impossible task.

The effect of the fall of Constantinople on Europe was a surprising one. The subsequent monopoly prices charged by the Turkish merchants for the products and spices of the East inspired western Europe to search for another way to trade with the Orient. Within thirty years the Portuguese were traveling around Africa, and exactly forty years later, Ferdinand and Isabella financed Christopher Columbus' first expedition. The fall of the city forced the beginning of the greatest period of exploration ever recorded. While Constantine XI's mistake of not hiring Urban doomed Constantinople and brought about the end of the Byzantine empire, that same loss led to the great Age of Exploration.

33

||||||||||||||||||||||||||||||||||||||||||||||||||||||||||||||||||||||||||||||||

SOME MISTAKES
HAVE TURNED
OUT WELL

A Math Error

1492

||||||||||||||||||||||||||||||||||||||||||||||||||||||||||||||||||||||||||||||||

I n 1491, a noted Spanish ship's captain and seaman made a math error when calculating the circumference of the earth. At the equator, a line drawn all the way around our planet is about 25,000 miles long. This has been known and verified by various forms of mathematics since the time of ancient Egypt. But Christopher Columbus was convinced based on his own calculations that this number was 15,000 miles. That is a 10,000-mile difference and the reason he was sure he could reach China by sailing westward from Spain. If he had been correct, it would have been an easy sail. The error appears to have come from Columbus using the wrong value for a degree of longitude when looking at Chinese maps. It is even possible he used the distances as shown on Ptolemy's maps, which were also far off.

At this time, the rivalry between Portugal, who had a painfully long but known route to the Orient around Africa, and Spain was intense. The Spanish monarchs were willing to do just about anything to find their own entry into the incredibly profitable trade. Many of us have heard the tale of Columbus convincing Queen Isabella that the earth was round by using an orange. There is no chance that really happened as just about every educated person in Europe already knew it was round. Columbus' math error explains why the advisers to Ferdinand and Isabella all opposed financing his expedition. It wasn't because they thought the earth was flat; it was because they had checked the sailor's calculations. The learned men of Spain's greatest court opposed financing the explorer because they had determined his math was wrong . . . and it was.

Even so, the Spanish monarchs decided to take a chance and in 1492 supplied three rather small ships to the mathematically challenged seaman. Or maybe it seemed a cheap way to just get rid of him after he had lobbied them for months on end. And so the rest is, as we say, history. Columbus sailed in the *Nina*, *Pinta*, and *Santa Maria*. Eventually, and rather heroically, he discovered the New World. Or at least he found a few islands in the Caribbean. The real importance of this being that Columbus showed everyone that something was there.

Incidentally, Columbus made another mistake while on his journeys. But this one was more fun. He mistook manatees for mermaids and recorded the finned women's presence in the newly found waters.

Believing his own math was vindicated, the captain called the native peoples "Indians" and called the islands he finally landed on the "Indies." Columbus died poor and would be amazed at how he has been revered today. He also might be a little upset to find out just how wrong he was. This math error may have been for Spain and Europe the most serendipitous mistake of all time. It brought the Spanish crown two centuries of plundered wealth and power while opening two continents to Europe.

34

OFF COURSE

Oh Yeah,
and a New Continent

1500

||||||||||||||||||||||||||||||||||||||||||||||||||||||||||||||||||||||||||||||||||

The Portuguese spice trade route to the Orient was the glory and the secret of that small nation. They had found a path, albeit a long one, that bypassed the Islamic merchants. The route they took was to sail around Africa and then up the eastern African coast before sailing across to India. Navigation was primitive, and techniques for preserving food were not much better. Spending any time in the open waters could get a ship lost and doom the crew to a death of thirst or starvation. Most merchants in the fifteenth century tried to always stay in sight of land. The long trip was risky, but immensely profitable. If one ship in ten returned full of spices, the profits were enough to cover the cost of the lost ships and give the investors 1000 percent return on their money.

In 1500, a Portuguese merchant named Pedro Alvares Cabral led his own fleet of fifteen ships attempting to trace the route of Vasco da Gama to India. But rounding the horn of West Africa, his ships caught some unusual winds and were pushed away from the coast. This likely caused everyone on board a good deal of concern. He sailed south and ran into an unfamiliar coastline. Cabral knew it was not part of Africa because it was on the wrong side of the ocean. It was to his west, and since he was supposed to be sailing down the coast of Africa, that would be to his east. It was a strange and wild land covered mostly by jungle. Today we call the country he found Brazil. Cabral had other business: He was after spices, not new continents. So after sailing along its coast for ten days and claiming the new land in the name of his king, Manuel I, (more or less standard procedure in his time), the Portuguese admiral wrote up a report and sailed east until he found a coast that was on the correct side of the ocean. Cabral finally did reach India, and four of his ships made it back to Portugal more than a year later.

Four ships filled with spices made Cabral, his investors, and the crown very happily rich. He filed his report with the king of the new land he had claimed for him and nobody cared. Cabral had not seen any golden cities or diamond mines, so it took an amazing twenty-five years before anyone sailed to Brazil again. In the centuries that followed, the riches of Brazil made tiny Portugal a wealthy and prosperous nation. When a pope later tried to make peace between Portugal and Spain as they competed in the New World, Cabral's accidental discovery while sailing off course gave his nation claim to Brazil. For Portugal, that unusual offshore wind pushing Pedro Cabral into strange waters was the best accident that ever happened. Even if at the time no one really cared.

||||||||||||||||||||||||||||||||||||||||||||||||||||||||||||||

35

BROKE THE RULES
ONCE TOO OFTEN

Dispensing with a Nation

1503

||||||||||||||||||||||||||||||||||||||||||||||||||||||||||||||

This is the tale of two Roman Catholic popes, one king, and several queens. The Roman Catholic Church, during much of the Dark Ages and Renaissance, was always short on money. Or perhaps more accurately, for most of that period before the riches of the New World poured in, most of Europe was always short of hard currency, and that was all there was. There was no paper money. The Church needed to support the clergy, the buildings, the Papal States (including their army), and its charities.

The Catholic Church used all of the tools it had to help raise money. One of these was its power to forgive sins or even decide if something was a sin. The really interesting part was that the Church could forgive sins before they were made. This led to the widespread sale of dispensations by the clergy. These were absolutions, or forgiveness, sometimes even in advance, for sinning. You paid your money in, and your sin was forgiven. These dispensations were one of the reasons for the Protestant Reformation. But at this time, if you were rich and important enough, you could get a dispensation for something as serious as murder. Even then, the Roman Catholic Church was working to reform itself. It was under pressure from the Protestants and just as much pressure from the reformers internally. Nevertheless, at the start of the 1500s, if the matter was serious enough and the donation (bribe) was large enough, a dispensation could still be bought. This was particularly true when kings and thrones were involved. As it had been for several centuries, the Catholic Church was very much both a political and a spiritual entity.

Pope Clement VII was in a difficult situation. Elected as pope in 1523, Clement inherited a volatile political situation in Europe, resulting from the Protestant Reformation. A series of miscues resulted in an inability for him to grant King Henry VIII of England concessions. Between 1523 and 1527, Clement's loyalty and support oscillated between France, Spain, the Holy Roman empire and various Italian princes. His wavering contributed to the mutinous invasion of Rome by the Holy Roman emperor Charles V's troops; Charles' men had even taken the pope prisoner for a brief time. While Charles V had not ordered the attack and was embarrassed by his troops' actions, he must have considered the political consequences to be palatable. Clement became subservient to Charles V and would spend the rest of his papacy as the emperor's lapdog.

In 1500, King Henry VII had two sons and two daughters. The oldest son was Arthur, expected to someday become king. His younger brother, Henry, was well-thought-of and well educated. A life in the Church as a priest was expected of Henry, with the advantage that he would not be breeding little nephews to the king who might someday become rivals for the throne. England was, at this time, a bastion of the Roman Catholic Church. In this it became the ally of Spain, ruled by the fanatically devout King Ferdinand (of Columbus fame). It was decided that rich Spain and England should draw even closer with the marriage of Arthur, heir to the English throne, to the youngest daughter of Ferdinand and Isabella, Catherine of Aragon. No one had any problems with this and when both of them were around fourteen years old (adult in those short-lived times) the two married. The problems began when Arthur died at age fifteen of tuberculosis. This left Catherine a very young widow, ten-year-old Henry the heir to the English crown, and a carefully planned political alliance that supported the pope weakened.

The solution seemed to be that Henry marry Catherine. But there was a problem. The Church had strict rules about marrying your brother's wife. For a range of social and practical reasons, this was a serious sin. There had been too many cases when a queen was forced to marry a cousin to add legitimacy after he had grabbed the throne. Catherine had been Henry's brother's wife first. But the union was just too good to pass up. So both Spain and England appealed to Pope Julius II for a dispensation to allow the marriage. Effectively, this waived the sin and allowed the Church to bless the union. With all that clout behind the appeal and for a substantial share of the dowry, Julius II issued the dispensation. At the time no one was concerned that this alone weakened the validity of the marriage.

The dispensation was duly issued in 1503, but due to Henry's youth, the wedding did not happen until June 1509. There were also rules about getting married before the marriage could be consummated. Henry had been king for two months when they married, and all seemed to be going as desired for everyone involved. At first the royal couple seemed happy. In the next nine years, Catherine bore Henry three sons and three daughters. All but one daughter, Mary, died very young. This created a problem because having a son who could inherit the throne was vital to the stability of England . . . and to Henry's ego. There still was no heir. Perhaps equally important to the young, energetic, rather brilliant, and very lusty Henry VIII was that Catherine had been worn and aged by the childbearing and losses. Now, if there had been an heir or two, this would not have mattered. As even the modern generation of royals has demonstrated, taking mistresses was an accepted practice. But there was no heir, and this complicated the situation. Henry and England needed an heir, and Catherine was no longer an appealing prospect. It was likely she was also no longer capable of conceiving.

Henry took an interest in a noted beauty in the court, Anne Boleyn. Anne was young, appealing, willing, and more. With her, Henry could have his heir, and a good time. But there was a kicker.

The heir could not be had from anyone but the queen. The illegitimate child of a king's mistress could be given honors, but he could never succeed to the throne. And Henry VIII was still married to Catherine, who just happened to still be the daughter of the king of Spain. This was a major political concern as Spain was then the richest and most powerful nation in Europe.

But where love, or lust, is involved, political considerations tend to be ignored. Henry wanted Anne, and he wanted an heir, so he sent his highest-ranking cleric, Cardinal Wolsey, to ask for another favor from the pope in Rome. This time he wanted the dispensation that let him marry Catherine revoked. He wanted a dispensation from the dispensation. If there had been no original dispensation, then his marriage to Catherine would not be valid. Henry would then be free, because Catherine's surviving daughter, Mary, would then be a bastard and no threat, and everyone would be happy . . . everyone except Catherine and all of Spain.

There had also been one change that complicated Henry's plan. There was a new pope. Julius II had died and Clement was now pope in Rome. But Clement took his religious duties much more seriously than had his predecessor. The new pope also was aware of which kingdom, Spain, donated far more funds to the Church than England ever could. So after months of arguments and political maneuvering, Pope Clement ruled that the dispensation stood. Henry was, in the eyes of Rome, still married to Catherine.

The pope's decision that he was still married put Henry in what he must have felt was a terrible position. Anne and he were already very active on a personal level, and she had pretty much put him on notice that she would stay on as queen, but not as lifetime mistress. There still remained the need to create a male heir. So Henry VIII found another way. If Rome would not allow him to dissolve his marriage, then he would dissolve his relationship with the pope. He and all of England would break away from the Roman Catholic Church. Countries and dukedoms all over Europe were doing the same thing that a part of the Protestant movement was doing.

Henry VIII would found a new church, the Church of England, which he controlled. The plan even had a second advantage. Henry needed money, and, among other things, powerful Spain was going to be angry (it was; see pages 147–152), so he was going to need a better navy and army. But England was always short of hard currency to pay for such things. If England broke with Rome, then it was okay for him to grab a fortune in Church lands and holdings. He could solve his budget problem and his marriage problem in one stroke. The new Church of England, of course, voided the dispensation, and Henry was free to marry Anne Boleyn, and four more wives later on. Henry VIII also went on to grab and sell just about every convent, monastery, and church in England.

While this new Church of England (or Anglican Church) still subscribed to many Catholic rituals and beliefs, anyone who remained a Catholic had to assume any heir he had with Anne had no right to the throne. So Catholics in England were almost immediately persecuted in the wake of Henry's decision. In fact, the Roman Catholic churches and the priests who remained in England were illegal until well into the nineteenth century. This violent and energetic persecution of Catholics included among its victims the venerable Sir Thomas More, who years earlier had helped Henry write that book defending the Catholic Church from Martin Luther's attacks. More was executed when he refused to attend Anne's coronation. This was but the beginning of a cycle of violence that would persist in England for hundreds of years.

Henry VIII ended up having six wives and three true heirs (Edward, son of Jane Seymour; Mary, daughter of Catherine of Aragon; and Elizabeth, daughter of Anne Boleyn). After Henry's demise, Edward VI took the throne but died of illness soon thereafter. Mary restored the nation to Catholicism and earned the nickname "Bloody Mary" for the hundreds of dissenters she ordered executed during her reign and the ensuing violence. Upon her death, Elizabeth took the throne, and she reestablished the Church of England.

Had Julius II not granted the dispensation, Henry would not have been married to Ferdinand's beloved daughter, whom he felt forced to divorce later. Spain might have remained friendly to England, reversing the course of Europe for two centuries. And with England supporting Catholicism, the Protestant Reformation would have been very different and far less sweeping. An England allied to Spain and France, rather than supporting the Protestant states, would have made a military difference that would have doomed Protestantism. Henry might even have met, married, and had the heir he so desired with a woman he truly loved. This alone would have made quite a difference to the women Henry VIII did marry, saving their heads and extending their lives if nothing else.

Except in the case of the French Revolution, Mel Brooks' humorous maxim "It's good to be the king" has held historically true. As a divine-right monarch, King Henry VIII got away with dumping two wives, beheading two others, and establishing the Church of England in opposition to Catholicism. Pope Clement VII's decision not to grant Henry an annulment caused a schism in his own Church that resulted in sectarian violence within England for decades. Had Clement simply acceded to Henry's demands, Anglicanism would have never existed and Catholicism would look vastly different. Two popes' mistakes dramatically altered the political and religious landscape of Europe and the world.

36

||||||||||||||||||||||||||||||||||||||||||||||||||||||||||||||||||||

SUPERSTITION

Gods and Gold

1521

||||||||||||||||||||||||||||||||||||||||||||||||||||||||||||||||||||

Superstition can get you into trouble. It doomed the Athenian expedition against Sicily in 415 BCE, made the Black Death worse in 1305, and in 1521 ensured the fall of an entire New World empire. A number of factors led to the conquest of the Aztecs by Hernando Cortes and his 500 soldiers of fortune. The Aztecs had been dominant over their large empire for less than a century. They had inherited, by way of a three-way alliance, the original empire of the Toltecs. It wasn't until 1431 that the Aztecs were in a position to begin expanding, and they did so with a vengeance. By 1465, their empire dominated all of Mexico and Central America as far as today's Guatemala. But this was never an easy occupation. Rome endured because it made the people they conquered part of their empire. The Aztec religion ensured that could never happen.

The faith of the Aztecs was the worship of sky deities, particularly the sun. But their sun god needed constant replenishment. That came in the form of blood and sacrificed prisoners. On a major Aztec religious holiday, thousands of humans would be sacrificed. The most common victims were prisoners. If there wasn't a war going on, the Aztecs often needed to start one to ensure a steady supply of sacrifices. This need for blood guaranteed a high degree of antipathy from the Aztecs' neighbors and subject peoples. Although this belief may have contributed to the dramatic downfall of the Aztec empire, it was not the primary cause. When Cortes landed in the New World, he found a land full of conflict and peoples who harbored a deep hatred for the dominant Aztecs. Almost from the beginning, he was able to recruit entire tribes into what quickly became a crusade against their oppressor. As much as anything, the conquistadors were a catalyst around which resentful Aztec enemies and subject tribes rallied. The superstition that encouraged the resentment and, at a key point, ultimately undermined Aztec resistance, was that of Quetzalcoatl, the white god.

Quetzalcoatl was a man with godlike powers who occasionally appeared among the Central American peoples, performing miracles and teaching them new skills. (Yes, modern UFO believers make much of this.) The myth was that when he next returned it would be the beginning of a golden age. Hernando Cortes was pale skinned, wearing armor far superior to any that could be made in the Americas, and was accompanied by horses and cannons. It is not surprising that he reminded so many Native Americans of the story. The Spaniard quickly saw the advantage this myth gave him and played it for all he could.

Tens of thousands of local warriors and chiefs joined the Spanish against the Aztecs. But the real edge that the legend of Quetzalcoatl gave to Cortes, and the one that made his conquest possible, was the fact that Montezuma, who had been the Aztecs' leader for more than a quarter century, was highly superstitious. In September 1521, as Cortes and his allies marched toward the Aztec capital, the guns and horses of the conquistadors proved decisive in several battles. When Cortes was warned of an ambush and avoided it, rather than looking for spies, Montezuma took this as a sign that the Spaniard really was Quetzalcoatl and could not be resisted. Rather than having to fight their way in, Cortes and his men were welcomed into Tenochtitlan, today's Mexico City, by Montezuma. They were then showered with gifts.

The city and empire were never the same. After Cortes went

back to the coast, the garrison he left behind was besieged in a palace. But the conquistador leader quickly returned and easily restored his control of the Aztec capital. From that time on, Montezuma, who mistook a greedy adventurer for a god, was just a puppet. When the Spanish tried to force Christianity on all the Aztecs and banned their old sun-worshiping religion, the Aztecs finally rose up against Cortes and their captive king. Montezuma's brother was elected to replace him, since he remained a prisoner of Cortes. For a while the Spanish were again besieged, but the real strength of the Aztecs was broken. Their hold over the more numerous tribes and even their unity was gone because one very important and even more superstitious man, Montezuma, mistook Hernando Cortes for Quetzalcoatl. If he had not been so superstitious, a powerful empire might not have fallen to a handful of adventurers. Spain would not have had the Aztec gold that for two centuries made it the most important nation in Europe, and the peoples of the Americas might very well have been treated quite differently had the Aztecs remained a power to be reckoned with.

37

JUST INCREDIBLY BAD JUDGMENT

A Turn for the Worse

1588

I t is perhaps difficult to analyze through the lens of history because we know how the invasion threat ended, but it can be reasonably argued that the Spanish Armada was actually winning against Sir Francis Drake and the other English sea dogs, even after the English fire ships broke up their anchorage on the French coast. It was later that Spain lost her armada, not by the action of the English navy but through the decisions of its own commander.

Many mistakes are made from ignorance. A lack of knowledge or experience can sometimes override natural talent, ability, and even a soaring intellect. The man the Spanish king chose to command the armada was not a naval officer, but he was one of their best and most experienced army commanders, Medina Sidonia. His failure demonstrates how the skills and assumptions that make you an effective leader in a land battle are different from those needed to command ships at sea. In this case, there were two differences that Medina Sidonia, commander of the Spanish Armada in 1588, did not know. That ignorance led to a mistake that made all the difference in the outcome.

The Spanish Armada had been built for the express purpose

of controlling the English Channel long enough to escort an invading Spanish army from the Netherlands to England. In 1588, the Spanish infantry was the best in the world, having defeated every foe they had met for half a century. If the Spanish managed to land in England, they would likely be able to overpower the island's small professional army and ill-trained militia. The only hope the British had was to prevent that landing to begin with.

So Philip II of Spain created an armada—an armed force made up of almost 100 ships, including approximately 40 large vessels, armed with massive cannons and carrying 19,000 soldiers. The plan was to sail north and meet up with an even larger Spanish army commanded by the duke of Parma. Parma had built barges along the coast that the ships of the armada would escort.

It took months to build and weeks to organize and bring together the armada. The English had plenty of warning, and its sailing date and mission came as no surprise to them. The sea dogs opposed the armada with just over 150 ships of their own. Many of these were actually armed merchant ships, and almost all of them were what today would be described as privately owned.

The real difference between the ships of Spain and England was the type of cannon they carried and the way the ships were constructed. The limiting factor in cannon size was weight. The bigger the cannon, the greater the weight, which increased much more than the caliber, and there was only so much weight a wooden ship could handle. Each of the opponents approached this limit in a different way. The large Spanish warships, and they had about forty of them, were slow, massive, and made of very thick wood. The cannons on all of the Spanish warships had a very large bore and were short in both length and range. In contrast, the English ships were much more lightly built and much more maneuverable. The cost of this was that they were made of thinner wood and could not carry as much "weight of metal" as the Spanish ships. The English vessels carried cannons that were smaller and much longer than those of the Spanish. This meant they could throw a small cannonball very far and accurately. The problem was that those cannonballs were relatively small and far too often they bounced off the thick sides of the armada's warships. In addition, size mattered, since the English crews were much smaller, and their ships carried no extra soldiers: This meant that there was no way for them to board and capture the much larger Spanish warships.

So the two battling fleets fought their way up the Channel. The dense mass of the armada made it suicidal for the English sea dogs to approach close enough that their smaller guns would have any effect on the thickly hulled armada. Only by staying at long range did they avoid any damage to themselves. Keeping a disciplined and tight formation, the Spanish Armada was able to sail up the Channel under constant, but ineffective, fire by the English. The armada's guns fired back as well, but they were unable to hurt the English ships as most of their shots fell short or were off target. This was a victory for the Spanish as their goal was not destruction of the English ships, but rather to transport an army across the Channel. Since the British were unable to stop the armada from sailing up the Channel, it appeared they would be equally unable to stop the same ships from crossing over with the duke of Parma's army on board. England seemed to be doomed, and Spanish morale soared.

The long fight had used up much of both the Spanish and the English powder and shot. But neither side knew just how low the enemy's supplies were. Then the weather turned rough. To the Spanish captains, more used to sailing in the relatively placid Mediterranean, a Channel storm, with the rocky French coast nearby, was a frightening threat. Even the English pulled back to give themselves more sea room. The armada anchored along a sheltered part of the French coast near Calais. They kept their tight formation and anchored close to each other for mutual protection. There was only a few hundred feet at most between ships when the first English fire ships appeared. Fire was one of the great dreads of any sailor in the age of wooden hulls and canvas sails. Just about every element of a sailing ship was flammable. One spark could doom a ship in minutes. Cutting their anchor cables, the ships of the armada rushed away from the tar-coated, burning, and possibly gun powder–filled vessels coming at them.

Their rapid rush out of the anchorage meant that the Spanish warships were no longer mutually supportive and in close forma-tion. They found themselves spread out in rough weather, with some ships too far away to be assisted by the others. English sea dogs, such as Francis Drake, gathered in groups of three to as many as ten, and they swarmed the isolated Spanish warships. More than a dozen of the big Spanish galleys were lost and most of the remaining ones were captured, before the armada was able to regroup into an effective defensive formation. Spanish morale was no longer soaring. A decision had to be made on what to do next.

The remaining thirty of the larger ships would likely have been able to escort Parma's army across the Channel. The ships cap-tured by the English were not going to be ready to fight against their former owners for some time. England could still be con-quered. Even if they had to wait a few weeks more than planned for Parma, the plan could still work. But Medina Sidonia made a different choice. He saw that their shot and powder were low and that the armada had nowhere to replenish. He had to suspect the English supply was also low—it was, actually, even worse than that. The English had effectively used the last of their shot and cannonballs attacking the stragglers. But Medina Sidonia did not take the chance that this was the case. The idea of another anchor-age with the sea dogs hovering just out of reach likely did not appeal to him.

The commander of the armada decided to abandon the inva-sion and just get his ships back to Spain. There was always next year. At this point no mistake had been made. The strategy would work, and there was no way for the commander of the armada to know the deplorable status of his opponent's lockers.

Then Medina Sidonia made a mistake that cost Spain her armada.

The bulk of the armada was sitting low on ammunition, hav-ing already lost many of their warships at the top of the English Channel. Below them and between them and Spain was a virtually undamaged mass of English ships whose own ammunition status was unknown. If they were as low on powder and shot as his ships were, the armada could wave as they passed by and reach Spain

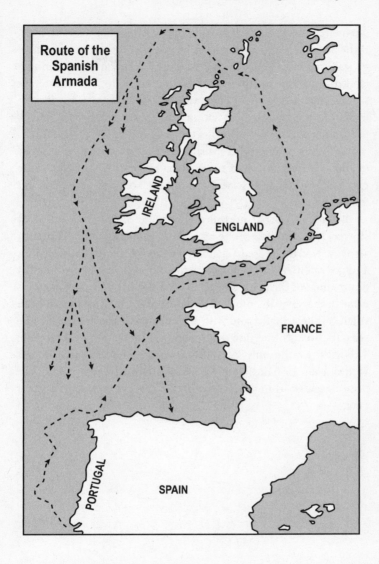

untouched. If the English had been able to get into their nearby ports and restock, then sailing toward those ships guaranteed the loss of the armada. So instead, Medina Sidonia chose to go the other way. He ordered sailors, experienced only at sailing in the calm and warm Mediterranean and South Atlantic waters, to sail north and return to Spain by sailing around Scotland and Ireland. If the armada had been a marching army, and they had a chance to walk back unopposed, this would have made sense. Being a land commander and looking at the maps, this decision must have seemed like an excellent choice to Medina Sidonia. But the armada was not an army just taking a different route to march back to friendly territory. It was a fleet sailing into unknown and unfamiliar waters. Waters where weather was a factor, and the weather in those North Sea waters was always fierce. A seemingly safe route that would have served an army well on land was a disaster for the armada.

Between the cold northern water and almost two weeks of storms, less than half of the remaining ships in Medina Sidonia's armada lived to see Spain again. His decision to avoid the sea dogs and go "safely" north changed history. It began the age of English dominance of the seas, and it marked the beginning of the collapse of the Spanish empire. Too much of Spain's wealth had been spent on the armada, and with the effective loss of control of the seas, the wealth that flowed in from the Indies began to dry up. This was not the only cause for Spain's economic collapse, but within a few decades after the armada turned north, Spain had been relegated from the leading power of Europe to an incidental player.

||||||||||||||||||||||||||||||||||||||||||||||||||||||||||||||||||||||||||||||

38

DEAD-END SCIENCE

Phlogiston

1694

||||||||||||||||||||||||||||||||||||||||||||||||||||||||||||||||||||||||||||||

Eminent scientists from the seventeenth and eighteenth centuries defended the phlogiston explanation of heat and chemical change. One of the best thinkers of his time, George Ernest Stahl, popularized the idea while a professor at the University of Halle from 1694 to 1716. Phlogiston was an "element" said to be contained in all substances that could be burned. It was often described as "inflammable earth." Phlogiston was used to explain and predict all things relating to heat and fire. Indeed, Joseph Priestley, considered the father of modern chemistry, went to his grave defending the phlogiston theory. It was thought to be a material that did not just contain heat but was itself the heat. Phlogiston was without color, smell, weight, or taste. When you burned something, you were dephlogisticating it—that is, driving all of the phlogiston out of the material. Often this left behind only ash.

Here is how phlogiston seemed to work: Such chemicals as charcoal and sulfur were thought to be made almost completely of phlogiston. This was because when you burn them there is nothing left except a little ash, which was explained as the impurities in the phlogiston. After all, if you dephlogisticate a material that was made up mostly of some form of the heat itself, there will be little left behind.

Take another illustrative example: If one room was warm and the other cool and you opened a door between them, then the phlogiston, like any gas or liquid, would seek to balance itself between the two rooms. Phlogiston would flow into the cool room and out of the warm, phlogiston-filled room; and since it's the essence of heat, it would raise the temperature of the cooler room and lower that in the warmer room. Eventually the amount of phlogiston would level out between the two rooms, and they would be the same temperature.

The remarkable thing about this amazing theory was that it seemed to have worked, and it had been used by eminent and respected early scientists for an entire century before it was finally proven wrong. It was not until science progressed to the point that researchers understood the fluid dynamics of the second example and Lavoisier explained the chemical changes that occurred in burning charcoal that the idea of phlogiston died out. This disproving was done by Antoine-Laurent de Lavoisier at the end of the eighteenth century. He did this when he discovered oxygen and determined the actual chemical reactions that occur during combustion. Phlogiston theory was perhaps the most persistent, widespread, and totally wrong mistake made by scientists all through the age when science, as we know it today, was developed.

39

||||||||||||||||||||||||||||||||||||||||||||||||||||||||||||||||||||||||||||||||||||

ALL COURAGE AND
NO PLAN

Culloden

1746

||||||||||||||||||||||||||||||||||||||||||||||||||||||||||||||||||||||||||||||||||||

On April 16, 1746, about six miles from Inverness, on the Drumossie moor, Bonnie Prince Charlie and his ragtag army of Highlanders faced the duke of Cumberland in what would be the decisive battle in the Jacobite cause. Charlie fought on behalf of his father, the Old Pretender, James Francis Edward Stuart, in a bid to seize power from George II. He was expected to lead the Jacobites into glory, thereby laying the ground for what might have been the rebirth of the Scottish nation under Stuart rule. Instead, he led his men to slaughter and forever buried any dreams of a ruling Stuart dynasty.

The Jacobite cause had its beginnings in the Tudor dynasty. When Elizabeth I of England failed to produce an heir, the Scottish king James VI came to rule as king of both England and Scotland. The Stuart dynasty, which traced its lineage back to the daughter of Robert the Bruce, became the supreme ruling power over a united English–Scottish empire. After the Cromwellian takeover and the beheading of Charles I, a new enemy of the people arose—the Catholics, who were viewed with great suspicion. The Anti-Catholic Test Acts, put into commission at the time of Charles II, required that all holders of public office be Protestant.

This posed certain problems for James II, brother and heir to Charles II. James lived in exile in France during the English Civil War and even served in the French army. If being raised as a Frenchman weren't bad enough, he was also a Catholic. Although his two daughters, Mary and Anne, grew up as Protestants, it was not enough to secure his popularity with the people. He did not have the charm and charisma that his brother had. He also seemed to lack a sense of humor and was even nicknamed "Dismal Jimmie" by the Scots. Suspicions grew when James issued the Declaration of Indulgence establishing freedom of worship for all Catholics.

Opponents of James invited his daughter Mary and her Dutch husband, William of Orange, to take over as joint rulers of England and Scotland. When William landed and advanced toward London, James fled the country. William and Mary took their oaths of coronation on April 21, 1689. Despite the newly established monarchy, James still had a small group of supporters, mostly in the Scottish Highlands. They were known as the Jacobites (from *Jacobus*, the Latin version of his name). His only real chance at regaining power came in 1690 in Boyne, Ireland. But James lost his nerve, turned tail, and ran. His lack of courage earned him the Irish nickname *Seamus an Chaca*, or James the Shite.

The defeat did not silence the Jacobite movement. For the next fifty years, there were plots, skirmishes, revolts, uprisings, and massacres all in the name of Dismal Jimmie. But in 1746 a new champion for the cause swept his way across the British Isles. Though James II had long been deceased, his grandson Charles Edward Stuart decided to take up the challenge. By this time, most of Scotland was apathetic toward the Jacobites. Support for them came mostly from the Highlanders, who were looked on by the city dwellers as being mostly bandits. The rest of the Scottish populace favored the Hanoverian king, George II. And, it should be noted that George was the great-great-grandson of James I, thereby making him a direct descendant of the Stuart line, a fact polished over by many historians. The main objection to him seemed to be more about the fact that he was German and less about his lineage. So, the Italian-born, French-speaking darling of the Highlanders sought to depose him.

The Bonnie prince teamed up with Lord George Murray, who became his field commander. Together, the two took Edinburgh and then trounced Hanoverian forces at Prestonpans. They pressed on to England, where the people feared the worst. There was a run on the bank in London and general panic ensued. The panic proved to be premature. When Charlie realized he had no support in England, he turned his forces around just 100 miles outside of London and headed back to Scotland. He decided to go head-to-head with the king's son, William Augustus, the duke of Cumberland. So far, Charlie had been considerably lucky. He controlled much of Scotland and had his followers convinced he could easily take the rest. But facing a force of 9,000 trained British soldiers with 5,000 untrained Highlanders was folly. Going against the advice of Lord Murray, the prince continued onward and concentrated his forces on the Drumossie moor near Culloden house. He lay in wait for the British army to arrive.

It seems the duke had better things to do than fight a battle with the rebellious Scots. He stopped eight miles away in Nairn to celebrate his twenty-fifth birthday. When Charlie heard this, he decided to surprise the duke. He gathered his troops and attempted to march over the moors at night. The march proved too challenging for the tired, starving Highlanders, so they turned around and went back to their original position. They had exhausted themselves on the long trek through the moors and were ill-prepared for the battle yet to come. The following morning, the duke met up with the Jacobite forces.

His actions were well calculated and well implemented. He began with a barrage of artillery aimed directly at the Highland infantry. To parry the onslaught, the infantry ran full-on toward the enemy. The British infantry made ready. They stood fast in three ranks, one kneeling, the next stooping, and the third standing. Cumberland had another trick up his sleeve. He had trained his men to attack to their left in order to evade the Highlanders'

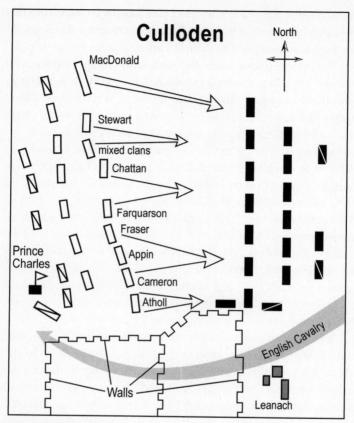

The Battle of Culloden

target, while thrusting under the sword arm. His plan was effective. Hanoverian forces rendered the Highlanders' assault on the left flank useless and managed to outflank them on the right. The Jacobites began a hasty retreat. In the end, 1,000 Highlanders lost their lives and 1,000 more were taken prisoner.

Charlie became a fugitive with a £30,000 price on his head. He eventually made his way back to France and died a rather anticlimactic death four decades later, after many years of drowning his sorrows in the bottle and reminiscing on what might have been.

Had he been more patient, the Bonnie prince might have become the reigning king of an independent Scottish nation. He needed only to concentrate his efforts in the north instead of trying to gather support in the staunchly Hanoverian English counties. Because of his poor judgment and lack of skills as a military leader, Charles ensured that the Jacobite cause would be lost in the annals of history forever.

40

||||||||||||||||||||||||||||||||||||||||||||||||||||||||||||||||||||

POOR PRIORITIES
Party Time
1776

||||||||||||||||||||||||||||||||||||||||||||||||||||||||||||||||||||

The revolution by the American colonists was just about over. The revolt had begun with a number of successes. When those victories failed to get the Coercive Acts, stamp tax, quartering of soldiers, and takeover of the courts rescinded by the British Parliament, the cry for rights changed into a demand for independence. But just as the Continental Congress passed the Declaration of Independence in July 1776, the tide turned.

On July 4, the first 10,000 of 30,000 veteran soldiers were carried to New York City by the Royal Navy. These were veteran redcoats who had conquered India, parts of China, a good portion of Africa, and the rest of the British empire. Lord Howe and his experienced regulars quickly won three battles and drove Washington's army from the colony's largest and most important city. Washington was driven from New York and then New Jersey. His army was broken and supplies were dwindling. Only the onset of winter forced Howe to go into winter quarters and allowed the rebels to escape to a primitive camp at Valley Forge, Pennsylvania.

Many of the soldiers at Valley Forge had enlisted with Washington after his capture of Boston that last spring. After months of defeat and retreat their morale was beyond poor. Desertion was a problem and hard to prevent. There seemed little risk in deserting a rebel army that was close to total defeat. The risk of staying with it and being punished by the victorious crown seemed a greater threat.

No one wanted to back a loser. The financiers of the revolution risked retaliation that included loss of their wealth and even hanging. The price was too high when defeat seemed all but certain. So the revolution's finances and credit were disappearing. The soldiers at Valley Forge were short everything from food to clothing.

The British, warm and comfortable in the nearby cities, expected there would not even be any more fighting. By the spring, what little remained of the colonial army was expected to dissolve. They were almost right. That might well have been the case if one of their most experienced officers had not handed the colonials a victory that restored their morale and changed the entire face of the war.

In 1776, there was no group more hated than the Hessian regiments. They were used to foraging, which meant taking what they needed, as was typical in European wars. The German soldiers spoke little English. Not being able to communicate, they had little sympathy for the "rebels" and often didn't bother to determine whether someone was a royalist or a rebel before treating them badly. The Hessians are today often called "mercenaries," but in reality they were from Hanover and so was the king of England, George III. They were German, not British, and they were not well paid. They were working under their own sovereign as well. So they were not true mercenaries.

Washington needed a victory, but no one in that time fought in the dead of winter. But right across the river were garrisons of the hated Hessian soldiers in their winter quarters. A victory over them would be doubly effective. Today we have often heard about how Washington crossed the Delaware River amid the ice floes and surprised the Hessians, and in hindsight it seemed as if the conclusion was foregone. This is very, very far from the truth.

Actually the plan called for two groups of rebel soldiers to attack across the river. The other failed to make the crossing at

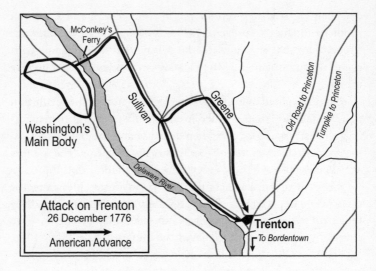

all. And the success of Washington's attack was far from guaranteed. He led 2,400 men, some poorly armed and partially trained, against nearly 1,500 crack troops who would be on the defensive.

The rebels' only edge would be surprise. To ensure they had this, the river crossing was done in darkness. The problem was that the same darkness and fierce cold that hid them also slowed the crossing. Instead of arriving at Trenton to attack at sunrise on December 26, 1776, the Americans were still marching toward the Hessians. Not all of the local people were rebels. In fact, at this point many were still loyal to the crown. As the army marched down the road toward Trenton in the very early-morning hours, a loyalist farmer realized who they were and hurried off to warn the Hessian commander, Colonel Johann Rall.

The farmer got as far as the colonel's door. There a guard stopped him and would not budge. Tradition says the colonel was deep into a game of either chess or cards and had left orders not to be disturbed. The farmer hurriedly scrawled a note to Colonel Rall. The note reached the colonel, but was in English. Rather than trying to summon a translator that early and leave his game, the colonel put the warning note, unread, into his pocket. From that point on victory was inevitable. Washington's 2,400 rebels surprised the Hessians, many of whom were asleep and mostly hungover or still drunk from the prior night's Christmas celebrations. For the loss of four wounded and no one killed, Washington's army killed 22 Hessians, wounded 94, and captured almost 1,000; the remaining 400 German soldiers scattered into the countryside. Just as important, Washington captured the food, clothing, and supplies of a well-equipped British regiment.

Had Colonel Rall bothered to read the farmer's note there is a high probability that the well-trained Hessians would have thrown back any rebel attack. Another defeat, combined with the ending of many of his men's enlistments, would have broken Washington's army. The Revolutionary War would have ended with a victory for Lord Howe, and today America might still be a British colony. The world would have been turned upside down.

41

||||||||||||||||||||||||||||||||||||||||||||||||||||||||||||||||||||

FINANCED HIS OWN WORST NIGHTMARE

Did unto Others

1776

||||||||||||||||||||||||||||||||||||||||||||||||||||||||||||||||||||

There are few records of someone in such a position of power that he managed, by his own decisions, to destroy himself and end a 1,000-year-old dynasty. This feat was accomplished by Louis XVI of France. Louis had taken the throne in 1774 and inherited his nation's antipathy toward Britain. His father, Louis XV, in 1771 had managed to reduce the power of France's parliament until it was nothing more than an advisory body. When the American colonies revolted, this seemed a good chance for France to hurt Britain at no risk to itself. Over the next five years, France sent aide and soldiers to assist the American colonists. This may well have made all the difference: The French fleet holding the bay outside Yorktown in 1881 ensured Cornwallis had to surrender and guaranteed American independence.

Louis XVI's American intervention was a foreign policy coup that greatly discomforted the British. But in the long run, it did more harm to his own monarchy. Supporting the American war was very expensive. It virtually bankrupted the royal treasury. This, in turn, meant that the French financial system had to be modernized and taxation changed so that the losses could be replaced. A specially summoned session of the Assembly of Notables was called to approve the changes. They refused to do so. This left the French king with only one more place to turn for approval of his financial plan. This was to summon the Estates General, the grand parliament with representatives from every level of French society. That was where his encouragement of the American Revolution and its popularity in France once more turned on the king who made it successful.

To justify their independence, the American rebels had to make the point that the rights of men were more important than the prerogatives of any monarch. The Americans meant the will of George III of Britain, but the ideas also took root among the intellectuals of France. When the Americans won, again with Louis XVI's help, the writings of such men as Paine and Adams were reflected in those of Rousseau and the leading minds of Paris.

Having financed and legitimized a revolution against a monarchy in the name of the rights of men, it should not have come as a surprise when the Estates General took the same view. Only this time, the king was Louis himself. The Estates General not only didn't pass the laws the king had summoned them to consider but instead began to rebuild the entire French government based on the philosophy begun by the leaders of the American Revolution. By 1787, the most powerful king in Europe had become a very limited, constitutional monarch who derived his power not from his throne but from the people. By 1789, Louis XVI, never an active leader, had withdrawn from involvement in the government and spent all his time on his hobbies of locksmithing and masonry. By 1793, the man who legitimized revolution in the name of the rights of men and financed the first one was beheaded in the name of the people of France.

For Louis XVI, financing and supporting the American Revolution put into motion results, attitudes, and actions that cost him first his throne and then his head. For him, and perhaps the thousands of those who died in the Terror of the French Revolution, it was a mistake that changed the world. It also was the mistake that ensured American independence and led to the rise of Napoleon.

42

||||||||||||||||||||||||||||||||||||||||||||||||||||||||||||||||||||||||||

DESTROYING THE ENVIRONMENT

Breeding Like a Rabbit

1788

||||||||||||||||||||||||||||||||||||||||||||||||||||||||||||||||||||||||||

We have seen how poor leadership and bad decisions can affect socioeconomic climates. Now let's look at what changes occur when a seemingly good idea alters the ecosystem of an entire continent.

When English sportsman Thomas Austin arrived in Australia to make a new life for himself, he was sorely disappointed. He had spent much of his leisure time back home hunting pheasants, quail, partridges, hares, and—his favorite—rabbits. Much to his dismay, Australia had no rabbits. So, Austin wrote to his nephew back in England and had twenty-four rabbits shipped to his home in Barwon Park in southern Victoria. After all, what harm could twenty-four little rabbits do? There had been earlier attempts to populate Australia with these furry critters. The first fleet brought them over in 1788, but they did not become feral, except in parts of Tasmania.

Other residents in Victoria took up the cause and had rabbits shipped over too. They were most likely enticed by Austin's own words, "The introduction of a few rabbits could do little harm and might provide a touch of home, in addition to a spot of hunting."

They listened well. The trend caught on, but Austin is the man who gets the credit, or rather the blame, for this enterprise.

Only seven years later, a recorded 14,253 rabbits were shot on Austin's property alone. The population had increased so much that 2 million could be shot or trapped without making the slightest dent in the growth of the species. Hunters prided themselves on being able to shoot 1,200 rabbits in just three and a half hours. This was a record unheard of back in England. It was the fastest growth of any mammal ever to be seen in the world. And yes, this is where the saying "breeding like rabbits" originates.

So, why had this accelerated growth taken place in Australia and not England? This is likely the same question that Austin and the other settlers asked themselves. First of all, the milder winters allowed the rabbits to breed all year round. This, coupled with the fact that much of the area had been converted to farmland, created the ideal conditions for a mass growth in population.

Because of this quick growth, the people of Australia experienced a turnaround in their thinking concerning the rabbits. Around the year 1850, a man was charged £10 for poaching rabbits on the property of a certain John Robertson of Glen Alvie. A few years later, Robertson's own son spent £5,000 trying to control the population. The effort proved futile. The rabbits caused irreversible damage. Rather than providing a "touch of home," they became a terrible nuisance.

In less than fifty years, the population stretched all the way to the New South Wales border, through Queensland, and across western Australia and the Northern Territory. This massive spread is still referred to as the "grey blanket." Ironically, the hunters themselves caused this mass migration. Socially, rabbits tend to stay together. Contrary to popular belief, rabbits are not rodents and are more closely related to horses than rats. And in some ways behave as such. Young bucks will leave to establish new territory only at the brink of starvation or a possible collapse in the population. Drastic events such as fires, floods, and other natural disasters may also cause a mass exodus. The hunters did not understand that the mere threat they posed to the growth of the species caused the rabbits to seek less-threatening territory.

Hunters also contributed to the migration by transporting the rabbits from shooting farms to establish them on their own properties for use as sporting game. Farmers became indignant over the practice, but the gentlemen hunters shrugged off the complaints, saying, "Farmers are the universal spoilers of a gentleman's sport." So, the continent-wide spread of these destructive creatures would not have taken place had it not been for the English gentleman and his love of hunting.

And why were the farmers so up in arms about something as harmless as rabbits? Well, farmers tend to be very practical and they saw the rabbits for what they really were—pests. They devastated crops and considerably reduced the carrying capacity of the land. They also posed a threat to the native wildlife. And, it became impossible to keep their populations under control. They tore through fences, they climbed fences, and they would often pile up on one side of a fence and act as a ladder for their fellows. Rabbits have even been known to climb trees up to five meters tall. One local Australian official described in his records the attempts at controlling the rabbits as "trying to hold back the tide with a pitchfork." Since the use of fences proved mostly useless, other methods of pest control were initiated.

Many people hired rabbiters to control populations on their properties. But these bunny bounty hunters had an agenda. If the rabbits were eliminated altogether, rabbiters would be out of a job. So, while seemingly eradicating a property of the pests, rabbiters often employed other tactics, such as releasing rabbits onto lands, freeing pregnant rabbits from traps, and allowing the young ones to simply carry on. In 1888, the New South Wales minister for lands decided to stop subsidizing farmers to pay bounties. Officials passed legislation to try to regulate the rabbit population, but to no avail. The onset of myxomatosis provided some hope at quelling the population. But, as it turns out, the disease that usually proves fatal to rabbits does not discriminate between species. It also proved fatal to some of the native Australian wildlife. The infection remains, but most rabbits today are immune.

Australia has been facing an invasion that has lasted more than 200 years. Her landscape has been devastated, her people have been forced into continuous hours of labor to deal with the problem, and the intruder has completely taken over. Some success has been achieved in limiting the rabbit population using traditional methods, but only at great effort and cost. A small mistake, by a few selfish hunters, has had a high cost in time, money, and environmental damage.

43

IMPATIENCE

With a Dash of Indecision

1798

Napoleon became emperor of France, and Europe fought almost twenty years of the Napoleonic Wars because Admiral Horatio Nelson blew it in 1798. While the British fleet led by Nelson eventually destroyed the French fleet that had carried General Napoleon Bonaparte and his army to Egypt, the operative word in that sentence is *eventually*.

The situation in 1798 was not good for Britain. It was at war with revolutionary France, and one by one its allies had been defeated or intimidated out of the war. Things had gotten so bad that by 1797 there was no British fleet in the Mediterranean for the first time in 150 years. In fact, there were only a few ports in the Mediterranean Sea that any British ship could even enter. Those friendly ports were Gibraltar, Malta, and Naples, among the hundreds of ports that were found on the shores of the Mediterranean, Adriatic, and connected waters.

The French were on a roll, and one general was definitely making a name for himself. He was Napoleon Bonaparte, who had conquered and revitalized the French army in Italy. Napoleon had effectively defeated the entire peninsula except for Naples: a conquest that came soon after that. Bonaparte had returned to Paris to be hailed by the masses, which made the members of the Directorate rather nervous. Fortunately for them, Napoleon began agitating in February 1798 for an army with which to conquer Egypt. The idea appealed to the French politicians on many levels.

Egypt, while technically part of the Ottoman empire (a French ally), had been, in reality, an independent nation ruled by the Mameluke horsemen for centuries. Placed where it was, if France could control Egypt, it had an easy route to India. Since the American Revolution, India had become a vital part of the trade empire that financed Britain and her allies. If India could be threatened, then England might be forced to accept a peace on France's terms. If Egypt were captured, the only route the British would have to India would involve going completely around Africa, taking months to send any reinforcements. With Egypt, French troops could reach India in a few weeks. Egypt would effectively give the French Republic interior lines in any expansion of the war to India or the Orient. It would put the British at such a disadvantage, there was a good chance of France taking over the entire subcontinent. Without the wealth of India, continuing the war would bankrupt Britain within months.

There also was another important factor that had to be on the minds of those who approved Napoleon's expedition to Egypt: It got him out of Paris. In fact it got him out of Europe entirely. Win or lose, the venture seemed to remove Bonaparte as a political threat.

By the spring of 1798, more than 31,000 soldiers and almost 200 scholars had gathered in Toulon for the invasion of Egypt. It was impossible to gather such a force without the British knowing. Word had reached the British weeks earlier, and in response, Nelson had reentered the Mediterranean. His fleet was hovering about seventy miles south of Toulon harbor, hoping to engage the French ships commanded by Admiral Baraguey as soon as they sailed. This was important because Nelson had no idea what the final destination of this powerful army would be. He knew only that from Toulon the fleet would be headed for an invasion. If Napoleon and more than 30,000 men got loose in the Mediterranean, the possible targets ranged from Ireland and Portugal to

Malta and Constantinople or Egypt. So the young admiral waited anxiously for the French to sail into his arms.

Most plans do not survive contact with the enemy, but Nelson's plan did not even have to wait for the enemy before it began to unravel. Weather scuttled any chance Nelson had of intercepting Napoleon near Toulon. A sudden and locally severe storm in early May swept across the Mediterranean and slammed through where the British fleet stood guard. It caught that fleet in the open waters. Nelson's flagship, the *Vanguard*, lost all of its masts. She had to be towed into a port and was nearly lost in the effort. The few frigates Nelson controlled were unavoidably scattered as they ran before the storm and were soon out of contact. Frigates were the scouts of the fleet and losing them proved costly later. All the British ships were separated and damaged. While the British were scattered and battered, the French sailed. Luck helped them avoid the storm. More than fifty merchant ships and a dozen men-of-war were able to slip south past the crippled British ships totally unobserved.

Nelson really had no choice but to put his hopes in meeting the French near their destination. This was because in the day of wooden ships and iron men, locating the enemy on the open sea was incredibly difficult. Today, with GPS and real-time satellite photography it can be hard to picture just how little a sea captain 200 years ago could observe. In an ocean that encompassed tens of thousands of square miles, a crewman perched on the top mast might be able to spot a ship ten or twelve miles away. His vision was greatly limited by the effective horizon. If they passed just a mile beyond the effective horizon of the enemy, a hundred ships, or in this case nearly eighty, were effectively invisible. Even sailing in a line at the normal speed, a ship's best speed was around ten miles per hour. Plus the warships could not separate too fully as they would have to be able to signal one another if anything was found. So all of Nelson's fleet, once it was reassembled and repaired, could search only a tiny portion of the sea at a time. Frigates, being faster and more able to stop merchant ships and ask questions, helped. But after the storm, Nelson's frigates mostly managed to find one another, not the main fleet. This meant that they were of no use to Nelson in the weeks just after the French sailed. Even if one of the frigates found the French vessels, its captain wouldn't know where Nelson's ships were to report that finding to him.

So Nelson had lost sight of Napoleon's army and protecting ships. But he knew that he had to find them. Everyone was in a panic as to what the already famous French general might do. Nelson got new orders and information from Gibraltar, but they were of no help. The orders made it clear that no one in England or Gibraltar had any better idea where Napoleon was going than Nelson did. The French fleet had vanished, and when it reappeared the cost to the British was likely to be high. Nelson's orders were for him to search the Mediterranean, the Adriatic, Greek waters, and even the Black Sea as needed. They also warned that the French could be planning to invade Ireland, or maybe grab Gibraltar, or Naples, or Sicily, or Malta. It is interesting that the list in his orders did not include Egypt, a tribute to the disinformation being put out by the French. So basically Admiral Nelson's orders read "look somewhere" but gave him no idea where to look.

By the time the British were repaired and ready to sail again as a fleet, ten days had passed. That meant the French could be as much as 300 miles away in about any direction. With no hard information on Napoleon's whereabouts, Nelson chose one of the possible invasion targets. He sailed for the port city of Naples. The Italian city had two advantages. It was a friendly port, one of the few, so supplies and more repairs were available. And there was a good chance that the British ambassador to that kingdom, Lord William Hamilton, might have obtained, from the many merchants who used the port, some idea of where the French fleet was.

Strangely, considering all the disinformation being spread by the French, France's ambassador in Naples had told the British ambassador that Napoleon's eventual destination was Egypt. But Lord Hamilton was unable to separate that nugget of truth from the many lies purposely spread by French agents, and so he put no faith in it. Instead he made his own best guess. When they sailed into Naples, Hamilton told Nelson's captains that he thought Napoleon's immediate destination was Malta.

On June 20, a month after the French had been lost, while sailing from Naples toward Malta Nelson's ships were met by the British consul from Messina as the fleet passed through the straits named for that city. The consul carried the news that Napoleon had indeed gone to Malta and the island had surrendered to his overwhelming force on June 9. It was too late to save Malta and probably too late to stop the French from sailing on.

So far, fate had intervened in Napoleon's favor. He would have approved of his luck, having once stated he always preferred a lucky general to a competent one. But once Horatio Nelson arrived at Malta on June 22, the French general didn't need luck anymore. From that point on, Nelson's own actions became the main cause of his own failure. While in Malta, Admiral Nelson was told that Napoleon had sailed away on the fifteenth or sixteenth. This meant the French again had almost a week's head start and could be hundreds of miles away in any direction. Actually, there was some confusion, likely due to translation, and the French had sailed less than two days earlier. But because of his incorrect assumption that the invasion fleet was at least a six days' sail away, Nelson ignored a report of four strange ships just to the southeast of Malta. These were actually four frigates that were trailing at the rear of the French fleet. Napoleon was just tens of miles away, not hundreds.

Nelson did not want to wait the few days that it would have taken to check out that report or order the entire fleet after the "strange ships." If they proved to be nothing, he would be even farther behind Napoleon. Having decided that if Napoleon's target had been relatively nearby Sicily, he would have heard of its fall by then, he correctly guessed Egypt had to be the target. The British fleet rushed south, making best speed to Alexandria harbor. In fact, Nelson was in so much of a hurry to get to Alexandria, he did not deploy the fleet in a wide line that would sweep the ocean as they sailed. He kept his ships together as this allowed them all to make greater speed.

Had the French actually had a six-day lead, everything Nelson did would have been correct. In fact, he would have probably arrived in Alexandria at just the right time. The problem was that the French fleet had really left Malta on June 19, not the sixteenth. The French fleet was also much slower moving. This is because the slow transports, full of soldiers, were by necessity setting the pace. So the French not only had left for Egypt later than the British thought, but were traveling at a much slower speed as well. Had Nelson made more inquiries, he might have found out the correct date for when the French had sailed. But fearing the worst, he rushed southeast to Alexandria (the main port of Egypt) so quickly, he never knew of the mistake.

Being able to sail toward Egypt much faster than the encumbered French fleet, Nelson actually passed that fleet on the way. He sailed past within a few dozen miles of the French without seeing them and arrived before they did. The British found the harbor at Alexandria empty. Had Nelson guessed wrong? He had to wonder. Napoleon could have landed anywhere and be wreaking real havoc on the few allies remaining in the area or could he have sailed off to Ireland? There could be dispatches on a sloop from London now blaming the admiral for the loss of Ireland or the capture of Gibraltar. Sitting in the empty harbor, Nelson's anxiety caused him to make the blunder that changed history. If he had just waited three days at the location he had correctly determined to be Napoleon's target, the British fleet would have been waiting when the highly vulnerable transports and their escorts arrived. The slaughter would have likely been terrible, and even if Napoleon himself survived, his invasion of Egypt would have been stopped before it was started. Without at least the illusion of that conquest, when Napoleon had returned to Paris, he would have come back as a failure and not a conquering hero worshiped by the masses. It is then likely his own coup and takeover of the government would have failed or never have been risked. There would have been no First Consul Napoleon and certainly not an Emperor Napoleon. Without the military genius of Napoleon, there would have been no war to conquer all of Europe. Peace might even have broken out as the French government by necessity moderated and the monarchies learned to live with it.

But Nelson could not sit still. After weeks of scuttling across the Mediterranean, he just kept going. Perhaps he lost confidence in his judgment that Egypt was the French's target. For whatever reason, on June 30, within hours of arriving, the British left Alexandria to sail up the coast of Syria (which included Palestine at this time). Twenty-five hours later, the French did arrive in Alexandria and instead of facing the Royal Navy, they met no real resistance. This allowed the entire army to be landed near the city. Nelson spent the next month frantically searching port after port for the French fleet. It was not until August first that he returned to Alexandria and found it.

In one of his most brilliant battles, Admiral Horatio Nelson crushed the anchored French defenders in Aboukir Bay. Only two of the French ships of the line and a few smaller vessels escaped destruction or capture. But Napoleon and his army were long gone. Ten days earlier, on July 21, Napoleon's army had destroyed the Mameluke cavalry army in the Battle of the Pyramids. After that victory, he had effectively conquered Egypt. With no fleet or reinforcements, the French were unable to hold Egypt. But a year later, in July 1799, Napoleon slipped back to France on a single frigate. Having carefully managed the news that reached Paris, he returned as a hero. In the coup d'état on 18 Brumaire (that is, November 9, 1799), Napoleon took control of the French government. It wasn't until after the Battle of Waterloo, sixteen years later, that Europe again knew any real peace.

Admiral Nelson correctly deduced the target of Napoleon's invasion and had actually beaten the French to Alexandria. But unable to just sit and wait, he then led the British fleet off on a monthlong search for a French fleet that arrived in the same city just twenty-five hours after Nelson left. It was a mistake that eventually made Napoleon the emperor of France and set the stage for sixteen years of war.

|||||||||||||||||||||||||||||||||||||||||||||||||||||||||||||||||||||||

44

TUNNEL VISION

A Battle of
Three Emperors

1805

|||||||||||||||||||||||||||||||||||||||||||||||||||||||||||||||||||||||

I n military history, few commanders have played as skillfully as the French emperor Napoleon Bonaparte, who manipulated both Emperor Francis II of Austria and Czar Alexander I of Russia at the Battle of Austerlitz.

In the months before the three emperors fought, the French had won battle after battle. Napoleon's army had even occupied the Austrian capital of Vienna. But now, despite the French general's maneuvering, two large Austrian and Russian armies had managed to unite. Napoleon's position was less than ideal. He was far from anywhere friendly at the end of long supply lines. His army was too deep into Austria to be able to pull back safely. One defeat, and the entire French army would be lost. Napoleon Bonaparte knew he was in a dangerous position. He was also aware that the two emperors opposing him knew this as well. In fact he was counting on it.

On December 2, Napoleon began a plan that took advantage of the two emperors' overconfidence. He not only had to win but also needed the battle to start soon. There was a good chance the Prussians would join the coalition against him within days. Only a decisive victory could keep them out of the war. The first step was to send his personal aide, a gentleman with the improbable name of Anne Jean Marie René Savary, to negotiate an armistice. While doing so, this officer carefully let it slip that the French morale was so bad that some of the army was unwilling to attack. This deception was supported by the allies' being able to see that the French soldiers had begun to build field defenses and were all digging in. Then, just to guarantee that the Russians and Austrians were sure the French soldiers were on their last legs, Napoleon conceded the highest and central position of the battlefield, the Pratzen Heights, to the allies as well. All this just whetted the appetite of his opponents to destroy the seemingly vulnerable invaders.

So far as the allies could see, they had 85,000 soldiers to 65,000 for the French. They held the heights that overlooked the whole battlefield, and they were sure that their enemy's morale was failing. All of the allied commanders were anxious to get on the attack and finish them off. The Austrian empire had recently been beaten in battle, had their capital captured, and been chased out of Italy. The normally cautious Austrians were more than anxious to even the score.

On the battlefield, Napoleon had set out irresistible bait. He had purposely weakened his right flank. Less than a corps was holding the right side of its position. This was the flank that protected the roads that led back to Vienna and then on to France. The emperors and their generals knew that if they could break through that thin line of defenders facing the left end of their army, it would force the surrender of the entire French army.

What the allies did not know was that Louis-Nicolas Davout, perhaps Napoleon's best marshal, was fast marching his entire corps toward that flank. But this was not entirely a sucker move: If the allies could smash through Soult's corps on the French right, then they could win the battle. Even the arrival of Davout would not repair the damage.

The Russian prince Bagration led a valiant attack on the French left in an effort to ensure no one there could go to assist the vulnerable French right. At the same time, massive columns of Austrians attacked on the far side of the battlefield. Badly outnumbered, the men of Legrand's division held the French right valiantly. Fighting behind barricades, they drove off charge after charge with musket volleys. The sheer number of attacking Austrians pushed them back, but it still did not yet break their line. Many times it appeared that a few more regiments were all that was needed for the allies to break through. Soon all the reserves behind the main attack were used up. But victory seemed so close that the allied commanders began to send in men who had been holding the Pratzen Heights.

As desired, all of the allied commanders had fixed their attention on the weak French flank. None noticed that Bonaparte was feeding just enough new men into the thin, slowly retreating line to maintain it. More and more troops attacked. More and more moved off the central position to join in the attack on their left. In the French center, two corps sat.

On the allied right, Bagration and the French had fought each other to a standstill. On their left, it still appeared that just one more attack, a few more regiments, and the allies would have their victory. So more men were ordered off the central heights and joined the attack. And still the French soldiers in front of the Pratzen Heights just sat and did nothing. This most likely proved to the Russian and Austrian emperors that the French morale had failed. Although that wouldn't have explained the dogged defense they were facing nearby. But confident there was no threat, more Russian and Austrian regiments moved off the heights. Still, the thin French line barely held on, always barely, but it held. It appeared they were ready to collapse under the weight of just one more assault. Between the fighting on both flanks, virtually all of the remaining allied divisions that had been on the Pratzen Heights since 9:00 AM were then marching up to behind the right side of the French line, where Soult's corps was still holding on against overwhelming numbers.

Victory for the Austrians and Russians seemed so close and to them everything seemed to be going almost according to their plan. But in reality the battle was going exactly as Napoleon had devised from the beginning. Then it was time. Suddenly Bonaparte unleashed his fresh divisions against the few troops remaining on the Pratzen Heights. They easily smashed the center of the allies' position. The combined Austrian and Russian army had been split. At the same time, Marshal Murat led the reserve cavalry against Bagration's horsemen, while the French infantry joined in to force the Russian prince's entire command away from the rest of the allied army.

The emperors of Russia and Austria and their generals had lost sight of what they were doing. By concentrating on accomplishing their original goal of breaking through the French right, they forgot the reason they wanted to do this was to win the battle. Trying too hard to win that tactical victory, they lost the battle. With virtually all of their men committed to attacking on the one flank, the Austrian and Russian generals had almost no one left to counterattack the French when they cut the joint army in half. The Russians threw what they could find at the French until they finally used their last reserve with no success. Finally, even the Russian Imperial Guard attacked in a glorious but doomed attempt to retake the heights. Then French cavalry rode that noble infantry unit down, and the battle was lost.

More French infantry went up the heights and then turned right. They took the same paths that the allied regiments had used to reinforce their attack. Coming down the heights, Napoleon's infantry tore into the vulnerable side and rear of the allied regiments that were still attacking the French flank. The entire allied line was "rolled up," even while the newly arrived Davout attacked through Soult's exhausted defenders. Within minutes, two-thirds of the allied army was routed. Bagration, seeing all was lost, managed to make a fighting retreat while Napoleon concentrated on the destruction of the thousands of panicky allied soldiers.

French casualties were under 7,000 killed and wounded with few captured. The Austrian and Russian armies had 15,000 killed and wounded and another 12,000 captured. The French also captured 180 cannons. Many of those who did escape were in no condition to fight again anytime soon. The Russian army did not stop its withdrawal until it was all the way back in Russia. The Austrian army was in worse shape and had nowhere to go. Peace, on Napoleon's terms, followed within weeks.

"Soldiers! I am content with you," the emperor stated in his Victory Bulletin. To show just how grateful he was, Napoleon personally adopted the children of every French soldier killed at Austerlitz. This included providing them with schools, homes, and the money to support them.

The allied army commanded by the two emperors started the battle with superior numbers and a strong position on the central heights. But they allowed themselves to be duped and led by Napoleon into doing what he wanted. The result of their mistake was a triumphant Napoleon Bonaparte able to rampage through Europe for another decade. The French emperor had taken a great chance. Had he lost this battle while so deep inside Austria, there is no question Napoleon would have become a prisoner and likely been executed. The Grande Armée would have been destroyed. But two emperors, and all of their generals, danced to a French tune at Austerlitz. It took another ten years and hundreds of thousands of deaths before Napoleon did meet his Waterloo.

45 and 46

||||||||||||||||||||||||||||||||||||||||||||||||||||||||||||||||||||||

NOT LEARNING
FROM HISTORY

Two Centuries and
Two Mistakes

1812 AND 1941

||||||||||||||||||||||||||||||||||||||||||||||||||||||||||||||||||||||

t is not impossible to successfully invade Russia, just really hard. This was accomplished many times in history. The Vikings did it, and they became the local lords. Later the Mongols invaded and controlled Russia for more than two centuries. It can be done, but in the last two centuries, two of the world's greatest conquerors have tried and failed. What there is to note here are the many similarities shared by the two invasions set more than a century apart: invasions staged by Napoleon Bonaparte and Adolf Hitler.

Both Napoleon and Hitler had been elected first, taking absolute power once in office.

Both invasions came while also at war with Britain. France had been at war with Britain for more than a decade when the Grande Armée entered Russia. Germany had failed to break the RAF in the summer of 1940 and invaded a year later.

Both were fighting a war on two fronts. France against the resistance and Wellington in Spain, and Hitler had sent the

Afrika Korps to bail out Italy six months before invading Russia.

Both times, invaders or their allies had control of virtually all of Europe except Russia and Britain.

Both invasions were the largest attack force ever seen up to that time. The Grande Armée consisted of more than 600,000 soldiers, hundreds of thousands of horses, and hundreds of cannons with contingents from all over Europe. The Nazi invasion, Operation Barbarossa, began with 3 million soldiers, 3,580 tanks, 7,184 artillery guns, 1,830 planes, and 750,000 horses.

Both invasions began in June: June 12 by Napoleon and June 22 for Barbarossa.

Both invasions sought a knock-out battle that would force a surrender on Russia. Neither managed to find one.

Both Hitler and Napoleon thought the invasion would be over fast, and the Russians would collapse even faster. Napoleon was quoted as saying he would defeat Russia in twenty days and be back in Warsaw within a month. Hitler and his generals expected such a quick victory that they did not even bother to stockpile winter clothing for the troops.

Both found themselves still fighting as that first winter began.

Both invaders saw Moscow as the key to victory. Bonaparte captured the city, but that did not force a Russian surrender. The German army got units to within fourteen miles of Moscow's city center, but they were still unable to take the Russian capital.

Napoleon was unwilling to give up Moscow and waited too long into the winter before trying to march back out of Russia. His men froze and were slaughtered along the march back to Poland. Hitler was unwilling to give up any conquered ground in Russia, issuing a no-retreat order to all of his units. This meant thousands of men were killed or captured who would be desperately needed in later years. Hitler was unwilling to allow a withdrawal from Stalingrad, and so a half million veteran soldiers ended up dead or captured.

Both badly overestimated the condition and usefulness of the Russian roads and the ability of the countryside to supply food for their troops.

Both armies were defeated as much by the winter as they were by the Russians. Napoleon's men died from a lack of supplies and the intense cold as they marched out; the German army lost men and were unable to fight effectively because of the rough Russian winter.

Partisan actions forced both invaders to assign a large part of their army to protecting the rear areas and supply lines.

During both invasions, the first winter was one of the coldest and fiercest of that century.

Both France under Napoleon and Germany under Hitler lost so many men in Russia that their empires were destroyed. Napoleon led 422,000 men into Russia in 1812; less than 10,000 returned. Of the almost 3 million men who invaded Russia in 1941, less than half remained by the spring of 1943.

Both nations never recovered from the losses taken in their Russian invasions.

Among the armies that invaded France in 1813 there was a very large Russian army. Among the armies that invaded Germany in 1944 the largest army was Russian.

For both leaders, the invasion of Russia ended an unbroken run of victories that had put them in control of most of Europe.

Hitler and Napoleon made many of the same mistakes invading Russia. Neither was prepared for a long war, both armies were broken by the harsh Russian winter, and both men failed to move quickly enough to save a vital army trapped there. But the biggest mistake has to be Hitler's alone, since he took almost exactly the same missteps as Napoleon had 130 years earlier while invading Russia. They say hindsight is 20/20, and Hitler was offered that hindsight had he picked up any world history book. He apparently hadn't studied his Russian history enough to pass that test.

47

||||||||||||||||||||||||||||||||||||||||||||||||||||||||||||||||||||

EGO OVER SURVIVAL

A Leipzig of Faith

1813

||||||||||||||||||||||||||||||||||||||||||||||||||||||||||||||||||||

I f one man's ego had not gotten in the way of his good sense, there would be someone named Napoleon VIII or IX who at least held the title emperor of France. The mistake that prevented this from happening was made by Napoleon Bonaparte himself. And he made this mistake not during but after the Battle of Nations fought in October 1813 in and around the city of Leipzig.

By October 16, more than 175,000 soldiers from Austria, Prussia, Russia, and Sweden had converged on the main French army consisting of about 160,000 soldiers. Napoleon had faced worse odds and won decisively, but something was different. This was after the massive losses incurred in the invasion of Russia, so the quality and training level of the French army was far below that of the Grande Armée before 1812. And if the French emperor's weapon was inferior, his foes had gotten smarter. The allies had finally learned from the many times Napoleon had defeated them over the past two decades.

Bonaparte had been doing well. In May, he defeated the main Prussian Army near Lützen, but a lack of cavalry meant he was unable to do more than drive them away. On May 20, 1813, he fought the Russians and gave them a beating as well. In fact, the French emperor was so successful that the allies all agreed to a truce that was mostly to the advantage of the French. This provided more time to train his new army and recruit new regiments. While the French trained, the allies concentrated their forces.

The truce was finally over on August 16, 1813, when Germany's fanatically anti-Napoleon diplomat Metternich demanded terms he knew would be unacceptable to any Frenchman. The general opposing Bonaparte had found a winning strategy. If they could not beat Napoleon in a battle, they wouldn't even try to. Instead, they would attack where he was not. Supply needs forced all armies of the period to separate a few days' march apart. There were not enough rations or wagons to bring in food to an army of 100,000 men staying for any time in one location. So the Austrians, Prussians, and even the Swedes went after the French army's dispersed corps.

First, the former French marshal who had become the Swedish king and changed sides, Bernadotte, defeated Oudinot that August 23. Then General von Blucher and his Prussians beat the Napoleonic marshal MacDonald's corps three days later. After that, Napoleon had no choice but to react to every move by any of the allied armies. For a while he held them all at bay, at the expense of exhausting his constantly marching soldiers. Marching as much as forty miles in a day, the French main army and Napoleon managed to reach Dresden, the capital of his Saxon ally, in time to drive off an Austrian attack. By October 15, Napoleon was preparing for yet another march, this time to meet von Blucher and his Prussian army, who were approaching Bonaparte's base in Leipzig from the north. But just as that move started, word came that an even larger Austrian army was marching toward the French army's position from the south. With far inferior numbers, Napoleon prepared to use a strategy he had successfully employed many times. He would defeat his enemies one at a time. This strategy at Leipzig, often called the Battle of Nations because just about every nation in Europe was involved, meant Napoleon had to first attack the Prussians in the north with the bulk of his army before the other forces approaching him could threaten the weak units facing them. If Napoleon could break through the Prussian line, scatter the army, and then turn south, he had a chance to roll up the allies' armies one after another from north to south. But the Prussians would not cooperate. Even though outnumbered and taking significant casualties, they refused to retreat.

When that attack failed, Napoleon used his central position to shift his forces and attempted to break through the Austrians in the south. That 180,000-man army was almost as many men as were under Napoleon's command. But the French had seen their emperor beat worse odds. Joachim Murat led 10,000 cavalry against the Austrians, and the horsemen tore through the line. But after the loss of horses in Russia there just weren't enough horsemen left to exploit the breakthrough. Before the French infantry could follow up, the Austrian cavalry countercharged. The fresh riders drove the blown French horses back, restoring the line. Another cavalry charge might have broken through since the Austrian horses were blown, but there was simply no more French cavalry left. At the same time as the cavalry were fighting, von Blucher's Prussians in the north pushed hard against the weak force left in front of them. Marshal Marmont and his soldiers fiercely defended their position. Around 9,000 soldiers from each side died that day fighting for the village of Mockern. The fighting ended when Marmont was seriously injured by the explosion of an ammunition wagon. Then the position being so stubbornly held by the badly outnumbered French infantry and gunners fell apart. But they had fought on until it was late in the day, too late for the Prussians to continue their attack.

The next day, both sides licked their wounds and waited for expected reinforcements. When the 6,000 men of the Saxon army changed sides and marched out to join the allies, French morale sagged. The Saxons had been the last ally fighting with them. When the Swedish army of more than 65,000 men also arrived to reinforce the allies, Napoleon decided on a fighting withdrawal. There were just too many allies for his tired and often poorly trained soldiers to stand off, much less attack. He was now outnumbered two to one. The first French units were able to pull out without any problem. Then the allies began to attack from all sides. In the end, none of the 30,000 men left as a rear guard made it out. Within a few days, Napoleon had barely 60,000 men in his retreating army, while the allies still had 300,000 soldiers on France's borders and more coming.

The defeated army slowly retreated to France. Three weeks after Leipzig, on November 8, 1813, the allies offered the greatly outnumbered French emperor a peace settlement. France would have immediate peace and retain almost all of the land it had held in 1789. That was the year that the war had started. Napoleon would retain his throne, and everyone would agree not to attack one another anymore. Outnumbered more than five to one, his economy collapsing, with no more men available to call up and train, even his most devoted allies having changed sides, and all of Europe joining against him, Napoleon had a chance to retain his throne and end the killing. The offer showed how much the allies still feared him. The French emperor's marshals urged him to accept the treaty. They felt that militarily there was no chance Napoleon could stop the inevitable. Bonaparte's unquestionably brilliant campaign over the next few months showed they were correct. A string of amazing victories did little but slow the overwhelming number of armies invading France from all sides. Even the English and Spanish had crossed the Pyrenees and were marching up from the south.

By turning down this final peace offer, Napoleon made the one mistake that he could not correct. A mistake that cost him his throne, and by March 1814, Paris was under siege. He tried to return to power one more time, but that ended with the Battle of Waterloo. It was at Waterloo where another decision he made reverberated into defeat, sending the French emperor into an exile he would never return from.

48

PUTTING THE WRONG MAN IN THE WRONG PLACE
Command Decision

1815

I n many ways, the British victory at Waterloo was very much as the duke of Wellington described it in his report to Parliament: "a near run thing." Until the last minutes, it could very well have been a French victory. When something is that close to succeeding, there are many things that could have been done differently that might have changed history. In the case of the Battle of Waterloo, perhaps the greatest factor was a personnel mistake made by Napoleon Bonaparte days earlier.

Newly returned from exile on Elba, Napoleon had just reformed his Grande Armée, though more than ever this army was made up of newly trained recruits. On France's border, every other nation in Europe was arming. Within days, the emperor would have to march out and defeat at least two armies as large as his. It was a time of decisions that would determine his future and that of France.

Before leading the new Grande Armée north from Paris, Napoleon had to fill a number of command positions. The most important two positions were those of commander of his new army and who would control Paris, which was under martial law. Two men were considered to be commander of the French army under Napoleon. These were two experienced marshals: Michel Ney and Louis-Nicolas Davout. A comparison shows that these two soldiers were very different men:

Michel Ney

Courageous to a fault and often wounded. He was known as "the bravest of the brave." He preferred to lead his men into the hottest part of the battle, often charging with his corps' cavalry.

Commanded a force that was sent to intercept Napoleon on his march toward Paris and instead joined his men to his emperor's.

Competent, but not intellectual. Impetuous and anxious to please. Not the best administrator.

Loyal to Napoleon, reacting to situations rather than planning for them. But for a moment he had hesitated before changing sides from the king to Bonaparte, and this bothered him. Perhaps putting extra pressure on him to be a hero once again.

Immensely popular with all of the soldiers.

Louis-Nicolas Davout

Brilliant, well organized, commanded the largest and best of Napoleon's corps, the Third, for years.

Loyal to Napoleon and equally so to France as a nation.

A thinker and planner. The most competent administrator but not at all flamboyant.

Commanded from the rear. Davout was very popular with his own men, but was not the common soldier's hero that Ney was.

Napoleon's decision was to put Davout in charge of Paris and have Ney command the army for him. When Davout protested,

Napoleon explained that he needed his best man to hold the heart of France for him while he was away with the army. Davout responded that if he won battles, Paris was his, and if Napoleon lost battles, no one could save Paris.

The only chance the French emperor had to defeat the massive number of soldiers being rallied against him all over Europe was to defeat them one army at a time. Napoleon and the French army of the north first met the Prussians at Ligny on June 16, 1815. Napoleon proceeded to defeat the Prussians in a hard-fought battle and turned west to confront Wellington. To ensure he did not have to deal with the Prussians again, Napoleon sent a third of his army, more than 30,000 men commanded by Marshal Emmanuel, Marquis de Grouchy, to harass them and drive them back to Germany. His plan to defeat the more numerous allies in detail, taking on each force individually before they could unite, was off to a good start.

The Battle of Waterloo took place on June 18, two days after the Prussian defeat. Fighting began late in the morning due to wet ground. Cannon was less effective and cavalry at a disadvantage in soft mud. So the two armies sat and waited for the battlefield to dry. There was another difference in this battle from Napoleon's victory at Ligny, beyond a slow start. Napoleon was ill. He had suffered from "piles," a painful and debilitating illness for years, and it flared up the day of Waterloo. Thus he was forced to leave much of the actual commanding to Ney as his field commander. If he had not had this unexpected problem, Napoleon himself might have been more active on the battlefield and his selection of Ney would have had less effect.

Until the midafternoon, the two equal-size armies fought and bled with no major effect. In a well-executed combined army attack, Ney captured La Haye Sainte, a fortified villa in the center of the battlefield. It was not until in the later afternoon that Wellington decided to march his infantry from their forward position to one behind a hill. This would protect them from the French artillery. As the day progressed, the ground had dried, allowing the round cannonballs to bounce and roll with deadly effect.

Napoleon was far behind the lines, and Ney, as usual, was

close to the fighting. When he saw the British infantry begin to pull back and out of sight over the hill, he drew the conclusion that they were retreating. The best way to shatter an army that was beginning to retreat was to slash into them with a force they could not outrun, the cavalry. Without checking with Napoleon first, he saw a way to win the battle. Marshal Ney put himself at the head of more than 10,000 horsemen and charged. It was virtually all the riders still able to charge, and he led them after the "retreating" British foot.

The normal response by infantry of the day was to form a square of men who stood with their bayonets facing out on all four sides. This kept the cavalry at a distance, allowing others in the square to shoot at them. But the cavalry square was vulnerable to any infantry also attacking since it had only a quarter of its men facing in any one direction. A square of infantry is even more vulnerable to artillery fire, as the cannonballs and canister rounds wreaked havoc on the closely packed and motionless formation.

But there were not many unengaged infantry battalions nearby when Ney ordered the charge. Ney, impetuous as always, was more anxious to catch the fleeing British than to ensure a well-rounded attack. He did ask Napoleon to send infantry to follow up the attack, but there were few divisions left in reserve after the Prussians had appeared. So Napoleon had no infantry he could send to support Ney's attack.

Ney's lack of infantry support would not have been a problem if Wellington had actually been retreating. But the British were not running. They were just over the hilltop and quickly formed squares. Ney, his fighting spirit up, led charge after charge against those squares. French horse guns did come up and punish the British, but not enough to break them. There was no infantry to deliver a final blow. By the fifteenth or sixteenth charge, the French cavalry was so exhausted their horses walked up to the squares. Even without French infantry support, a few squares were broken and the soldiers in them slaughtered. Many of the British squares had as many wounded men sheltered in their centers as healthy ones who held the sides. It was recorded that some British units had lost so many men while facing the French cavalry that when they finally moved away, the location of the infantry square was marked clearly by the bodies left behind.

Napoleon was said to be furious when informed of the charge. With the Prussians approaching, he knew he had no infantry to support it. However, he and his guard were not ready to commit his last reserve. But there was no way to call back the attack and no way to stop Ney from charging time after time until the French horses were too blown to fight further.

Grouchy had pushed the Prussians from their rear, but was now tied up fighting a quarter of von Blucher's Prussians with his third of the French army at Wavre. This left the rest of the Prussians to march toward Waterloo. When they appeared, Napoleon responded by sending his Young Guard to slow them. As the cavalry charges were ended due to the complete exhaustion of the horses, there still seemed a chance to at least drive off Wellington before enough Prussians arrived to guarantee defeat. So Napoleon Bonaparte turned to his last reserve. The Old Guard formed into massive columns and charged up the hill and toward the battered British and their Dutch allies.

At this point the Anglo-Dutch army was in bad shape. Some units were at less than half strength. Few British cavalry were capable of attacking, and the heart was gone from the Dutch units. It has to be remembered that less than two years before, these Dutch soldiers had been part of the Grande Armée, idolizing the French emperor they now fought. Wellington was quoted as saying all was lost unless they soon had the Prussians or sunset. Sunset was still a few hours away. He had no reserves left at all.

The Old Guard marched forward, hoping to smash through the punished British infantry. If they did, it was likely Wellington's entire army would fall apart. Instead of breaking through, the guard's massive columns were shot apart, and they were finally forced to retreat. When word spread that the Prussians had arrived and that the guard was retreating, it was Napoleon's army of the north that dissolved. Victory or defeat had come down to the last fight between the French reserve and desperate British regiments.

An ill Napoleon had not been able to keep his impetuous

second-in-command under control. Marshal Ney had ordered a charge with the last of the French uncommitted formation, its cavalry. Ignoring the fact that he was supposed to be commanding the entire French army, Ney charged over a hill and into the unknown. He expected to seal a victory and instead rode to defeat. If Napoleon had chosen the more competent and less impulsive Davout to lead his army, the Battle of Waterloo might well have ended as "a near run thing" that was a French victory. Had Napoleon Bonaparte won at Waterloo, he might well have been able to dictate a peace that could have kept him on the throne of France.

49

INVITING IN THE ANGLOS

Welcome to Texas

1821

When Mexican authorities allowed Anglo settlers into Texas in 1821, they believed it would be in their best interest. By letting outsiders develop land that the Spanish settlers did not want, the state would benefit from the cotton and cattle industries that were so prevalent in the southern areas of the United States. It seemed like an amicable arrangement, but Mexico got more than it bargained for.

For the most part, Mexico had a "no foreigners" policy, but they saw nothing wrong in allowing foreigners to populate remote areas. They adopted an "out of sight, out of mind" attitude toward the new settlers. This attitude was nothing new. In 1790, Anglo settlers moved to Spanish-owned Upper Louisiana. They were looking for a new life, and the Spanish were looking for people who could keep the Comanche and Kiowa at bay. There were three requirements for newcomers: They had to be Catholic, hardworking, and willing to become Spanish citizens. In 1821, when Mexico won its independence from Spain, the new government adopted the same policy.

Anglo settlers came from all over the United States, enticed by cheap land and the promise of a better future. Back home, they had to pay dearly for land. The going rate in the United States was $1.25 per acre for a minimum of eighty acres. In Hispanic-owned Texas, settlers could purchase land for $0.04 per acre. In addition, the head of the family, whether man or woman, could claim 4,605 acres. The $184 needed to purchase the land could be paid over a six-year period.

As if this alone weren't reason enough to lure settlers into Texas, there were others. Back in the United States, many settlers suffered foreclosures due to crop failures, or they were seriously in debt. Since there were no extradition laws between Mexico and the United States, people could escape their creditors by moving and settling in Mexican territory. Like the settlers on previously owned Spanish lands, new settlers in Texas had to become Catholic, and they had to take an oath of allegiance to Mexico. To most this seemed a small price to pay for a new life with a clean slate.

One man in particular, Moses Austin, saw great potential to make money by applying for an empresario grant, which involved bringing in new settlers. He planned on charging each settler $0.125 per acre and using the profit to restore his family's finances. He received permission from the Spanish government to settle 300 families in Texas. Unfortunately, Austin died before he could even get the ball rolling on the venture. So, his son, Stephen F. Austin, inherited the contract.

After going through a great deal of bureaucratic red tape, the younger Austin finally received the go-ahead to bring families across the border. He encountered problems shortly after the colony settled. Texas had a shift in government. The Mexicans won independence from Spain in 1821. The former Spanish territory became Mexican owned. The settlers had a whole new government to deal with. The new government did not carry forward every policy.

For example, the African slave trade had been banned in Mexican-held lands. This posed problems for the white settlers in Texas who were used to making their profits off the backs of the African slaves. The settlers found a loophole. They were allowed to bring their family slaves into Texas, where they bought and sold them. This practice continued for years until it was finally banned.

When the settlers heard rumors that the slaves might be emancipated altogether, they took the precaution of having their illiterate slaves sign ninety-year indenture contracts. They need not have worried. In 1829, when President Vicente Ramón Guerrero finally emancipated the slaves, Austin spoke to his politically savvy Mexican friends and got a government exemption for his settlers.

Austin's payback for his attitude toward the slaves came in the form of a financial letdown. It turned out that empresarios did not own the land within their land grants and therefore were not allowed to make a profit from the land. So, the plan of charging settlers $0.125 per acre was foiled. He did find another way to make money. The perk of being an empresario came with the bonus of 23,000 acres per each 100 families that settled. By 1834, near the end of the empresario era, Austin settled 966 families and received 197,000 acres in bonus land. Since the bonus land legally belonged to him, he could sell it to the highest bidder.

Austin was not the only empresario in Texas. Many others came but were not willing to follow the restrictions laid down by Mexican authorities. You know the saying "Give them an inch and they take a mile"? Well, the white settlers took more than a mile. They treated the Mexican inhabitants as foreigners in their own land. They used any excuse they could to incite the Mexican government and cause trouble. However, credit must be given where due. Austin did send a militia group to help the Mexicans put down one rebellious empresario.

The Mexicans grew more and more nervous about the growing number of settlers coming into Texas. So, in 1830, the Mexican government passed a law prohibiting any further Anglo immigration. They also taxed the settlers heavily. This was likely to encourage as many as possible to leave again. All over Texas, settlers protested. Although Austin had usually sided with Mexico during these hostilities, he was arrested outside Mexico City. He had been petitioning the newly appointed general, Antonio López de Santa Anna, to reopen the borders to immigrants and lower the taxes. Austin spent almost a year in a Mexican prison for trying to incite insurrection.

Santa Anna proved to be a vindictive despot who antagonized

just about everyone in Texas, regardless of race. When he arrived back in Texas in 1835, Stephen Austin found the state in near rebellion. Even though he had occasionally sided with the Mexican authorities, spending a year in prison established his credentials. Leading landholders held a convention and appointed Austin as their leader. After many battles against their Mexican overlords, the Anglo settlers finally won their independence at the Battle of San Jacinto in 1836.

Mexico lost a lucrative province when it lost Texas. They lost it because the majority of its residents had no loyalty to that country. Even in protest to Santa Anna's restrictions on their liberties and high taxes, without the American settlers there would have been little chance the province would have separated. Perhaps instead of paying Anglos to settle Texas, they should have offered better incentives to their own people. It was a mistake that cost Mexico the territory of Texas and turned the United States' gaze on that nation's other northern territories. The world would be very different if everywhere from Texas to California were still part of Mexico.

50

||||||||||||||||||||||||||||||||||||||||||||||||||||||||||||||||

DO NOTHING

Executive Inaction Dooms
the United States

1850

||||||||||||||||||||||||||||||||||||||||||||||||||||||||||||||||

lmost all of the mistakes in this book are actions. They tell about someone doing something wrong or having an accident that changed history. Along with commission there is also omission. Not doing something can be just as great a mistake as doing something very wrong.

In the decade before the American Civil War, the United States endured three presidents in a row who were simply not up to the job. The question of slavery, which was wrapped in the problem of states' rights and federal jurisdiction, was the major issue of the 1850s. Yet despite the obvious importance of the problem, amazingly little was done to address it. Slavery was just not a topic that could be ignored or about which any agreement could easily be found. The United States was just about the last place in the modern world where slavery was still legal. Britain, France, and most of Europe had banned it. A look at the record of the three presidents who served from 1850 until Lincoln was elected demonstrates what a mistake it can be when you do nothing.

Millard Fillmore took office because Zachary Taylor made some stupid choices. On the Fourth of July 1850, President Taylor spent hours in the hot sun at the dedication of the Washington

Memorial. He then went back to the White House and helped himself to a lot of cold water, a large bowl of cherries, and finally some iced milk. The problem with this was that Washington, D.C., was in the midst of a particularly virulent cholera epidemic. Cholera is transmitted through tainted water. Everyone had been warned not to drink the water, eat fruit washed in the city's water, or have anything containing ice made from the city's water. Taylor did all three and was dead four days later. This made his vice president head of the nation in one of its most troubling times. Fillmore was not as strong a leader or as decisive as his predecessor. Where Taylor had stopped the Clay Compromise, Fillmore saw it as a needed solution. This admitted California as a free state and tightened the laws in the north regarding the return of fugitive slaves. Since the Fugitive Slave Act was unenforceable in the abolitionist north, the south felt betrayed. The Clay Compromise ended up doing more harm than good. That was it. Fillmore did nothing else and was dropped by his party in 1852. More than two years were lost through inaction.

Franklin Pierce was a last-minute candidate who first appeared on the thirty-fifth nomination vote at the Democratic Convention. That party was split between proslavery southern representatives and those who were just as vehemently abolitionists. Pierce was a doughface, a northerner who favored slavery. Pierce won the nomination and the presidency. But once in office, he proved totally ineffective in dealing with the slavery problem on any level.

Actually Pierce did more damage to what had been already worked out when he did try to act. When the issue of expansion of the United States into its western territories blew up over which would be free and which slave states, he helped Frederick Douglass destroy the Missouri Compromise. The citizens of Kansas and Nebraska were allowed to vote, slave or free. The resulting violence gave rise to the term "Bleeding Kansas," and the split between north and south became greater. President Pierce was never again able to deal with the issue of slavery or much else. Mostly he went drinking and argued with his critics. By the end of his term, Pierce had proved himself abysmal at diplomacy and had a habit of substituting bluster for action. He alienated even his own party. In

1856 the motto of the Democratic Convention was "Anybody but Pierce." When James Buchanan took office everyone forgot to get President Pierce to ride in the inaugural parade. He never did get to it. Because of Pierce, four more crucial years were lost, and the nation became more divided.

James Buchanan had been a really good trial lawyer and made a fortune at it. This was good as it gave him something to live on after being one of the worst U.S. presidents ever. He could not have come along at a worse time. When the problem of slavery had begun to overwhelm all other issues and split the nation, he proved to be a weak hand on the rudder of the ship of state. The former lawyer really got elected more for where he was during the election of 1856 than for who he was or what he stood for. While everyone else had gotten soiled over the violence resulting from the Kansas-Nebraska Act, Buchanan was ambassador to England. This made him just about the only generally popular and untarnished candidate the Democrats could field. The new Republican Party did well, but the Democratic machine managed to win just one more time. The problem then was that Buchanan had no idea what was going on. Once president, he was indecisive, and he fluctuated between proslavery and antislavery positions until he had alienated both sides. One is hard put to find any substantial accomplishments in any area by Buchanan, even at a time when the United States was tearing itself apart.

In a list of the worst presidents in history, all three from the 1850s make the top ten. Some argue James Buchanan was the worst while other historians hold out for Franklin Pierce. All three were totally ineffective at dealing with the most pressing problem of their day. By the time Abraham Lincoln replaced Buchanan as president, the nation was divided and was soon at war with itself. Three men who led the nation did nothing, and by doing nothing, they doomed the United States to a civil war and hundreds of thousands of deaths.

51

||||||||||||||||||||||||||||||||||||||||||||||||||||||||||||||||||||||||

STUBBORN

The Man Who Prolonged
the Civil War

1861

||||||||||||||||||||||||||||||||||||||||||||||||||||||||||||||||||||||||||

More than 600,000 men on both sides died in the American Civil War. The war lasted nearly five years and devastated much of the southern United States. Had the Union won the first battle of the war, there is a good chance that the war might have ended within weeks when compromises were still possible. In the first battles of the Civil War, both sides struggled to understand command and maneuver. But one side was better armed than the other, and that helped make a difference.

Because of the Union's greater industrial capabilities, most people today are under the impression that the Union Army was always better equipped. This was certainly the case by 1862, but due to a mistake made by James Wolfe Ripley, as the chief of ordnance, this was not true at the start of the war.

In July 1861, Ripley took over the office that purchased all of the weapons and equipment used by the Union Army and Navy. He was sixty-seven years old at the time he was appointed chief. He had fought in the War of 1812, against the Creek and Seminole tribes under Andrew Jackson, and more recently in the Mexican War. He also had been working with ordnance and supply for more than thirty years before he became the top decision maker in that office. He was brought in because his predecessor was inefficient and unable to change with the times. Unfortunately for the Union armies, Ripley proved worse.

Just as the war started and before the Battle of Bull Run (Manassas Creek), the British had completed changing over most of their army to using a new Enfield rifle. This left them with warehouses full of almost 100,000 perfectly usable rifled muskets. The British immediately contacted Ripley, as it was apparent that the U.S. government was going to need a lot of weapons quickly, and offered them to him. The mistake was that Ripley immediately and adamantly turned down the offer.

There were probably a number of reasons that the chief of ordnance did not take the British muskets. It cannot be forgotten that he had actually fought against the British in the War of 1812. Also, there was national pride. The stated reason that he turned down the weapons was "Buy American." There is also the suspicion that Ripley stood to personally gain by limiting all purchases to American-made weapons. He held some ownership in a U.S.-based weapons company. But the real reason, his later actions showed, was that the man who determined for two years what the Union Army fought with was simply hidebound and opposed to any change.

When Ripley turned down the British weapons, they were quickly snatched up by the Confederacy. This meant that for the first months of the war, while Union units struggled with getting the right ammunition for a range of mismatched muskets, the Confederate troops were almost all armed with fairly modern muskets of the same caliber. They were, for those first months, better armed and more easily supplied than the Union soldiers they fought.

James Wolfe Ripley continued in his stubborn resistance to new ideas and weapons until removed from the top position in September 1863. In those two years, he resisted breech-loading weapons, refused to buy the Spencer or other repeating rifles, and kept the army from purchasing any substantial number of Gatling guns. Ripley did not cost the North a victory, but he made it harder to achieve by denying his side the most modern weapons and equipment. And it seemed he did this for no reason other than his own aversion to anything new or different. In a war that marked the beginning of modern technological warfare, Chief of Ordnance Ripley's decisions slowed a Union victory more than the mistakes of any one general.

52

||||||||||||||||||||||||||||||||||||||||||||||||||||||||||||||||||||||

TECH FAILURE
AND PANIC

Fear of the Unknown

1863

||||||||||||||||||||||||||||||||||||||||||||||||||||||||||||||||||||||

I f it had not been for a lightning strike, the American Civil War
might have ended in 1863 with Joseph Hooker considered one
of the great generals in history. The problem that helped doom
Hooker, and partially cost the Union a victory at Chancellorsville,
is one that is also a cautionary tale of depending on new and untested technology in battle.

The Army of the Potomac went through a lot of generals in the
first years of the American Civil War. Among those generals was
"Fighting" Joseph Hooker. He was in command at the Battle of
Chancellorsville, which took place in late April 1863. There were
a lot of reasons for the Union defeat, including the brilliant flank
march in which Stonewall Jackson died. But preeminent among
the reasons for the Union Army being defeated, historians agree,
was a loss of nerve by General Hooker.

Hooker's battle plan was excellent and had a good chance of
defeating Robert E. Lee. It made use of the Union's superior numbers to pin the bulk of the Army of Virginia while flanking it with
the rest of the larger army. Hooker had been given a number of
the new Beardslee Patent Magneto-Electric Field Telegraph Machines to send commands. These early telegraph units used a

hand crank and no battery. One of the problems with these almost untested devices was that they used a visual display on a moving dial to send letters and not Morse Code. Because of this, the telegraphs were easily thrown out of adjustment, making all future messages gibberish. They also had a range of only seven miles between machines. The short range meant that messages had to be relayed between stations established along the line of march. Every seven miles there had to be an operator who read a message and then passed it on to the next machine. For a twenty-one-mile message, they needed four trained operators. Setting up a string of sensitive Beardslees during a battle was no easy task, considering the machine itself weighed a hundred pounds, and it used a heavy copper cable that was easily grounded and decayed over a matter of just weeks. During the Chancellorsville battle, in their haste to get a line set up, old cable had been reused. This further garbled signals, and then one of the awkward machines was found to have been hit by lightning and could not be repaired anywhere closer than New York City. Hooker had been led to believe his communications with his generals would be almost instantaneous; instead, they proved to be almost nonexistent.

Things started well with three corps of Hooker's army crossing both the Rappahannock River and Rapidan River undetected. Within a day, the Army of the Potomac began to concentrate at Chancellorsville. That placed it in a position to attack Fredericksburg. Lee met this threat by leaving a small force, under Jubal Early, in Fredericksburg and moving to meet Hooker with most of his army. Hearing that Lee was approaching, Hooker halted and prepared to meet him. The plan was to wait until attacked and then move unengaged units to stop or flank the Army of Virginia. This was ceding the initiative to the Southern commander.

This might have worked for Hooker if his primary means of communications had not broken down almost from the start. He had begun the battle with machines that were supposed to allow him instant communications with his commanders. But his Beardslee telegraphs very quickly either ceased to work at all or sent unintelligible messages. This left the Union Army with only signal flags and couriers for getting information to and from its spread-out commanders. But most of those commanders had correctly realized that the Southern soldiers were reading their signals, so they refused to use the flag semaphores. With Lee approaching and Hooker's communications collapsed, it is not surprising that Hooker was worried. He had been given the expectation of leading a carefully controlled defense; instead he found himself shadowboxing in an information blackout.

Just at the point where Jackson was turning his flank, Hooker could get information only by courier. By the time he was notified of the flank attack, entire regiments were retreating. When Jackson's troops smashed the Union XI Corps, Hooker wrongly concluded that Lee had somehow outnumbered him by two to one. It is easy to see bogeymen everywhere when you are being kept in the dark. Simply put, for a variety of reasons, General Fighting Joe Hooker was losing his nerve. The next day, the Confederate forces attacked both of Hooker's flanks. He withdrew to a defensive position and by the next day he was back across the rivers to where the Army of the Potomac had started, leaving thousands of dead and captured behind.

Fighting Joe Hooker's army lost the Battle of Chancellorsville because their commander lost his nerve. The flank attack and holding action make this one of Robert E. Lee's most brilliant battles. But Hooker's failure was certainly helped by what was one of the Union Army's first, but hardly the last, technological failures in battle. Incidentally, the Union never again trusted or used in battle the Beardslee telegraph.

53

||||||||||||||||||||||||||||||||||||||||||||||||||||||||||||||||||||||||||

GETTING CARRIED
AWAY COSTS
THE WAR

A Ride Too Far

1863

||||||||||||||||||||||||||||||||||||||||||||||||||||||||||||||||||||||||||

The Confederacy needed a dramatic victory. There had been some serious losses in the west, but the larger Union Army had been kept at bay in Virginia. What was needed in June 1863 was a victory that showed that the South could not only defend itself but could take the war into the North. They needed to show that they had some chance of actually winning the war, not just holding on longer. This would provide the impetus for England and France to recognize them as a nation. Then the European navies would break the Union blockade, and it would be a whole new war. Robert E. Lee's decision to take the Army of Virginia north into Pennsylvania was a political, not a military, one. But this one mistake started a series of events that had the opposite effect. It ultimately doomed the Confederate cause because of very uncharacteristic mistakes he made near a small town named Gettysburg.

The mistake came about because the Gray Ghost, irregular cavalry commander John Mosby, sneaked into the center of the Union Army and came away with a copy of their current plans. What the plans showed was that there were gaps in the Union positions that could be exploited by J. E. B. Stuart's cavalry. This

took place at the beginning of what was one of Lee's most audacious maneuvers: invading Pennsylvania. It was the job of Civil
War cavalry to protect the supply lines of their army and dis-
guise (cover) its movements. At the same time, they had to disrupt
the supplies and report the movements of the enemy forces. While
the Union cavalry had markedly improved, because of their confidence and courage the Confederate mounted army was still a
very dominant force.

Unquestionably one of the most daring leaders of the Southern cause was J. E. B. (Jeb) Stuart. Time and again his raids and
other exploits had earned him accolades from his commanders
and respect from both sides of the war. Mosby finished his formal
report to Lee on what he had found with the recommendation
that the best way to protect Lee's communications was to assail
Hooker's own supply lines. (General Joe Hooker was then in command of the Army of the Potomac.) In response, Stuart presented
a plan to General Lee that involved a raid by a large part of his
command, effectively a majority of the cavalry of the Army of
Virginia. They would move behind the Yankee forces and to
nearby Washington, D.C. Stuart was sure that this would, as it had
in the past, create a panic that forced most of the Union horses to
pull back and chase him, and likely force thousands of blue-clad
infantry who might otherwise face Lee to stand on the defensive
to protect the Union capital.

A lot of people blame the absence of Stuart's cavalry before
and for the first days of Gettysburg for there being a battle there
at all. In the recriminations after the war, some said that Stuart
was more interested in headlines and raiding than in doing his
job. This was not really the case. Stuart's plan to ride around much
of the Union Army appealed to Lee, who sent General Longstreet,
Stuart's direct commander, a note expressing his conditional
approval. This order from Lee read that if Stuart could get across
the Potomac River without alerting the Federals to Lee's plan to
strike North into the Shenandoah Valley, he should do so. While
the Confederate cavalry was waiting to cross into Pennsylvania,
Stuart received orders to that effect from Robert E. Lee on June 23.
These read in part:

If General Hooker's army remains inactive, you can leave two brigades to watch him, and withdraw with the three others, but should he not appear to be moving northward, I think you had better withdraw this side of the mountain tomorrow night, cross at Shepherdstown next day, and move over to Fredericktown.

You will, however, be able to judge whether you can pass around their army without hindrance, doing them all the damage you can, and cross the river east of the mountains. In either case, after crossing the river, you must move on and feel the right of Ewell's troops.

The result of this order was that Stuart and most of his cavalry were missing for the first days of the Battle of Gettysburg. As a consequence, Lee had virtually no intelligence as to the location of the Army of the Potomac before the battle. But Stuart was not AWOL, gallivanting on his own; he was in obedience to Lee's direct order. So mistake number one has to be Lee's willingness to send off most of his horsemen just as he was beginning to move into hostile territory. His intent in doing so, distraction and forcing the withdrawal of Union troops to defend against the raiders, was valid. Whether that was more important than the less glorious role of gathering intelligence is what we are judging here. Since the real goal of moving North was to demonstrate to the European nations the strength and viability of the Confederacy, the publicity of such a raid combined with a victory against a portion of the Union Army would have been doubly beneficial. So perhaps this was a worthy risk, but the devil is in the details.

Stuart actually left behind more than half of his mounted command. The risk came from the fact that with nearly half the mounted strength of his army gone, Lee had just enough horsemen to cover his own movements. He did not have enough to also maintain reliable information on the many Union corps that were moving, under Hooker and then Meade, to intercept his army.

After taking some time to gather the 2,000 horsemen who would accompany him on the raid, Stuart crossed the Potomac where ordered to and passed through the Bull Run Mountains.

Then things began to go wrong. At the town of Haymarket, Confederate scouts discovered Hancock's entire infantry corps moving north. At this point, there was no choice: Stuart's mounted force had to avoid the much larger infantry corps. So on June 26, Stuart ordered his entire force to go south, which resulted in being behind the entire Army of the Potomac. This also meant that a large part of the Union Army was between him and Lee. Communications with the Army of Virginia became, at best, difficult.

Then things began to slow down for Stuart's normally rapidly moving horsemen. Troops in this period carried few supplies. This was particularly true of cavalry. Simply put, horses eat a lot. They had to purchase, or take, virtually all the food, grain, and so on they needed from local sources. Living off the land normally allowed cavalry to move much more quickly because they were without the slow supply wagons to hold them back. The dark side of this equation was that it meant Stuart's force had very few supplies with it, and virtually no feed for their horses. The countryside they rode through had already been picked clean by the Union Army just days before. There was no more grain or fodder of any sort at the farms the raiders passed near. This lack of fodder meant that on June 27 Stuart's cavalry lost several hours to grazing and foraging. On some earlier raids, Stuart's cavalry had moved as much as fifty miles per day, but now in two days they had moved a total of only thirty-five miles and much of it in an unplanned direction that took them farther away from the Army of Virginia. More important, Lee had begun to move north, and Stuart's raiders no longer had any way to even know where their main army was located. Stuart could not report what he saw to Lee because he didn't know where General Lee was located. In fact, a messenger sent to Lee on the twenty-eighth, with the intelligence Stuart had gained thus far, never was able to deliver the information.

Because of the need to again cross the Potomac unobserved, Stuart's force next had to use an inferior and dangerous crossing known as Rowser's Ford. At this point, the river was nearly a mile wide and chest deep on the horses. It took a good portion of the night of the twenty-seventh before the crossing was completed.

It was late in the morning of June 28 before the exhausted

Southern horsemen were again moving. Later that day, they reached Rockville, which created the consternation Stuart desired by being only fifteen miles from Washington, D.C. There the Confederates spent the day paroling more than 400 captives while resting and feeding men and horses. After a twenty-mile night march on June 29, one of Stuart's Confederate brigades under Fitz Lee began tearing up the B&O Railroad tracks. Since the Union Army moved most of its supplies by rail, this was also a slow but very effective action. The loss of the railroad diminished both the supplies and reinforcements that could be sent to Meade, who had by then taken over from Hooker as Union commander. A train of 125 supply-laden wagons, a real prize, was next captured intact. These seem to have been new wagons in great condition by later accounts. They were piled high with all sorts of supplies Lee could use. The wagons were added to the cavalry column. These spoils of war were too good to pass up but also had the effect of slowing Stuart.

On that same day, Early and some Union cavalry were camped in a small town named Gettysburg. Unaware that the entire Union Army had marched north and were near, Lee had ordered his separated divisions to gather in that same Pennsylvania town.

After he had captured the supply wagons, Stuart's entire column overcame the stiff resistance of a small Union force at the town of Westminster and camped for the night to take advantage of the plentiful supplies stored there. Neither Stuart nor Lee knew where the other Southern commander was. More important, without enough cavalry to scout for him, Lee was just learning that the entire Army of the Potomac was nearby.

By this time there were several columns of Union cavalry hunting for the raiders, and one was encountered at the city of Hanover. The Union force was driven from the town, then countercharged and chased the foremost Confederate troopers back onto their main column. That Union countercharge was then stopped. Stuart formed a defensive line on a nearby hilltop. Here both cavalry forces sat until Stuart was able to send the captured wagons safely ahead. The Confederates then slipped away. The next day, July 1, Stuart turned north and camped near the town of

Dover. From there, he sent out two troops of riders hoping to locate Lee. One of these rode toward Gettysburg, the others toward Shippensburg.

This was on the first day of what is now called the Battle of Gettysburg.

Stuart left Dover later in the day and in Carlisle, Pennsylvania, encountered stiff resistance from a brigade of Union infantry commanded by William "Baldy" Smith. The Confederate commander called on the infantry to surrender and threatened to bombard the town with his horse-drawn cannon. Smith replied, "Shell away." So the Confederate horsemen did. The fighting at Carlisle continued late into the night, with Smith refusing yet another demand to surrender.

The next day, the troopers he had sent to Gettysburg found Stuart and passed on Lee's order that he hurry with his entire column to join the battle there. It was now in its second day. On July 2, Stuart led his already exhausted riders toward Gettysburg.

Eight very active days after separating Stuart's brigades, he rejoined the Army of Virginia. Having been forced away twice, the raid had taken much longer than expected. Lee's first words were "Stuart, where have you been?"

The Confederate Army lost the Battle of Gettysburg, and with it, virtually all hope of winning the American Civil War. Would Lee have fought that battle there if he had been given good intelligence as to the position of the Union Army? Would Lee have won if he had instead retreated and fought the defensive battle he had told his commanders earlier that he desired? There is no way to tell. What is certain is that Lee allowing his "eyes and ears" to be absent at such a vital time meant that both armies blundered into the Battle of Gettysburg. That need not have been the case. And Stuart's mistake of turning away and moving slowly out of contact for several extra days meant that his cavalry could not be there for Lee when they were needed. There were a lot of other mistakes made by both sides at Gettysburg during the battle, but these two mistakes, Lee's order and Stuart's detours, combined to ensure the battle itself happened. And after Gettysburg, the Confederacy was never again able to do more than slow its inevitable defeat.

54

OVERCONFIDENCE

The Last Measure

1863

t was the night of the second day of Gettysburg. Thousands of men had died on both sides. Lee needed a victory, and the Union Army was dug in on the hills. Lee could not just retreat intact. He needed to win, preferably big. The war had been going on for three years, and from a strong beginning marked by remarkable victories, the Confederacy was now being ground down. Much of the West had been lost and Vicksburg, the South's last bastion on the Mississippi, was under siege. The Union blockade had isolated the rebels from Europe and the European powers. France and England were anxious to support the Southern cause, but not until it was shown that the Confederacy would survive. Just defending was not enough. There was no hope of winning a battle of attrition against the more populous and prosperous North. A victory over the Union in Pennsylvania would show that no part of the North was safe. It would prove that the Southern cause was able to defend itself, and a victory might put enough pressure on Lincoln that he would have to accept a separate peace. Then France and England would have a reason to recognize the Confederacy, and their navies would open the blockaded ports. With European weapons and financial support, the tide of victory would again favor the South. As an added bonus, a big win would likely mean defeat for their most hated enemy, President Abraham Lincoln, in the fall election.

Lee had led his army into Pennsylvania to find just that victory. He had planned to fight a defensive battle following the classic strategy of threatening the enemy in their own land and then forcing them to attack you to drive you out. Lee had scouted a perfect defensive position near the town of Cashtown. But this was not to happen: Both armies had stumbled into each other two days earlier near Gettysburg, Pennsylvania. Beginning as a meeting engagement by a few units, it had escalated until both entire armies now faced each other.

The Union had stood to the defensive. In other times Robert E. Lee would have moved around it or withdrawn, but he needed to win. He was confident as well; in three years, the men of the Army of Virginia had worked miracles defeating larger armies time after time. He was counting on the high morale of his soldiers and the brittle morale the Union troops had so often shown to give him his victory. But times had changed, and the Army of the Potomac had matured. Its veteran corps were no longer prone to run when charged, and the firepower of its artillery was much more deadly than it had been even a year before.

Lee could sense a victory was possible. Stuart had returned, and the Union forces had been battered. Lee's losses were also large, but the morale of those left and their faith in him were high. As he rode along the Seminary Ridge, Lee described his plan for that morning. It would be a massive charge of the entire line against what he felt was a weakened Union Army that was just barely holding on. That was his first mistake. He had fought on his home ground too long. Men fight better in defense of their homes. It had given him an edge in Virginia, but now it was the Union soldiers who were defending their homes. This day they would not panic and break at the sound of the rebel yell.

Longstreet pointed out to Lee that three of his divisions had attacked the day before and lost half their numbers. They simply were not going to be effective in another such attack. Lee had to agree, but in spite of that warning, he ordered the remaining six

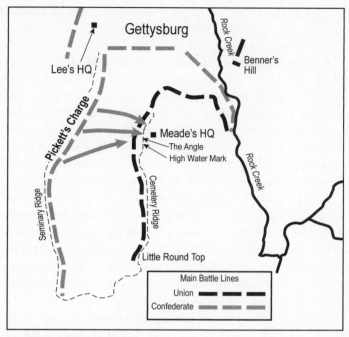

The Battle of Gettysburg

divisions to prepare to attack. But the commander of half the remaining soldiers jumped the gun. Confederate general Richard
Ewell, whose corps on the first day of the three-day battle had
driven back both the Yankee First and XI Corps, led his three
divisions in an attack on the highly fortified Union position on
Culp's Hill hours before he was supposed to. If he had taken the
hill, that might have allowed him to roll up the Union line or
break through. The position was much too strong, and all Ewell
took was a lot of casualties. His divisions were too damaged and
disrupted to attack again that day.

The need for a victory remained and Lee, having broken the
center of the Union's position in the past, was determined to do it
again. Even though he was diminished by two-thirds, he ordered
Pickett's Charge to continue. Part of Lee's hope lay in the massed
battery he had gathered. Ammunition for the cannons was lim-

ited, and all that remained was to be used for a grand barrage that would terrify and defeat the Union troops in front of General Pickett's three divisions before their attack even began.

Because they were firing mostly muzzle-loading cannons up a hill with direct fire, hitting a single thin line of Yankees behind a stone fence was difficult at best. The Confederate artillerists fired and endured counter battery fire until their ammunition ran low. But unfortunately for the men who were about to charge, almost all of their cannonballs flew high over the fence line, where the Union infantry waited in the rear. Horses and ammunition wagons were punished but not the men who would meet the attack.

Lee also had a hidden card he was counting on. He had sent the recently returned J. E. B. Stuart to make an end run around the Union Army and attack the same part of the line as Pickett was, but from behind. If attacked from the front and the rear, there was no question that the Union line would shatter. With the Union Army split, it would turn and run as it had done so many times before. He would have the victory he needed.

As the column of Confederate horsemen approached the back of the Union position, they were attacked by a regiment of Michigan cavalry led by the aggressive young general George Armstrong Custer. The Michigan unit was not large enough to defeat five times their number of horsemen, but they could delay them. Then more Union riders arrived, and it soon became clear to Stuart that he could advance no farther. He withdrew. There would be no attack from the rear to support Pickett's division.

When the artillery stopped firing, the order was given, reluctantly, by James Longstreet, for the charge. More than 10,000 men, virtually the last intact divisions in Lee's armies, moved out. The First Artillery began to punish the neatly formed lines, then musket fire from the front and flanks. The entire charge started just before 4:00 PM and was over in less than an hour. Southern soldiers fell in droves and yet many came on, a handful reaching the stone fences that sheltered the Union infantry. Those few too died quickly or were captured. Only remnants of those brave divisions stumbled back. Pickett lost half of his men and all fifteen of his regimental commanders. Barely a quarter of those who had charged were able to return to the ranks. As Pickett's men re-treated, Lee ordered General Pickett to re-form his division. Pickett is said to have replied that he had no division left.

In a desperate effort to win, Lee had expended his last reserve and fought a most uncharacteristic offensive, frontal battle and lost it. There was nothing left to do but retreat. Lee's mistake cost the Confederacy its last chance at foreign intervention and inde-pendence. Perhaps he was just too confident that the soldiers who had given him miracle victories before would do so again. Most certainly, Robert E. Lee's most dramatic and final mistake, on the third day of the Battle of Gettysburg, was to order Pickett's Charge. The dramatic end result proved what Lee should have known all along: It never had a chance of success to begin with. With its failure, the Army of Virginia was never again able to take the offensive.

‖‖‖

55

RACIAL BIGOTRY

Last Chance Lost

1864

‖‖‖

The Confederacy's last chance for victory in the American Civil War was not lost on the battlefield. The mistake that ensured the South would lose occurred in a meeting room in Richmond, the Confederate capital. The Confederates were being ground down by the sheer number of Union soldiers arrayed against them. For years, Robert E. Lee had won almost every battle, and still the Union pressed on every front. The entire Mississippi River was in Union hands. The problem was manpower. The Union could replace its losses and still have enough manpower to work in its factories. The South was desperately short of both soldiers and skilled workers. Even Lee's victories had cost them heavily, and there were simply no more replacements to be found.

In January 1864, two of the most important men in the Confederacy proposed a solution to the manpower problem. These were Secretary of State Judah Benjamin and General Patrick Cleburne. The two men proposed a plan in which slaves who volunteered to fight for the Confederacy would be given freedom for themselves and their families when the war was won. There were already perhaps 30,000 men of color serving with the Confederate

Army, often as servants, but many were of mixed blood. What the two men proposed was also an answer to Lincoln's Emancipation Proclamation.

This letter, from the highly respected veteran General Patrick Cleburne, was sent first to the general commanding the Army of Tennessee, General Thomas, in March 1864. It was then forwarded to the Confederate Congress. It eloquently argued for the enlistment and freeing of black soldiers:

> *Moved by the exigency in which our country is now placed, we take the liberty of laying before you, unofficially, our views on the present state of affairs . . . We have now been fighting for nearly three years, have spilled much of our best blood, and lost, consumed, or thrown to the flames an amount of property equal in value to the specie currency of the world. Through some lack in our system the fruits of our struggles and sacrifices have invariably slipped away from us and left us nothing but long lists of dead and mangled. Instead of standing defiantly on the borders of our territory or harassing those of the enemy, we are hemmed in today into less than two-thirds of it, and still the enemy menacingly confronts us at every point with superior forces. Our soldiers can see no end to this state of affairs except in our own exhaustion; hence, instead of rising to the occasion, they are sinking into a fatal apathy, growing weary of hardships and slaughters which promise no results . . .*
>
> *The President of the United States announces that "he has already in training an army of 100,000 negroes as good as any troops," and every fresh raid he makes and new slice of territory he wrests from us will add to this force. Every soldier in our army already knows and feels our numerical inferiority to the enemy . . . Our single source of supply is that portion of our white men fit for duty and not now in the ranks. The enemy has three sources of supply: First, his own motley population; secondly, our slaves; and thirdly, Europeans whose hearts are fired into a crusade against us by fictitious pictures of the atrocities of slavery . . . Like past years, 1864 will dimin-*

*ish our ranks by the casualties of war, and what source of re-
pair is there left us? . . .*

*The Constitution of the Southern States has reserved to
their respective governments the power to free slaves for mer-
itorious services to the State. It is politic besides. For many
years, ever since the agitation of the subject of slavery com-
menced, the negro has been dreaming of freedom, and his
vivid imagination has surrounded that condition with so
many gratifications that it has become the paradise of his
hopes. To attain it he will tempt dangers and difficulties not
exceeded by the bravest soldier in the field . . . The slaves are
dangerous now, but armed, trained, and collected in an army
they would be a thousand fold more dangerous; therefore
when we make soldiers of them we must make free men of
them beyond all question, and thus enlist their sympathies
also . . .*

Many of the officers who were fighting supported such a plan.
General Robert E. Lee supported the enlistment of black men into
the ranks. This solution solved many problems. It would have provided tens of thousands of new Confederate soldiers when they
were desperately needed. By giving a way out to those slaves willing to fight for it, the Confederacy would have taken away from
the Union Army a major source of recruits. The people of the
Union were tired of the war and the high casualties. Draft riots
were common, and after three years of conflict, recruiting was
difficult. More than 100,000 black volunteer soldiers were serving
with the Union Army by the end of the Civil War. Many of them
were runaway slaves, and they relieved the pressure that conscription caused. Had these men seen a way to freedom that did not
require a dangerous flight and risk to their families, many might
well have fought for the Confederacy instead. That would have
meant as many as 50,000 more Confederate soldiers and 50,000
fewer Union soldiers as well.

Beginning to free the slaves would also have gone a long way
toward getting recognition from Britain and France. It had always
been to the economic advantage of both European nations for the

Confederacy to win since the South was their main supplier of tobacco and cotton, while the Union was their chief competitor for manufactured goods. But the question of slavery, which had been long banned by both countries, forced them to maintain a distance.

The mistake was simply to not even consider offering freedom to the slaves in exchange for fighting for the Confederacy. The reaction of the Southern press and politicians was loud and emotional. The idea was universally condemned by the Confederate Congress and the Davis administration. Racism and the desire to not let the war force what the Union Army was now striving to achieve overcame even desperation. By June 1864, Richmond was under siege, and by November, Union general W. Tecumseh Sherman's independent army was cutting a swath through the heart of what remained of the Confederacy. There simply were not enough men to stop Sherman, but it did not have to turn out that way.

On the bright side, had the South implemented the policy suggested by two highly respected leaders in the Confederacy, we would possibly have had two separate and weakened nations, rather than one fifty-state unified superpower.

||||||||||||||||||||||||||||||||||||||||||||||||||||||||||||||

56

AIDING THE ENEMY

The Ultimate Weed

1876

||||||||||||||||||||||||||||||||||||||||||||||||||||||||||||||

So what is a story about a common plant doing in a list of 100 of the world's greatest mistakes? If you live anywhere in the southern United States, where there are no hard frosts, you already know the answer.

Kudzu is a vine that originally grew on the rocky mountainsides of Japan. There it had to struggle with poor soil and cool weather. This made it an aggressive and hardy plant. In good soil and warm weather kudzu grows incredibly fast, often several inches per day. The joke in the southern United States today is that you have to close your windows at night to keep the kudzu from growing in overnight.

Kudzu was first introduced into North America in 1876. It was popular with a small number of gardeners, and just a few plants were grown until the 1920s. In those days, the ecological concern was not global warming, but soil erosion. This was the era leading into the Dust Bowl and anything that held the soil in place was popular. It also helped the plant's popularity when it was discovered that kudzu was suitable for grazing as well. Its only drawback was that it could not survive a hard frost.

In the 1920s and early 1930s kudzu was the wonder plant.

There were kudzu cookbooks and even kudzu clubs. Competitions were held to find new ways to use the tough vines and the broad leaves of the plant. In the early 1930s the U.S. government work programs paid workers to plant almost 2 million acres with kudzu. Then one day someone looked around and realized that wherever kudzu grew it killed off every other plant. The vine will climb and steal the sunlight from the tallest tree and grow so thickly not a single blade of grass survives. It was not saving the soil; it was threatening the entire ecology. Since that revelation, the government has spent tens of millions of dollars trying to kill off or slow the spread of the vine they had formerly been paying to have planted.

Today, even after years of eradication efforts, kudzu covers 7 million acres of land. Its range is limited only by frost and snow. A patch was even found in Canada in July 2009. The plants were growing in an area where Lake Erie kept the soil warm all year round. Kudzu has changed the face of the South. Drive along any highway, and you will see an area where the blanket of Kudzu leaves crawls like a green flood completely covering forests and fields. The killer plant can be easily recognized as it covers even the highest branches with its broad leaves. Today, kudzu is becoming a problem outside of the United States. The invasive plant is now being fought in northeastern Australia and northern Italy. Kudzu is a mistake that just keeps on growing and growing and growing some more.

57

|||||||||||||||||||||||||||||||||||||||||||||||||||||||||||||

EVERYONE LOSES

Little Big Horn

1877

|||||||||||||||||||||||||||||||||||||||||||||||||||||||||||||||||

T he honor of the first mistakes in this series of errors that
doomed a people goes to Lieutenant Colonel George Armstrong Custer. If there were a single cause for the many
lapses in judgment that led to the death of Custer and nearly 300
troopers of the Seventh Cavalry, it was frustration. Just plain,
simple frustration.

Custer could not get the enemy to face him, and he needed a
victory. George Armstrong Custer was an unquestioned Civil War
hero. His greatest moment came when Jeb Stuart was leading the
bulk of the Confederate cavalry behind the Union lines at Gettysburg. Stuart was going to attack from behind the same units
and artillery that Pickett's Charge would face. General Custer led
his Wolverine Cavalry against ten times their number. It held Stuart up until more Union horses arrived and the Southern riders
were forced to retreat. Had Stuart's attack succeeded, Gettysburg
might well have been a Southern victory and so Custer's courage
may have saved the Union. This and the fact that he was the
youngest brigadier general in the Union Army helped the young
officer develop an ego and ambition. General Grant had become
president and other war heroes saw their chance. What Custer

needed was a win that would get national coverage and advance his political prospects. But the Indian war dragged on, and the great victory he needed eluded him.

Custer commanded the Seventh Cavalry in the Dakotas. The different style of fighting employed by the tribes, hit-and-run tactics and withdrawals when confronted by a strong force, gave him the wrong impression of their determination and courage. He felt they were cowards who would run when faced with any serious opposition. Subsequent encounters encouraged this view.

After months of trying unsuccessfully to bring the tribes in the Dakota territories to battle, a strategy was devised to force a battle. The plan was that the army would invade in three columns from three directions. The three were to converge and force the "hostiles" ahead of them until they could be beaten by the combined forces. The Seventh Cavalry was one of those columns. It was commanded by Lieutenant Colonel Custer, who like most officers had taken a demotion from general when the U.S. Army downsized after the war.

The plan quickly fell apart. The northern force was met, stopped, and driven back. So the other two columns continued with the invasion. Once the three columns were riding across the Indian lands, they were out of contact with one another and the telegraph. This meant that Custer did not know of the northern column being driven back or that the third column was delayed. He did not know he was unsupported. What he was mostly concerned about was not support but that the hostiles would once again slip away.

So the former general made a number of decisions, all of which were intended to allow his cavalry to ride faster and so bring to battle an elusive opponent. The first of these decisions was to leave behind the wagons and similar horse-drawn items that might slow his troopers down. This included the new Gatling guns, which alone might have given Custer's Last Stand a new name. These early machine guns had been used by the Union Navy in the American Civil War, but a decade later they were still distrusted by army officers. The second decision George Custer made was to disregard the scouting reports of how many hostiles he was facing. This may have been partially inspired by the disdain in which he held the Sioux and Cheyenne warriors. Finally, Custer broke one of the basic rules by splitting his own command into three parts. Once more the reason for this was to ensure that the hostiles did not escape. This was not likely to happen since the camp he was approaching contained more than 5,000 women and children. The 2,000 armed warriors guarding it had no choice but to defend their families.

One column, commanded by Captain Benteen, was sent to prevent any retreat. The other two columns under Major Reno and Custer himself would hit the village from both north and south. This would force the warriors to stay and fight. Before it got close to the village, Major Reno's column was confronted by hundreds of Sioux and Cheyenne warriors. They drove Reno back across a river and up a bluff. The blocking column was also under pressure and forced to withdraw as well. When Custer and 210 men attacked the village, it took most of the pressure off Reno's column, which was later able to unite with Benteen's men and withdraw. But that left no one to reinforce Custer's force.

As he led his 210 men down toward the encampment, the Civil War hero realized that there were well over a thousand tepees in it. His small force would have little effect on so large a village and would quickly be broken up as they rode through the maze of dwellings. So he diverted his attack off to one side, but that took him out to the rolling ground beyond. There they met more than a thousand warriors who were riding hard to meet what they justifiably saw as an attack on their wives and children. Custer had to stand and fight. He spread his men in an extended formation, hoping their Spencer repeating rifles would be enough. They weren't. Without the artillery or Gatling guns, which Custer had left behind, they were quickly overwhelmed. Custer's command died to the last man.

The men of the Seventh Cavalry certainly paid a high price for George Armstrong Custer's mistakes. It was the most one-sided defeat in American history. The victory also reinforced the white opinion that Indians were violent savages. After the defeat at Little Big Horn, the U.S. Army reinforced and increased their efforts all through the Dakotas. Within a few years, the only Native Americans not starving on reservations were the few hundred that remained exiled in Canada.

The final mistake that doomed the Sioux and other tribes was a betrayal. The Oglala Sioux chief Crazy Horse was perhaps their most respected leader. A competing chief told General Crook, who commanded the U.S. cavalry in the territory, that Crazy Horse planned to kill him during a parley. On the basis of this statement, Crook issued an arrest warrant for the Oglala chief. Ironically, after successfully leading warriors in many battles, Crazy Horse may have become convinced that war was not the best route for his people. In early September, the chief had refused to join a small band of warriors led by Chief Red Cloud, and then later that month, he convinced Chief Spotted Tail and hundreds of his warriors to return peacefully to the reservation. When asked by Colonel Luther Bradley to come to Camp Robinson on a promise that no harm would befall him, Crazy Horse agreed. It was a mistake.

Thousands of Lakotas were already gathered at Camp Robinson when Crazy Horse arrived. Many of them were families he had personally led there that May. He entered the camp with Indian agent Jesse Lee accompanying him. Lee pleaded that the chief be allowed to speak his piece. His request was refused. Chief Crazy Horse was too influential and this made him a threat. Bradley ordered his immediate arrest. Being arrested virtually guaranteed that the chief would be killed or shipped off to die at a desolate prison in the Florida Keys.

At first Crazy Horse went willingly with the officer of the day. When they entered the building and he realized he was being taken in the camp jail, the old warrior pulled a knife and ran back out. One Lakota warrior who had fought with Crazy Horse earlier was now working for the army. His name was Little Big Man, though his story is very different from the Dustin Hoffman movie by that name. As Crazy Horse ran out the door, Little Big Man grabbed his arm. Crazy Horse stabbed the Indian scout and ran a few steps farther.

Armed only with a knife, Crazy Horse found himself surrounded by soldiers. Dozens ran toward the fleeing chief, and one officer yelled, "Kill him, kill him." Crazy Horse was bayoneted and died that evening. With his death went the best hope for a peaceful resolution of the problems in the Indian Territories. It was the final act that guaranteed the near destruction of the Cheyenne and Sioux cultures.

Custer's mistakes in command led to a massacre that reinforced public opinion that the tribes were savages whose violent way of life needed to be exterminated. The results were increased efforts and massacres of women and children, such as the revenge taken by the Seventh Cavalry at Wounded Knee. With the death of Crazy Horse, the loss was guaranteed. It is a terrible irony that the Sioux and Cheyenne paid such a terrible price for their one-sided victory. George Armstrong Custer may have made the mistakes, but both his troopers and the Native Americans felt the repercussions.

‖‖‖

58

ONE WRONG TURN

How to Start a War

1914

‖‖‖

Rarely has one driver making a wrong turn affected history more than in Sarajevo in 1914. It all really started in about 1859 as Germany struggled to become a nation. The result of that unification was that the traditional balance of power in Europe was disrupted. By 1870 and the Franco-Prussian War, there was no balance and no one doing any balancing. Rather, the balance was replaced by interweaving alliances, often based on treaties that contained several secret clauses.

By 1914, racial and political tensions were high all over Europe. This was particularly true in the Austro-Hungarian empire. This Hapsburg empire had a number of problems. Most of the trouble was because it was made up of several nations and even more ethnic groups. Many of those racial groups distrusted or hated one another even more than they did any of Austria's external enemies. The Austrians lorded over the rest, the Germanic Austrians even more so, while the Serbs hated the Slavs, the Slavic groups all resented everyone else, and less numerous minorities were all exploited and persecuted. Adding to the problems of Austria was Emperor Franz Joseph. He had been on the throne for fifty years and was totally out of touch with both his subjects and the times. Complicating this volatile mix was the fact that dozens of different ethnic groups inside Austria were being supported by nations such as Russia and Germany. So the situation in the Austrian empire was unstable at best and getting worse.

Instability bred chaos and extremism. In parts of the empire, such as Serbia, dozens of radical groups existed, all capable of violent terrorism. Some wanted national freedom, some were ready to kill in the name of democracy; anarchists bombed everyone else in the hope of eliminating all governments. Many groups simply hated and feared all of the other ethnic minorities and religions who were their neighbors. Christians and Muslims continued centuries of antipathy. Almost every group strove to make sure their minority took control of their local area once the inevitable happened and the Hapsburg empire collapsed.

It was in the middle of this volatile and unstable situation that it was decided that the heir to the throne, Archduke Franz Ferdinand, should visit Sarajevo. Now this may sound like a mistake, then again it may not have been. Sarajevo was probably one of the most dangerous centers of radicalism in the empire. The archduke was a moderate and publicly stated that as emperor he would allow the Slavic states to form their own internal governments. This was anathema to the internal police forces of the empire, who spent most of their time putting down plots by those same Slavs. Or perhaps Ferdinand simply wanted to reassure those friendly to his empire, in one of its most hostile provinces, that he cared. So the son of the emperor made a state visit to Serbia. This is the same Serbia that has spent the last few decades dealing with civil war and ethnic cleansing. It might also be added that in the opinion of most governments, the emperor's son was not the sharpest point on the crown, at best.

In any case, Ferdinand was advised not to go to Serbia, but insisted. So at the end of June 1914, the heir to the Hapsburg throne went to Sarajevo. Knowing that this was going to be a problem, the empire's secret police went on overtime in all of Serbia and arrested many suspected terrorists. But there were so many that they were unable to get the majority of them. They left virtually untouched one group: the Slavic nationalist fanatics known as the Black Hand.

The route that the caravan of open cars carrying the Austrian archduke would take from the train station to city hall was known. In fact, it was announced so that people would be able to line up and cheer, or at least see their future emperor. Young Black Hand terrorists were spaced along that route. Each terrorist was armed with whatever they could obtain, from grenades to pistols and even a few bombs.

At the beginning of the marked route the first few waiting Black Hand had no chance to attack as the cars sped past before they were ready. Then one, a typesetter named Cabrinovic, threw a grenade. It bounced off the car carrying the archduke. When the grenade did explode, the blast injured those riding in the auto behind Ferdinand's. Some were hurt seriously enough to be hospitalized. After this incident, the auto caravan sped up again and rushed to the city hall. There the archduke reaffirmed his faith in Serbia's markedly dubious friendship with the empire and his appreciation of those who served his father's empire there.

The Austrian military commander for Serbia, General Potiorek, urged the heir to get out of the city as quickly as possible. Instead Ferdinand insisted that he first go visit those who had been injured by the grenade meant for him. A two-car caravan was formed, with the mayor of Sarajevo's vehicle leading the way to the hospital. And here is the mistake. The first car took a wrong turn. It went the wrong way at a fork in the road. As a result of their wrong turn, the open-topped auto carrying the archduke and his wife slowed to a near stop. It may have even pulled partway into an alley to turn around and get back onto the correct route.

By sheer coincidence one of the would-be assassins, Gavrilo Princip, who had failed to get a shot earlier, happened to be standing where they stopped. He had been standing in the wrong place. Princip still had his loaded pistol. When he found himself standing just a few feet from the royal couple, he quickly fired two shots. One hit Ferdinand near his heart and the other struck Duchess Sophia in the stomach. While the terrorist was quickly subdued, the damage was done. Both royals died soon after.

Within days, the Austrian army was invading Serbia. This meant that Russia, committed to support their fellow Slavic nation, declared war on Austria. So Austria turned to Germany with the expectation that Russia would back off rather than face the two of them. Russia did not back off, but instead invoked its treaty with France, who also declared war on Germany. So Germany, who already had armies on the French border ready to act, attacked into northern France. They attacked across neutral Belgium in an attempt to outflank the French army. Britain had a mutual defense treaty with Belgium and so declared war on Germany when that small nation was overrun. World War I had begun.

The mayor's driver took a wrong turn, and as a result, two weeks later, all of Europe was at war. World War I might have been inevitable anyway. But given more time and different circumstances, it may have started months or even years later. Without the fuse being lit in Sarajevo, there might have been a chance for peace. But because of that wrong turn, World War I broke out, and over the next five years, millions died.

‖‖‖

59

TOO SUCCESSFUL A
DEVIOUS PLAN

The Enemy of My Enemy

1917

‖‖‖

This mistake is one of a lack of foresight. In April 1917 a truck, sealed almost airtight, entered Germany from Bern, Switzerland. In that truck were nineteen Russians. All nineteen had been considered too dangerous to allow to travel through, or even enter, virtually any nation in Europe. Only adamantly neutral Switzerland would tolerate them. Now they were going home. One of the nineteen men in that truck was Vladimir Lenin. The Russian revolutionary had fled the czar's secret police and eventually ended up in Switzerland. From there he coordinated the actions of his outlawed and small, but fanatical, Bolshevik Party.

The start of World War I had made any communications with Russia difficult. It was a most frustrating time for a revolutionary being cut off and far from the action. Finally, Lenin approached the ambassador to Switzerland from one of the nations where he had been one of the most wanted enemies of the state, Germany. The kaiser's government did not like revolutionaries. But Germany was three years at war, and losing. One of the nations allied against Germany was controlled by the same Russian government Lenin wished to overthrow. His promise of leading a revolution and then taking Russia out of the war was enough to interest the hard-pressed Germans. They agreed to return him to his native country. It is unlikely that anyone in the German army actually expected Lenin and the Bolsheviks to really seize power. There were barely 50,000 Bolsheviks spread across dozens of cities among the tens of millions of people living in Russia. But obviously anything that distracted the new Menshevik or Kerensky government, who had kept Russia in the war after the czar abdicated, would benefit Germany.

So Vladimir Ilyich Lenin was sneaked into Russia by the German army. He was even given some operating money. To the surprise and dismay of Germany, by November Lenin had succeeded. Alexander Kerensky, a middle-class moderate, had made a number of poor decisions, including keeping Russia in the unpopular war, allowing food costs to remain so high few soldiers or workers could afford to eat, and not redistributing land to the desperate peasants who had reluctantly supported him. When the Bolsheviks finally acted, only one small military unit, the Petrograd Women's Battalion, actually fought to defend the unpopular Menshevik government.

In the short term, the German army got what it wanted. Lenin kept his word and withdrew Russia from the alliance fighting Germany. The German government then demanded a high price for what they had already done. They wanted to be given Poland, the Baltic nations, and Ukraine. Lenin and Russia refused, and with those demands and refusal, any slight goodwill between the two nations was lost. Germany assisted Poland and the White armies to battle the Red Army for almost another decade.

But by the time Russia had withdrawn from the war, it was too late to save the kaiser's war effort. The German troops who hurried west arrived in time to die in the Verdun offensive. That offensive had been the last hope for Germany to defeat the Allies before the power of the United States could affect the war. The Germans were stopped at Verdun, and soon fresh and enthusiastic American soldiers had more than balanced out any German reinforcements from the Eastern Front.

It was years until the Red Army actually controlled all of

Russia. By the time it did, the enmity with Germany was mutual and intense. Stalin now led Russia, and communists were aggressively pursuing world domination. It is surprising that Russia was almost as self-defeating when it assisted in the secret training of the German army. But that is a mistake of its own.

So while in the short term the German army got what they wanted by smuggling Lenin back into Russia, doing so may have been one of the worst judgment calls ever made in the twentieth century. The Bolsheviks were one of the smallest and most radical of all the many revolutionary movements in Russia. Without Lenin's genius, the Bolsheviks would likely have remained a minor, extremist group of no importance. The much more moderate Mensheviks, or at least a less reasonable populist government, would instead have emerged.

No Lenin, then no Stalin. The millions of Ukrainians and Kulaks Stalin killed to allow the collectivization of the farms and factories would have lived. In Germany, the strong Communist Party led to a political reaction that in 1933 put the Nazi Party in power. So if those German intelligence officials had not decided to send Lenin back to Russia, there might not have been the mass programs and starvation in Russia in the 1930s: no Nazis, no Holocaust, no World War II, no Cold War, no Mao Zedong, no Castro. Assisting Lenin and enabling the Bolshevik revolution that gave rise to communism just may be one of the worst, world-changing mistakes in this book.

60

||||||||||||||||||||||||||||||||||||||||||||||||||||||||||||||||||

THINKING SHORT
TERM

A Fine Crop of Dust

1917

||||||||||||||||||||||||||||||||||||||||||||||||||||||||||||||||||

Europe was hungry. World War I was raging, and many European farmers were now in the army. The nitrates that would have gone into fertilizer were being used to make munitions. So it was decided that the United States needed to grow more food. The way to do that was to plow formerly unused lands and plant wheat or corn on them. This came at a time when there was also a period of unusually high rainfall. That was fortunate in that it made a lot of marginal land productive. It was unfortunate because the extra rainfall didn't last.

The encouragement to plant came from the U.S. Food Administration (USFA), which was founded as part of the Food and Fuel Control Act passed August 10, 1917. The USFA was created to encourage more food production and to control the distribution of agricultural products. So the USFA turned to the most traditional way to encourage an activity. They offered a bonus payment for every acre on which corn was planted. The bonus was enough to make corn growing profitable even on marginal land. Even less fertile soil in normally dryer states was used to grow wheat. The guaranteed high prices from the USFA subsidized the plowing of new lands in such states as Kansas, Oklahoma, Texas, and New

Mexico. The soil in those states was normally too dry for wheat, but thanks to a few seasons of unusually high rains, large crops of wheat were possible.

When World War I ended so did the subsidies. A few of the new farms were able to get in several more good wheat crops, but many others were abandoned. Within a decade, there were only a few of the new farms left. They were replaced by ranchers raising cattle and horses, just like the farmers had replaced those ranchers when the land was first converted to crops. But there was a difference now. Before the land was farmed, the soil had been held together by the roots of sturdy, slow-growing grass. But that grass had all been plowed under. So with that ground cover gone, the hooves of the animals chewed up the unprotected soil.

Then in 1934, strong winds blew for weeks across the Southwest. Millions of acres of already pulverized soil turned to dust. Dust clouds, know as dusters or black blizzards, covered the skies. When they had ended, what little fertility the dry land once had was gone. So badly had the soil been ruined that any period of high winds created mini dust bowls up to as late as the 1950s.

For a few years, American wheat was able to feed the doughboys and our allies. The cost of that wheat was millions of acres of grazing land lost. The lives of tens of thousands of farmers were ruined and the Great Depression was made even worse. The drama was so tragic and widespread that it was the theme of one of John Steinbeck's greatest novels, *The Grapes of Wrath*.

This pattern is recurring again today. In China the need for food led to the plowing of the lands adjoining their northern deserts. Today those deserts grow at a rate of 1,500 square miles per year and on some days the red dust clouds over Beijing are so thick that you cannot breathe without a mask. It appears this is one world-changing mistake we keep on making.

61

RIGHTEOUSNESS
OVER REALITY

Prohibition: The Noble
Experiment?

1917

The reign of tears is over. The slums will soon be a memory. We will turn our prisons into factories and our jails into storehouses and corncribs. Men will walk upright now, women will smile, and children will laugh. Hell will be forever for rent." Such was the opinion of the Reverend Billy Sunday, a proponent of Prohibition, one of the biggest domestic mistakes in U.S. History. Despite Sunday's hyperbolic assertion that it was the panacea to all of society's ills, it was not long before Prohibition came to be seen as an abysmal failure.

Prohibition, commonly called the "Noble Experiment," was the anti-alcohol movement that gained steam throughout the nineteenth century and became a staple of the progressive movement at the start of the twentieth century. By 1900, more than half of the states had become dry states, which prohibited the sale of alcohol. The Prohibitionists believed that there was no way a person in a dry state could obtain liquor. However, they overlooked the postal service, which was run by the federal government, not the states. So alcohol could be purchased from a wet state and sent to a dry state.

When that loophole was discovered, the Interstate Liquor Act was passed in 1913, making it illegal to send alcohol to any dry state. Again, that caused more problems for the "dries" because after that law was enacted, there was no longer a legal way to get alcohol in a dry state. Soon illegal methods were proliferating, with crime syndicates and the liquor industry partnering up.

Though neither Woodrow Wilson nor his opponent, Charles Hughes, prioritized the Prohibition issue in the 1916 election, the forces of the temperance movement gained enough congressional and public support to propose the Eighteenth Amendment to the Constitution in 1917, banning the sale and manufacture of liquor in the United States. Many states did not agree with the proposed amendment, so it was debated for two more years. The Prohibition movement had support from an array of sources, from various Protestant groups, to the Women's Christian Temperance Union, to the KKK; the opposition was spearheaded by immigrant groups and Catholics. Sympathizers for each position could be found in both political parties.

On January 29, 1919, the Eighteenth Amendment was ratified, but it was not to take effect until a year later. It banned all hard liquor with more than 40 percent alcohol content (80 proof). Many of the amendment's original supporters were under the impression that it banned only hard liquor and thought they could still legally consume wine and beer. But in October 1919, the Volstead Act was passed prohibiting the sale and manufacture of all drinks with more than 0.5 percent alcohol content. Basically, any beverage with any alcohol content at all was banned.

The aim of Prohibition was obviously to reduce or eliminate the consumption of alcohol, but proponents believed the societal benefits would extend far beyond that goal. However, the end result was far from beneficial. During the years between 1920 and 1933 when the national prohibition of alcohol was in effect, the United States saw a dramatic increase in violence, organized crime, and corruption. The Prohibition of alcohol created a lucrative black market that crime lords, such as Al Capone, took advantage of. The Mafia grew in strength during Prohibition, and the rate of robbery also increased markedly. During those years, the homicide rate shot up by an alarming 78 percent. Saloons were replaced by speakeasies, illegal alcohol distribution centers that became increasingly common during the Prohibition era. These institutions became particularly prevalent in large cities, where the majority were run by crime syndicates. Violent crime peaked in 1933, the year Prohibition was repealed, and steadily declined in the years after that. When you criminalize the common man, crime becomes common and even accepted.

Even in the area of reducing alcohol consumption, Prohibition failed. While there was a small initial decrease in consumption, this decrease was short-lived. It was not long before consumption levels were higher than pre-Prohibition levels. Arrests of drunk drivers increased by 81 percent during the Prohibition years. Increases in consumption were mirrored by similar increases in money spent on enforcement. While speakeasies were frequently broken up by law enforcement, the black market was simply too profitable to stop the spread of alcohol. Moreover, corruption was rampant at all levels of government, be it in the form of a crooked cop or a bribe-taking politician. Millions of dollars were wasted in an ineffective attempt at eliminating alcohol; this lost money was compounded by the lost revenue that would have been generated via taxation and continued even into the Great Depression.

A quality problem lay beyond the increase in consumption. Alcohol became more frequently adulterated by toxic substances. If you make something illegal, you can't protect the public from harmful forms of it. In addition, alcoholic beverages became substantially more potent; estimates suggest alcohol products on average contained 50 percent more alcohol than before Prohibition. Moonshine, white mule whiskey, and other dangerous beverages became common. A consequence of this was that the death rate from alcohol poisoning nearly quadrupled during the Prohibition era. While some Prohibitionists disregarded the effect on alcoholics and instead expressed hope that they were reaching out to younger populations through education, the average age of individuals dying from alcoholism fell by six months during Prohibition. Moreover, Prohibition encouraged the use of drugs, such as opium, marijuana, and cocaine as a substitute for alcohol.

These are substances that many people would have never come in contact with until Prohibition.

The cumulative effect of Prohibition's numerous failings was a shift in public opinion in favor of repealing the amendment. Repeal was particularly popular in cities. Despite Senator Morris Sheppard's famous assertion that "there is as much chance of repealing the Eighteenth Amendment as there is for a hummingbird to fly to the planet Mars with the Washington Monument tied to its tail," opposition became heated during the Roaring Twenties and at the start of the Great Depression. Eventually Franklin Roosevelt was forced to moderate the federal position on alcohol; he allowed the brewing of certain beers and light wines. This paved the way for full-fledged repeal in December 1933 with the ratification of the Twenty-first Amendment. Roosevelt famously quipped, "I think this would be a good time for a beer." The decision to prohibit alcohol was restored to individual state legislatures.

After the repeal of Prohibition, many of the problems it created were reversed. While many state and local dry laws stayed intact through the era of federal regulation, others were gone forever with the obvious failure of Prohibition. Crime syndicates and all of their related evils remained. The widespread use of illegal drugs continued to stay an increasing problem that has yet to find a solution.

The Noble Experiment of Prohibition was a mistake completely self-inflicted on the country by the federal government. It had consequences that still reverberate throughout American society. Prohibition was one of the largest domestic mistakes in American legislative history, and it negatively changed the United States forever.

62

||||||||||||||||||||||||||||||||||||||||||||||||||||||||||||||||||||

MEANINGLESS GESTURE

When the United States Invaded Russia

1918

||||||||||||||||||||||||||||||||||||||||||||||||||||||||||||||||||||

You will never hear about it in the United States, but be assured anytime you discuss relations between the two countries with a Russian, the American army's invasion of Russia will come up. Yep, that is correct, the time that the United States really did invade Russia. We landed, occupied a major city, and stayed for months. The entire fiasco started in 1918 during the last months of World War I.

In 1917, the new Bolshevik government basically surrendered to Germany and dropped out of the war. This upset the Allies as it potentially freed about seventy divisions of German troops that could be moved to the Western Front. President Woodrow Wilson decided that he needed to do something about this, preferably replacing the Bolsheviks with someone who would rejoin the war effort. Things were very unstable in all of Russia with the White Army fighting the Red and private armies fighting everyone. So it was decided to send a military force to Russia.

The expedition would consist of 9,000 soldiers commanded by a rather confused and soon frustrated Major General William Graves. General Graves' previous position had been protecting San Francisco from German attack. This was not a job that prepared him for the task, but his appointment was convenient as the ships would sail from that city. Normally, sending thousands of troops halfway across the world involves meticulous planning and detailed orders. What Graves got was a short note. Vague and without specific orders, the note listed goals like "overthrow the Russian government" and instructions to avoid conflict when possible. Graves' final orders came from the secretary of war, given in a Kansas train station and consisting of only "God bless you and goodbye." With that, Graves rode to San Francisco, gathered up 9,000 men, most of whom had been garrison troops, and with virtually no heavy artillery sailed for Russia.

The purported excuse for the United States sending in the army was that they were there to assist in the evacuation of 30,000 anti-German Czech soldiers who had become unemployed when Russia dropped out of the war. They were known as the Czech Legion and were Austrian deserters who had been willing to fight against Germany and Austria for Russia. The men of the Legion were known to be making their way along the Trans-Siberian railway west toward its terminus at the city of Vladivostok on the Kamchatka Peninsula.

When General Graves and the doughboys arrived in Vladivostok, they discovered that there were just over a thousand British and another thousand French soldiers already there for the same purpose. There were also nearby about 72,000 Japanese soldiers who weren't even faking a good reason. They were admittedly on the peninsula for the purpose of grabbing large tracts of Siberia for Japan. Japan in World War I was allied to Britain, France, and the United States. Also among the many groups running around with lots of guns was a Cossack army of more than 15,000 horsemen and a fluctuating number of other White Russian troops of widely varying quality.

The Czech Legion was there as well, but it hardly needed anyone's help. The legion was not only firmly in control of the city of Vladivostok itself, but it had units occupying most of the stations and cities that the Trans-Siberian Railroad passed through. They were effectively running and maintaining the railroad and protecting it from everyone else. Made up of highly competent and well-armed veterans, no one wanted to antagonize the Czechs. This arrangement suited everyone as it meant the trains kept running and remained effectively neutral. However, it did enrage Trotsky, who issued an unenforceable order for the legion to surrender its weapons. The few times Red units had attacked the Czech Legion, they had suffered heavy losses and accomplished nothing. Once the legion had moved west along the railroad, there was little Moscow could do to them. So the last thing the Czechs wanted was help from the Americans. They had things completely under control and even provided the police who patrolled Vladivostok.

That all rather begged the question of what 9,000 American soldiers were doing in a city 5,000 miles from Moscow. To get any farther away from the capital while still being in Russia, the Americans would have had to have been treading water in the Pacific. Worse yet, the Yanks were under vague orders to overthrow the Bolshevik government, but the Bolsheviks didn't control any territory within a thousand miles of them. But it was just as well since they weren't supposed to shoot at anyone while overthrowing the government of a nation spanning nine time zones with a population of more than 20 million. So for months, Graves and his troopers did nothing. Well, they actually did a lot, but it all involved bars and brothels.

Eventually, some U.S. troops did assist in patrolling some of the railroad line and even had a few tense scenes with the local Cossack warlords. Finally, months after World War I had ended, the Czech Legion all gathered in Vladivostok and boarded ships sent by the French to transport them home. This left Graves and his Americans in charge of the city. But with the war over, their secret mission of regime change was meaningless. But the Americans hung on until they had been there for more than a year. Finally in November 1919, following the example of the British and French, Graves and his invasion force boarded boats and returned to the States. Casualties had been 137 dead in action, mostly from Cossack snipers and outright bandits, and 216 from other causes. These included accidents, illness, and a range of sexually transmitted diseases.

There never was a clear purpose to sending over thousands of doughboys and even less of a reason for keeping them in Russia for more than a year after the Great War had ended. All that Graves' expedition accomplished was to enrich Vladivostok's red-light district and antagonize the Bolsheviks by rubbing in their faces that they could do nothing about the foreign occupation of their largest Pacific port. What the expedition did accomplish was to cement a permanent distrust of all Western governments toward communist ideology.

||||||||||||||||||||||||||||||||||||||||||||||||||||||||||||||||

63

POLITICAL SCIENCE
Lamarckism
1920

||||||||||||||||||||||||||||||||||||||||||||||||||||||||||||||||||||

Even after Charles Darwin's *On the Origin of Species* was published, there was a good deal to be discovered about how animals evolved over time. Along with Darwin's approach, which stated that nature favored variations that helped the individual survive long enough to reproduce, there was also Lamarck's theory. He believed something that was subtly, but significantly, different. Jean-Baptiste Lamarck believed that animals inherited traits that were acquired by their parents. What he believed was that if an animal changed due to its environment, its children would inherit that change. This was no slow process of natural selection over millions of years, but one that could take place in a fraction of that period. For example, Lamarckism says that if you cut the tail off a lizard, that lizard's offspring will have slightly shorter tails. If you cut the tails off that generation, the next generation of lizards would have tails that were even shorter. Eventually, if you cut off enough tails, the baby lizards will be born without one. This contrasts with how Darwin explained the giraffe's long neck by stating that the giraffe's longer necks gave them an edge in eating, and so they were healthier and had more babies who shared their long neck characteristic. Lamarck said that because the parents stretched their necks by trying to eat leaves high on a tree, their offspring were born with longer necks.

Almost every real scientist rejected Lamarckism because it simply does not test out in the laboratory: The tails stay long. Changing the body of an animal or the attitudes of one person does not change his or her genes. But the theory found acceptance in one nation in the 1920s. This was Soviet Russia. Lenin was aware of it and favored it. Lamarckism underlay his theories of how a state evolved and how communism could bring about a paradise on earth. In the 1920s, another leader decided that Lamarckism, no matter how scientifically bad, was correct. That made all the difference because that one man was Joseph Stalin. Why Stalin preferred Lamarck's theory is obvious. Communism intended to change humanity and make it into something better. Under Lamarckism, all the horrors of the Stalin era were acceptable if they changed the next generation to be more communist, to be more aware and group-minded. And the generation after that would be even more communist thinking because their parents were forced to be. And in just a few generations everyone would be born good, selfless communists, and the need for the state would go away. If millions died being shipped to Siberia so that their farms could be collectivized, that was okay because in a few generations the descendants of those who remained would be perfect collective thinkers. This theory justified any action, because if you stressed or pushed humans in the right way, you could quickly change their very nature. The end justified the means.

By the 1940s, Lamarckism was the only acceptable view of evolution and genetics allowed in the Soviet Union. Pushed by a poorly educated animal breeder named Lysenko, any scientist who disagreed with the theory or attempted to use any other theory in their laboratories was fired or even sent to a gulag, where most died. With Lysenko in charge, politics, not science, was the basis of all scientific papers and teaching. Real genetics was effectively banned and ideology replaced experimentation. Another destructive result Lamarckism had on Russia came from its having been the basis of the techniques used to improve crops and in animal husbandry. This invalid basis guaranteed failures, which had to have added to the food shortages that recurred throughout the Stalin era. It was not until a full decade after Stalin died, in 1965, that Lamarckism was finally condemned publicly by scientists in Russia. The theory of Lamarckism was known to be just bad science by 1900, but its theories suited Stalin and justified his murdering millions of humans.

64

AIDING THE ENEMY

Irony

1926

|||||||||||||||||||||||||||||||||||||||||||||||||||||||||||||||||||||||||||||||||||||

The Treaty of Versailles severely limited the size and nature of the German army. The intention was to make sure that Germany was never able to again attack its neighbors. In this, the treaty failed miserably. The main reason was Germany quickly found a way to circumvent the restrictions. The irony of how they did this is that Germany and Russia both gained and lost terribly by cooperating. Not to mention the tragedy their actions later thrust on the rest of the world.

Within a few years of being forced to sign the Versailles Treaty, the German army chafed unbearably under its restrictions. Soon, they began to find a way around virtually every clause. The real breakthrough for the Wehrmacht was the Treaty of Rapallo signed in 1922 between Russia and Germany. The inspiration for the treaty was that both nations were being treated like pariahs by the rest of Europe. The Germans were maligned due to World War I, and Russia was hated for being communist. This new treaty called on both Russia and Germany to "co-operate in a spirit of mutual goodwill in meeting the economic needs of both countries." While the treaty was publicly signed on April 16, 1922, the important part was the secret annex to that treaty signed the following July 29.

One of the Versailles restrictions was that the Wehrmacht could not have any tanks. The secret agreements in the Treaty of Rapallo provided a way for the German army to have and train with tanks. The German army could not make or use tanks in Germany without being caught by France or England, and the Soviets wanted to learn tank building and tank warfare. Thus the Germans were given the use of a tank school and test ground in Russia near the city of Kazan in trade for knowledge. Starting in 1926, the German army trained hundreds of men in tank warfare and refined their combat techniques with live war games. It could be said that the Blitzkrieg was birthed not in Germany but on those dusty Russian fields. Of course, the Russians benefited as well. German engineers helped them modernize their tank production, and the Kazan school became a vital part of their World War II armored training. Both sides even tested new tank designs and weapons there.

The German army was also forbidden to have or train in most types of aircraft. By 1923, the German army was training Soviet officers and pilots in exchange for the use of aircraft and the opportunity to train its own pilots as well. German engineers were assisting in many areas in the industrialization of Russia. Hundreds of German pilots flew and practiced in forbidden aircraft in the late 1920s and early 1930s at joint air schools near Lipetsk, Russia. Both sides also even developed poison gasses near the Volga River town of Saratov.

By 1930, because of German assistance and guidance, the first Soviet mechanized brigade was formed. In 1933, Adolf Hitler became chancellor and announced that Germany would no longer accept the restrictions of the Versailles Treaty. Cooperation slowed, then ended. Eight years later, the armored columns of the Wehrmacht tore into Russia at the beginning of Operation Barbarossa. Four years later, hundreds of victorious Soviet tanks swarmed Berlin. Allowing the Germans to train in their country was certainly a disastrous mistake for the Russians as viewed in 1941. Russia took an estimated 20 million casualties, civilian and military, before the German invasion, spearheaded by armored officers who first learned their trade near Kazan. Teaching the Russians tank warfare and how to manufacture better tanks was perhaps an even greater mistake. By 1944, the German army was being overwhelmed by thousands of T34 and KV Russian tanks. Each side made a great mistake in assisting the other. Who paid the higher price is open to debate.

65

A SLOB SAVES LIVES

Mold

1928

This is perhaps the classic example of a mistake that changed the world for the better. In this case, the world benefited as a result of bad laboratory technique. It was technique at its worst followed by science at its best.

To be able to connect a result with an action or reaction in science you try to eliminate as many outside variables as possible. In chemistry, this means making sure no outside chemical or organic material contaminates your samples. In 1928, Alexander Fleming, an otherwise brilliant scientist, accidentally left a bacteria sample uncovered by an open window. Fleming's lab was notoriously disorganized, and this was likely not the first time his samples had been contaminated. By the time he had discovered the mistake, which of course should have rendered the sample useless, a number of mold spores had begun to grow in the rich solution in the petri dish. This one happened to be used to grow the deadly staphylococcus bacteria.

There were several ruined samples in petri dishes, but one was different. Fortunately for the world, Fleming took a careful look at the results of his mistake. Upon detailed examination, he saw that one of the molds was doing something no one had ever seen anything do before. It was killing the bacteria near it. Later, he was able to determine that this particular mold grew on, among other things, bread left out too long. Finding the mold in the petri dish led Fleming and his team to create the first antibiotic. This was penicillin, which has since saved tens of millions of lives.

66

||||||||||||||||||||||||||||||||||||||||||||||||||||||||||||||||

DOING NOTHING

Herbert Hoover and the
Great Depression

1929

||||||||||||||||||||||||||||||||||||||||||||||||||||||||||||||||

As Herbert Hoover assumed the mantle of president in 1929, one of his most famous assertions had been "We in America today are nearer to the final triumph over poverty than ever before in the history of any land." Less than a year later the country was in the throes of recession, witnessing a financial crisis that was to cause poverty and unemployment rates to skyrocket. The recession was precipitated by a cyclical downturn in the market but exacerbated by misguided economic policies. It was Hoover's ineptitude that deepened the crisis. While he somewhat justifiably became a scapegoat for the economic crisis, his failures were not reversed by his successor, Roosevelt, and their combined actions extended the duration of and worsened the intensity of the Great Depression.

Hoover had secured the Republican nomination for presidency in 1928 despite never having been elected to public office. He had attained great fame under President Woodrow Wilson by organizing the rationing of food for World War I and for his humanitarian efforts on behalf of persons starving in the wake of the war. His mystique was enhanced by his extensive role in the Harding and Coolidge administrations as the secretary of commerce, a previously unimportant cabinet position that attained great significance under his watch. He became one of the most instrumental figures in the economic boom of the early to middle 1920s, a period that oversaw an overextension of credit that portended ill for the future. Nonetheless, Hoover was viewed as a wallet-friendly candidate and surged to the presidency despite Coolidge's lukewarm opinion of him.

While there are many competing theories for the origin of the Great Depression, it is apparent that Hoover did not particularly err in the months leading up to its beginning. In October 1929, on Black Tuesday, the stock market experienced a monumental collapse that precipitated the most severe economic downturn of the twentieth century. While the stock market modestly rebounded in successive months, the crash had a tremendous negative effect on consumer confidence. The decline in stock prices facilitated the bankruptcies of many lenders. Many economic historians suggest the inaction of the Federal Reserve in preventing the collapse of these banks massively exacerbated the crisis.

In June 1930, Hoover signed into law the Smoot-Hawley Tariff Act. This protectionist gesture resulted in a deepening economic crisis worldwide. Hoover's miscues extended beyond the tariff. Various policies aimed at encouraging job sharing and propping up wages have since been determined to be responsible for close to two-thirds of the drop in gross domestic product (GDP) in the two years that followed the crash. Hoover tried to keep industrial wages too high; the result was that unemployment increased and the GDP suffered. Contrary to many historical critics of Hoover, he rejected the arguments of his treasury secretary, Andrew Mellon, in favor of a laissez-faire response to the crisis that would treat it as a cyclical event from which the economy would naturally rebound. Roosevelt's policies based on this model are often considered to have increased the duration of the depression by several years.

On Hoover's watch, unemployment reached almost 25 percent. The number of homeless Americans dramatically increased. This resulted in a proliferation of shantytowns across the country, which were derisively referred to as "Hoovervilles." Hoover championed the Federal Home Loan Bank Act in an effort to spur the construction of new homes and reverse the tide of homelessness, but his actions were too little, too late. Before the downturn, Mellon had overseen a tremendous decrease in taxes on the upper economic echelon of society—the top income tax rate had been cut from 73 percent to 24 percent. To finance various public works projects later in his term, Hoover largely reversed these cuts; the consequence of such a considerable tax increase was substantially mitigated economic growth.

In 1931, Hoover urged major banks to form a consortium called the National Credit Corporation (NCC). Hoover encouraged but did not force major banks to loan money to smaller banks that were experiencing difficulties. NCC members were understandably leery of taking such actions, and loans were rarely given. A year later, Hoover helped secure the Emergency Relief and Construction Act, a last-ditch effort to increase loans to financial institutions, farmers, and railroads. Though it had little effect at the time, its efforts were extended by Roosevelt.

In 1932, Hoover lost in a landslide to Franklin D. Roosevelt due to his failings on the economy and on Prohibition. The election was pivotal from the perspective that it ushered in a realignment of political views. Roosevelt would be elected four times and oversee a period of Democratic domination in American politics. Considering the crises Roosevelt faced as president (including the Depression and World War II), it is difficult to imagine what the world would look like had Hoover's ineptitude not assisted in this political revolution. Nonetheless, Hoover's failings should not absolve his successor. Roosevelt continued many of Hoover's economically ruinous policies, and in so doing extended the duration of the Depression. Unemployment remained high throughout Roosevelt's New Deal policies. It was only after the onset of World War II that the United States truly dug itself out of its rut. Nonetheless, Hoover became the electoral scapegoat for his actions; then he later became the historical scapegoat due to the favorable impression many had of Roosevelt's economic policies. It is for these reasons that Hoover will always be remembered as a humanitarian who became an abysmal president whose economic mistakes changed America and the world forever.

67

BAD BUSINESS

Smoot-Hawley

1930

F ew bits of legislation have managed to do the damage that the Smoot-Hawley Tariff Act, passed in 1930, did to the American and world economy. The bill was introduced by the chair of the House Ways and Means Committee, Willis Hawley, and the chair of the Senate Finance Committee, Reed Smoot. The preceding fall, the stock market had crashed, and this bill was an attempt to revive the American economy. To do this, the act created a stiff tariff on more than 20,000 foreign imports. The plan was to suck money from Europe in the form of tariffs and to make European goods more expensive so that American-made items would have a distinct sales advantage. The bill easily passed a panicky Congress and doubled the effective duties on many manufactured and agricultural products.

The real effect of Smoot-Hawley was almost exactly the opposite of its intent. The European nations, seeing their products being virtually locked out of the U.S. market, passed their own protective tariff bills in retaliation. This meant that most American goods up to doubled in price all over Europe. By 1932, the trade war Smoot-Hawley had started was in full swing.

In 1929, the United States had exported about $4.5 million

worth of goods to Europe. A million dollars went pretty far in 1930, when a loaf of bread cost $0.09. By 1931, all U.S. exports there totaled only $1.5 million. Two-thirds of all imports from the United States had been blocked out by the protective tariffs passed between 1930 and 1932. Imports to the States diminished just as quickly, going from $5.5 million to just over $2 million by 1932.

But no one bought new American goods from new American factories to replace the more expensive European imports that the Smoot-Hawley bill blocked out. Had they been able to do so, it might have worked. The reason they could not was that many of the consumers no longer had the money to buy much of anything. This was because of the millions of jobs lost as factories closed because they no longer could export their products to Europe. The unemployed were unable to buy American-made goods, much less more. Job losses made the Depression much worse. Not only were the jobs at the exporters lost, but many American jobs were gone as well. The American agricultural sector also largely depended on exports, and so protectionism made it impossible for farmers to sell their crops. This forced down the price paid for agricultural products. Lower prices put many farmers and farm workers out of work and cost thousands of families their farms.

When a quarter of the buyers of your product suddenly have no money, then your sales are down 25 percent. So you have to lay off some of your workers, cut wages, or eliminate benefits to enable your business to survive. But increasing the number of employed and paying workers less mean that sales for everyone are down again. The unemployed or financially strapped workers have less money to spend. As they continue to spend less, domestic sales continue to plummet and more workers lose their jobs. This cycle of unemployment creating more unemployment, which Smoot-Hawley reinforced, continued until World War II and wartime spending ended it.

The Smoot-Hawley Act had exactly the opposite effect of what was intended. Rather than helping to end a depression, which was started mostly by bad monetary policies, the tariffs it created made the financial situation much worse. Those tariffs caused a trade war that guaranteed that the 1930s saw not just another recession, but the Great Depression.

Reed Smoot and Willis Hawley were soundly defeated in the 1932 elections. Those workers whose jobs they had destroyed voted them out. By 1944, most nations had done away with the worst of the tariffs the bill had created and the postwar recovery became the greatest expansion of wealth in recorded history. It is only in the last few years that a return to protective tariffs for some businesses have reappeared. They were a mistake that changed the world and made a bad economic situation terrible. Let us hope today's leaders have learned from history.

68

TASTY MISTAKE

A Failed Recipe

1930

One day in 1930, the innkeeper of the Toll House Inn wanted to make something different as a dessert. Her name was Ruth Wakefield, which I mention because we should all be grateful to her. She was making a type of butter cookie that had been around since the colonial times. To make these cookies different, she decided to add a chocolate flavor to them. Normally, a baker would accomplish this by adding cocoa powder. The problem was Mrs. Wakefield was out of cocoa powder. So she decided to substitute what she had on hand. The innkeeper and baker cut up a Nestle's chocolate bar and dropped the pieces into her dough. After all, the temperature at which cookies bake is hot enough to melt chocolate, or so she thought. She later admitted that she assumed the chocolate would melt into the cookies, giving them a nice, even chocolate flavor. The innkeeper had expected to pull out chocolate cookies, but to her surprise the pieces of chocolate remained intact. Though they were a bit melted, rather than chocolate cookies, she had butter cookies with pieces of chocolate in them. She called them her Toll House crunch cookies, but they are known today as chocolate chip cookies. Her reward from Nestle, whose sales skyrocketed after they put her recipe on their packaging, was a lifetime supply of chocolate. Here is one mistake that definitely changed the world for the better. Yumm.

||||||||||||||||||||||||||||||||||||||||||||||||||||||||||||||||||||||

69

FAILURE TO ACT

The Schwarze Kapelle

1938

||||||||||||||||||||||||||||||||||||||||||||||||||||||||||||||||||||||

This mistake was probably the greatest missed opportunity in the twentieth century. It occurred in August 1938 and involved the British prime minister, Neville Chamberlain. Those who have read any history of World War II have already heard about how appeasement instead of strength eventually led to the shooting part of World War II, when Hitler invaded Czechoslovakia later that year. What is less well-known is the tremendous opportunity Chamberlain had laid at his door and passed up. Though in making this blunder he had help from many others, including Winston Churchill.

It was in August 1938 that a well-respected noble and land-owner, Ewald von Kleist-Schmenzin, arrived in England. He represented a secret organization in Germany known as the Schwarze Kapelle, the Black Orchestra. This organization included a number of important and prominent German leaders, notably General Ludwig Beck, who had run the general staff since 1935 and supervised the resurgence of the German army. Beck had resigned because he feared, correctly, that Hitler was going to lead Germany into a disastrous war. This conspiracy also included Admiral Canaris, the head of the Abwehr and other powerful individuals. The purpose of the Schwarze Kapelle was to eliminate Hitler and re-store democracy to Germany. There was every reason to think that the coup, for it was a coup, would work. Many of the German generals felt unready for war and were concerned about the highly aggressive stand Adolf Hitler was taking on almost every foreign question. The group also included important business leaders.

The plan was to capture Hitler, so as not to make him a martyr and start a civil war. Once they had him in custody they would put him on trial for crimes against the German people. There were several other important Nazi leaders to be imprisoned as well, including Hermann Goering, recently made a field marshal; Hein-rich Himmler, the head of the SS; and Reinhard Heydrich, who controlled the SD, the security service of the SS. There was a strong expectation that the generals would rally behind their re-moval. All the conspirators needed was a strong sign of outside support. This would expose the error of Hitler's opportunism. It would also show the undecided that Germany itself was being placed in an unnecessarily risky position by Hitler and that under-standing would provide the impetus to guarantee the revolt's success. All they needed was a strong stand by Britain and World War II would be averted. In Beck's words, "If you can bring me positive proof that the British will make war if [Hitler] invades Czechoslovakia, I will put an end to the Nazi regime!"

Kleist-Schmenzin arrived and was hustled past customs by six MI6 agents. All that was needed was a public statement by the British government that if Hitler went through with his plans to occupy Czechoslovakia, they would declare war; then he could act. The plans for this invasion were complete, troops were being placed, and orders distributed to the German commanders. We now see that this visit was quite literally the last opportunity to stop the plunge of Europe into war. It must not have been that clear then.

The first meeting Kleist-Schmenzin had was with a Lord Lloyd, an influential member of the ruling party. It is likely this was a sort of initial screening that the Schwarze Kapelle passed. A meeting occurred the next day between Kleist-Schmenzin and Robert Vansittart, an important adviser to the government on foreign affairs. Vansittart was more concerned about what would happen to things like Germany's borders after the coup, rather than in assisting with the coup itself. But the next day, Kleist-Schmenzin met with the first lord of the navy, Winston Churchill. He again recounted the plans of the conspirators to a silent Churchill. The future wartime prime minister stayed noncommittal until the German was about to leave, and then he said only that he would be interested in working with them only after they brought down Hitler. This was the position that the Chamberlain government chose to take. They would do nothing until the coup was already a success.

In fact, quite the opposite occurred. A few weeks later, on September 13, Neville Chamberlain sent Hitler a note asking for a meeting. Hitler was enthused that he was being given the recognition from the British and that they had come to him. They met in Munich on September 30, and rather than confront Hitler, Chamberlain made every effort to appease him. They signed an agreement to guarantee "peace for our time," which most certainly didn't occur. What it did allow was the occupation of Czechoslovakia by the Nazis, with no resistance from Britain or France. The Schwarze Kapelle was helpless. With Hitler having been triumphant in a bloodless takeover and the Allies showing they had no stomach for challenging the Nazis, the conspiracy was unable to act.

A few harsh words about the invasion of Czechoslovakia, and there might not have been a World War II and nearly a hundred million lives would have been saved. Rather than supporting the Schwarze Kapelle, the British government chose appeasement. The world was never the same again.

‖‖

70

DEALING WITH
THE DEVIL
Green Light
1939

‖‖

In August 1939 Joseph Stalin made a mistake, one that deeply affected not only the Soviet Union but also the rest of the world. The mistake was that on August 23, 1939, the dictator of the communist empire signed a secret protocol with Adolf Hitler. The document was a clear blueprint for a political alliance between Russia and Germany. It included economic exchanges, cultural exchanges, and even military cooperation. Effectively, this agreement laid the basis for the two nations to divide eastern Europe between them. One provision stated that should Germany invade Poland, Stalin would order the now-infamous "stab in the back." Russia promised to also invade the already prostrate nation from the east and occupy a large part of it.

There was a very good argument to be made that it was to Russia's advantage. Their army had been crippled by purges and the failures of a botched invasion of Finland. But by signing this pact with Germany, Joseph Stalin also guaranteed the start of World War II. One of the Nazis' greatest fears was a two-front war. This had proved disastrous for Germany only a few decades before in World War I. This pact guaranteed that would not happen again. Ironically, they were right, and when Hitler chose to disregard the agreement two years later, it began a series of events that resulted in the total defeat of the Third Reich. The pact removed the last real check on German aggression. Britain and France maintained a continuing attitude of appeasement. America's stand was one of adamant neutrality that even a concerned Franklin Roosevelt could not change. With Russia neutralized, there simply was no one else strong enough to stop the Nazis.

Stalin had many reasons to think this protocol was a good idea. One was that it left his own occupation of Ukraine, Belarus, the Baltic states, and the eastern part of Russia's old nemesis, Poland, unchallenged. Another appeal was that it played to Stalin's need to create a buffer zone that reached about 200 kilometers from the actual Russian border. Perhaps most important, Adolf Hitler had been working hard on the Western democracies to join with him in a crusade against the communists. Stalin had a real fear Hitler might succeed. It had been barely twenty years since most of the Western nations and Japan had sent military units into Russia to support the White Russian, anti-Bolshevik armies. Finally, it appears from the now-available records that Stalin actually believed that any war between Germany and Russia could be avoided. This was, in retrospect, wishful thinking, but that belief not only caused him to sign the protocol but also led to orders that crippled the Russian army when the Wehrmacht invaded two years later. So desperately did Stalin hold on to the belief that Hitler would obey the terms of this pact that German troops passed trains of raw materials from Russia still delivering resources as agreed, hours after Operation Barbarossa had begun in 1941. Leopold Unger, a Polish-Belgian author and historian, is unquestionably correct in calling the 1939 protocol the "most cynical operation of the World War II, and the founding document of the post-war Soviet empire in Europe." This agreement also effectively ended discussions on another pact, the Tripartite Pact between Britain, France, and Russia, which was also designed to ensure peace and hold Hitler at bay. So, effectively, Stalin decided to believe Adolf Hitler and Germany—which had attacked Russia in World War I—instead of trusting his allies from that same war.

In the lens of history, there are fewer more obvious, world-changing mistakes than Joseph Stalin cutting a deal with the devil. Perhaps the only greater mistake Stalin made was believing that the agreement was anything but Realpolitik: something cynically done by Hitler only for passing expediency. So while the Nazi–Soviet pact of 1939 gave Russia the illusion of security, in reality it gave the Nazis a green light to attack Poland and then France. It was a major factor in the start of World War II. Believing the assurances of peace with Russia, which Hitler betrayed the first chance he got, was more than just a mistake. It sold out not only Poland and western Europe but, in the end, was even more costly to Russia itself. Almost exactly two years after signing the nonaggression and cooperation pact, Hitler attacked Russia. Stalin was so dismayed that he had a virtual breakdown and was ineffective for the crucial first days of the invasion. The result of his mistake was the loss of millions of Russian lives, half the Russian population suffering from Nazi occupation, and the destruction of much of the manufacturing base of the Soviet Union. It was a terrible price for a short-term agreement. Rarely has anyone's judgment proven so wrong.

71

||||||||||||||||||||||||||||||||||||||||||||||||||||||||||||||||

HALFWAY RIGHT

Totally Wrong

1939

||||||||||||||||||||||||||||||||||||||||||||||||||||||||||||||||

The Maginot Line was built by France in reaction to the slaughter of more than 1 million French soldiers in World War I. Before that war, the French military doctrine had been unchanged from when Napoleon I was emperor. If you wanted to win a battle, you attacked. Courage would overcome any enemy and guarantee victory. Admittedly, the doctrine had not worked so well even for Napoleon at the Battle of Nations or Waterloo, but France stuck with it. Then came World War I and the trenches. Attacking through barbed wire against modern artillery and machine guns proved fatal and useless. But it took the French generals almost two years and a mutiny to understand this.

The result of the French people's revulsion to the horrific losses in World War I was to go to the other extreme. The leaders of postwar France decided that if total offense was a disaster, total defense must be the answer. France, since Vauban and Louis XIV, had been the leader in building fortresses, so fortresses it would be. The result was the construction of the Maginot Line at the cost of more than 3 billion francs. That amount today, were it an equivalent portion of the U.S. annual budget, would be more than $3,000,000,000: That's *$3 trillion*. But the problem was not cost. The mistake that the French made was that the French built only half of the line.

The Maginot Line was not a single line of forts. It was rather a continuous series of defensive positions. The line included everything from small machine gun bunkers, some remote-controlled using periscopes, to massive artillery cupolas that would have been impressive on a battleship. In places, the defenses ran more than ten miles in depth. The forts were well stocked with everything from artillery shells to vintage wines and were ready to hold off any German attack for weeks without resupply. The Maginot Line was originally planned to run the entire length of the northern border of France. Half that border was with Germany. The other half ran along the border with Belgium. The first half, the portion that ran along the German border, was completed in the 1930s.

When construction of the Maginot Line reached the 150-mile border between France and Belgium, the government of Belgium objected. They refused to accept anything on the border because it inferred they would be abandoned by the French in the event of a German attack. But they also refused to allow the French to help them build anything along their border because it might serve as a provocation to the Germans. Belgium threatened that if the French built anything at all, they would ally themselves with Germany.

The French reaction was to do nothing. Even after Poland was invaded, there was no effort to add even the most rudimentary fortifications to the border that ran from the Ardennes to the Channel. Half of the French border was solidly fortified. The northern half, the route German armies had used almost every time they invaded France in the past thousand years, was left undefended. Eventually, the leaders of France justified stopping halfway by explaining that now they knew where the Germans had to attack since the Maginot Line was impregnable. Unfortunately for them, they were so right and so very wrong.

With half the border defenseless, the French and British agreed on a new strategy. When the Germans invaded Belgium, and only *after* they invaded, massive armies, waiting along the French border, would rush north and reinforce the Belgian army.

The plan even worked. When the Sitzkrieg ended and the fighting between France and Germany began, the Nazis did attack northern Belgium; and like everyone expected, a day later the British Expeditionary Force and a substantial part of the French army hurried past the undefended French border and into defensive positions along Belgium's waterways. While they did so, the Germans pressed only a little and mostly waited.

Once the British and French had committed dozens of divisions in Belgium, the Wehrmacht attacked through the virtually undefended Ardennes Forest. Undefended because the Maginot Line stopped short of it, and the French incorrectly assumed the forest was too dense for a major offensive to push through. They were wrong about it being impassable, and within weeks the main German offensive had reached the Channel. Hundreds of thousands of Allied soldiers were now trapped in Belgium. About 300,000 were eventually evacuated from Dunkirk, but more than that were left surrounded in northern Belgium while the panzers poured over the undefended portions of the French border and tore through France. Exactly one month after the Ardennes attack, the Nazis occupied Paris.

The part of the Maginot Line that was completed worked; what few Nazi assaults were made along it from Germany failed. But once France fell, most of the defenders had to surrender. Their guns faced the wrong way and many of their families were in German hands. The few fortresses that held out were not even attacked. Bulldozers were used to simply cover the turrets, ventilation shafts, and entrances with yards of dirt that turned the underground defenses into tombs.

But by allowing politics to overcome military sense, the incredibly expensive fortification failed to be more than a trap for the men manning it. Had the national wealth spent on constructing the Maginot Line been spent on tanks, planes, and artillery, the French army would have been immeasurably stronger. But the postwar wealth of France was squandered on a defensive line that by being incomplete accomplished nothing.

Had France ignored the irrational objections of Belgium and completed the Maginot Line, it might well have fulfilled its purpose. If, in 1940, the German panzer spearheads had to fight through a completed Maginot Line, their losses would have been staggering. The Nazis might still have defeated France in a much longer war, or they might not have, as the Blitzkrieg would have had little effect on mutually supporting and highly fortified positions. France might even have survived long enough to learn how to fight a modern war or force yet another stalemate on her German invaders.

72

STOPPING SHORT OF VICTORY

Miracle by Mistake

1940

Blitzkrieg was smashing France. The Wehrmacht had sailed through the "impassable" Ardennes Forest and bypassed the Maginot Line. German panzer divisions had spearheaded a push to the Channel that had effectively cut the British forces off from the French army and was pushing them back to the coast. On May 24, 1940, the British Expeditionary Force (BEF) was deeply engaged with the German Second Army. On that same day, the foremost of Heinz Guderian's panzer units were thirty miles from the port of Dunkirk. This put a substantial amount of Nazi armored and highly mobile units close to Dunkirk, the last continental channel port in Allied hands. The Nazis had more units near the port than almost all of the BEF combined. Worse yet, the BEF was totally engaged and could spare nothing to meet the threat in their rear. They were saved only because on that same day the order was received from Field Marshal Gerd von Rundstedt to the panzer divisions in Army Group A, which included all of the forces facing the BEF, to halt and re-form on the Lens to Gravelines canals. That move not only stopped Guderian from going for the port but relieved the pressure on the rest of the BEF

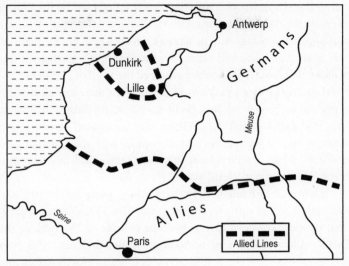

The Dunkirk evacuation

as well. This order may well have lost Germany its last chance to force a peace on Britain.

There has since been a lot of speculation as to why the decision to halt the panzers was made. No one after the war was sure why this order was given. It certainly wasn't because the armored units needed to stop. Diaries from the battle showed that the men and equipment were capable of continuing to attack, and they were frustrated at not being able to do so. Often speculation turns to the theory that Hermann Goering wanted the glory of giving the BEF its coup de grace to go to the Luftwaffe alone. Reichsmarschall Goering was also effectively the number two authority in the Nazi government and had Hitler's ear, so he could easily have made such a demand.

This stop order came from the highest level and may have been influenced by Hitler's desire to seek a quick peace with Britain to leave his entire army free to deal with Russia. Planning for the attack that actually occurred the next summer was already being developed. Allowing the BEF to escape, or at least surrender rather than be destroyed, may have been a ploy used by the Führer to encourage better relations with the British. At this point, he still had hopes of joining with his fellow English Aryans in his planned war against all Slavs and other *untermenschen*. Or perhaps it was ordered because Hitler had experienced the mud of Flanders first-hand in World War I and was afraid that the armored elite of his army would bog down and be of no use in finishing off France. What is certain is that the decision was not caused by any action taken by the Allies nor was it at all popular with the German general staff. Whatever the reason, this mistake may well have changed the entire course of World War II.

If Dunkirk had fallen, then there was no place for the BEF and associated Allied units to retreat from. The 338,000 men evacuated would have been lost or become prisoners. The bulk of the British officer corps and noncommissioned officers, who later formed the core of the British army fighting in North Africa and landing in Normandy, would have been lost.

One of the likely effects of such a loss on Britain would have been the collapse of civilian morale. If that happened, there was a high probability that Britain would have entered into the peace talks Hitler so desired. And in those talks the British empire might well have been represented by the less-determined Clement Attlee and not the then sea lord Winston Churchill. Churchill gained his premiership partially by riding the burst of confidence that came from the successful withdrawal of the BEF. If the bulk of the Royal Army had been lost, the more timid and conciliatory Attlee might well have accepted the premiership instead. In reality, Clement Attlee was offered the leadership of Britain, but he declined in Churchill's favor. Since Hitler publicly stated that he thought of the British as being fellow Aryans, this might well have encouraged a peace agreement or at least a British openness to a negotiated peace that preserved their empire. Avoiding a two-front war was a tenet of German strategy. That doctrine combined with Hitler's determination to attack communist Russia suggests that the terms the Führer might have offered Britain would certainly have been very generous.

Even if the loss of the BEF had not forced a peace on Britain, it would have drastically changed how that nation could fight in the next few years. It may well have meant a complete withdrawal from the Mediterranean basin, leaving it to the Axis. Many of the men who fought and eventually stopped Rommel in North Africa were survivors of the Dunkirk evacuation. With the BEF lost, it would have been unlikely that tens of thousands of men could be spared from England to go defend the Suez Canal and Egypt. Lacking enough troops to fend off their assault, Africa might well have fallen to the Italians even without an Afrika Korps being needed.

Even more dramatically affecting the course of the entire war would have been the lack of troops available to assist Greece in 1941. When the Italians attacked Greece, the British rushed several divisions to support the successfully defending Greek army. With that support, the Italians were stopped and pushed back. The Greeks were actually on the offensive in Albania within a month of Italy's attack. Because of the Anglo-Greek success, the German army had to intervene with significant forces. That intervention delayed the kickoff of Operation Barbarossa, the invasion of Russia. In Russia, later that year, the German army's successes slowed and then stopped as the weather worsened. Without the British forces sent to Greece, the German intervention may not have been needed, or not needed on a scale that delayed Barbarossa. It was only the early winter weather in 1941 that stopped the shift of several panzer divisions back to the attack on Moscow. With no delay and another month of good weather after the invasion had started, the Russian capital might well have fallen. The capture of Dunkirk and the BEF in 1940 might well have meant that Germany in 1941 would have been able to attack Russia earlier in the summer. They would then have had enough good weather to capture, as the Wehrmacht almost did, the political and transport center of the entire Soviet Union: Moscow. Had they done so, it would have crippled, if not outright defeated, Russia before the onset of the bitter cold. The decision to stop Guderian's panzers short of Dunkirk may well have been a mistake that lost Germany World War II.

||||||||||||||||||||||||||||||||||||||||||||||||||||||||||

73

RENAISSANCE MAN

Whom Do You Trust?

1940

||||||||||||||||||||||||||||||||||||||||||||||||||||||||||||||

Here is a "what if": If you were the leader of a nation at war, whom would you trust as your second-in-command? A man who:

1. May have stopped the panzers short just so that his aircraft could get credit for destroying the trapped British in Belgium and then instead allowed more than 300,000 enemy soldiers to be evacuated from Dunkirk?

2. Had failed you in the Battle of Britain even though his Luftwaffe far outnumbered the Royal Air Force? Then he blamed his pilots and called them cowards.

3. Bragged publicly and continually that his Luftwaffe would never allow a single British aircraft over Berlin? In a radio interview, he said that if one bomb fell, you "could call him Meier," which was contemporary slang for "I would be a fool," and a week later, seventy-five British bombers attacked the German capital with few losses.

4. Guaranteed that if the surrounded Sixth Army stayed in Stalingrad, his aircraft could deliver 750 tons of supplies a

day? This promise was made even though his own officers informed him that they had barely enough planes to deliver a third of that amount. The army was ordered to hold the city and not to break out when it could. Eventually starved for ammunition and just plain starved, more than half a million German and allied Axis soldiers were lost at Stalingrad.

5. Forbade the head of his fighters, Adolf Galland, to report to anyone that the new American fighters were now accompanying the bombers deep into Germany?

6. Even as the Allies bombed Germany's cities, continued to extend the Goering Works manufacturing empire until it employed 700,000 workers, many of them prisoner labor? Most of what the Goering Works made were items under contract to the Nazi government or the Luftwaffe. You can bet those were no-bid contracts. During the war, his company made him one of the richest men in Germany.

7. Regularly used morphine and had been effectively addicted to the drug since 1923? Because of this addiction the Reichsmarschall gained more than 100 pounds by 1943.

8. Was notorious as the greatest art thief in history, assigning entire military units to loot thousands of art treasures from all of Europe for his personal collection?

Who would trust and rely on such a man? Hitler did. The man, of course, was Hermann Goering. He became Hitler's war minister, commander of the Luftwaffe and, as Reichsmarschall, the number two head of the Nazi government. He was even Hitler's designated successor almost to the very end of the war. No matter how often Hermann Goering failed, Hitler made the mistake of continuing to trust "Fat Hermann," the self-proclaimed Renaissance man. Perhaps we should be very grateful for this mistake. How frightening might the world be today if the Führer had instead found a competent right-hand man?

74

BLINDED BY REVENGE

A Jettisoned Victory

1940

wo mistakes in August 1940 may have changed the entire war that followed. One was made by the lead aircraft in a small flight of Heinkel bombers on August 24. It was night, and accurate bombing at night was difficult. In 1940, there was no GPS or any other way for a pilot to know where he was. The only available method was simply to follow landmarks. This was a dicey proposition on a dark night. Even in daylight, following any flight plan over enemy territory while being fired on from the ground and threatened by fighters was difficult. In the dark, it became incredibly easy to be dozens of miles off course. So it was not unusual for a flight of Heinkels, over blacked-out England, to go astray. The only real difference between the situation that night was that they had strayed over central London.

That was during the peak of the Battle of Britain. If Germany could gain air dominance, it could control the Channel and invade England. Their army had been shattered on the Continent and those who had escaped had left their artillery, tanks, and even weapons behind. The only thing protecting Britain from invasion was the Royal Air Force (RAF) and the Royal Navy. But without control of the air over the English Channel, the ships of the Royal

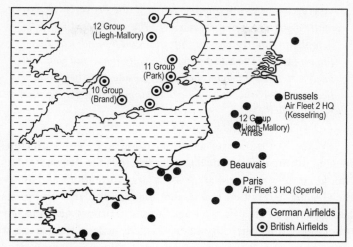

The Battle of Britain

Navy would be easily sunk in the narrow waters. If that occurred, there was virtually no chance the battered Royal Army could hold the island against a determined German landing. Since August 13, the Luftwaffe had been constantly challenging the RAF. Their targets had been the RAF itself. German bombers had struck at the English airfields, aircraft production plants, and occasionally the strange radar towers along the coast. This forced the Hurricanes and Spitfires of the RAF to meet every attack or be destroyed on the ground.

The German's normal technique was to send over bombers protected by fighters during the day and unprotected bombers at night. The strategy was working. When the British fighters rose to attack the daytime bombers, the Nazi fighters could attack them. Since the RAF was outnumbered more than two to one in fighters, this created a steady attrition that favored the Germans.

In a message to the secretary of state for air on June 3, Winston Churchill stated that

> *the Cabinet were distressed to hear from you that you were now running short of pilots for fighters, and that they had*

now become the limiting factor . . . Lord Beaverbrook has
made a surprising improvement in the supply and repair of
aeroplanes, and in clearing up the muddle and scandal of
the aircraft production branch. I greatly hope that you will
be able to do as much on the personnel side, for it will indeed
be lamentable if we have machines standing idle for want of
pilots to fly them.

By August 19, a concerned Vice Air Marshal Keith Park commented during a heated debate as to whether the British fighters should go in as they arrived or form large formations and attack the German aircraft en masse, that the loss of planes and pilots had become so great it no longer was a pertinent question. He observed that a larger formation was still better, "but we are at moment in no position to implement it anyway." There weren't enough pilots left flying to use in any large formations. To the British, it was becoming clear that the Luftwaffe was winning what was later known as the Battle of Britain. And the Germans knew they were winning. Just the day before those Heinkel bombers wandered over London, Air Marshal Hermann Goering had ordered that the Luftwaffe was

to continue the fight against the enemy air force until further
notice, with the aim of weakening the British fighter forces.
The enemy is to be forced to use his fighters by means of cease-
less attacks. In addition the aircraft industry and the ground
organization of the air force are to be attacked by means of
individual aircraft by night and day, if weather conditions do
not permit the use of complete formations.

So as things stood, with the RAF at the edge of exhaustion and running low on pilots, Operation Seelowe, the invasion of England, seemed inevitable. Then those few Heinkel bombers went off course. Not seeing their designated targets and deciding it was time to turn back toward their airfields in France, they did what they were supposed to do. They simply dropped their bombs without aiming at anything in particular. Without bombs it was easier for the aircraft to dodge enemy fighters. This clearing out of bombs was the common practice by both sides throughout the war. It just happened, unknown to the Heinkel pilots, that they were over London. The bombs themselves did little damage to the city, but the reaction was great.

After the German bombing of Rotterdam on May 15, 1940, the official policy of the RAF became to bomb all military targets even when the target was located somewhere that guaranteed civilian casualties. But such bombings had been rare. Both sides had avoided bombing the other's cities. But with the Germans seemingly beginning to attack London, this changed. The British reacted by sending up ninety-five RAF bombers who flew to the edge of their range. Their mission was to bomb Tempelhof air base. This base is located near the center of Berlin. Eighty-one of those bombers reached Berlin, but as was common throughout the war, their bombing accuracy was terrible, and that night, their bombs fell all over the German capital.

Goering, who had been bragging about how well the air war over England was going, was more than embarrassed. He had publicly and personally promised the citizens of Berlin that they would never even see a British aircraft over the city. Himmler had featured him making this promise on the radio several times in the weeks before the British reprisal raid. Adolf Hitler too was infuriated. In what seemed to have been an emotional reaction, they ordered the emphasis of the attacks on Britain to change from concentrating on the RAF to the bombing of London and the other British manufacturing and population centers.

By this time, most of the RAF coastal air bases had been rendered unusable. The RAF had plenty of aircraft, but was desperately short of trained pilots. The pilots they did have had been flying constantly for weeks and were exhausted. Some German bombing raids were beginning to get through without any aircraft intercepting them at all. Churchill's valiant "few" were on the ropes and the count had begun. Britain was days away from losing control of the air over the Channel and England.

But the German decision, in reaction to the Berlin raid, changed everything. London began to suffer, but the pressure was off the RAF. While the German bombers wreaked havoc on London in the first days of what became known as the Blitz, the Royal Air Force's pilots got needed rest, aircraft were serviced correctly, and new pilots were brought in. Air bases could be repaired and all of the radar stations put back on line. While the Battle of Britain continued for several more weeks, never again was the RAF so close to total defeat. By September, Hitler was forced to accept that an invasion of England was impossible.

If those Heinkel bombers had not mistakenly dropped bombs on London on August 24, it is possible that the Third Reich might have won World War II. The United States was not yet involved and would not be for more than a year. With England forced to surrender or be occupied, even if the United States had entered the conflict, there was no easy base near occupied Europe to stage an invasion from. More important, if the RAF, who had been days from collapse as an effective force, had been defeated and England forced to sue for peace, then the half million soldiers guarding western Europe would have been free to participate in the invasion of Russia a year later. With that many more men and tanks, the ability of Russia to survive those first months was questionable. Without them, German units penetrated to within fourteen miles of Moscow.

The Heinkel bomber pilots made an ordinary mistake following the standard procedure, by jettisoning their bombs without realizing London was below them. But the reaction of Hitler and Goering to the reprisal raid that bombing generated lost Germany the Battle of Britain and a chance to knock Britain out of the war. The prideful, emotional decision to change tactics to bombing London in August 1940 may well have cost the Nazis victory in World War II.

75

NOT PREPARED

Left out in the Cold

The history of warfare has shown many times that overconfidence can kill, and this case of misjudgment killed hundreds of thousands.

If anyone had a reason to be confident in 1941, it was the Nazis and Adolf Hitler. In 1939, Germany had overrun Poland in a matter of a few weeks. In 1940, France fell in just over a month. Not only did the Blitzkrieg ensure victory, but it seemed to guarantee a quick one as well. Then came Operation Barbarossa, the German invasion of Russia. Attacking Russia, they bet everything. The consequences of failure, even failing to win a quick victory, are shown by history. But in 1941, Hitler considered himself a military genius and, so far, appeared to have lived up to the claim. All of Europe, from Poland to the Pyrenees, was occupied by Germany or was her ally. On June 22, 3 million German and allied soldiers attacked Russia. Somehow, mostly because Stalin refused to believe it was going to happen and executed those who disagreed, the Wehrmacht achieved surprise.

In the first months of the invasion, hundreds of thousands of Russian soldiers were captured. In one case alone nearly 700,000 men surrendered or were killed when a large part of Ukraine was surrounded. Then it began to get cold, and a mistake that is very uncharacteristic of the meticulous planning normally attributed to the German general staff became apparent. The mistake was that Hitler and others were so confident of a fast victory, such as had occurred in Poland and France, that there had been no provision for equipping the army to continue fighting in the cold Russian winter.

Now, this means much more than a lack of overcoats and long underwear. Trucks and tanks were not winterized. The radiators would freeze up and even the diesel fuel took on a wax-like consistency in the subzero temperatures. Weapons froze solid in the middle of a battle and water-cooled machine guns became useless. On a personal side, there were no sleeping bags or insulated tents, so thousands of German soldiers literally froze to death in their sleep.

As quoted earlier, there is an old axiom that no battle plan survives contact with the enemy, but winter can be predicted. Through overconfidence or mistaking the open reaches of Russia for being similar to densely populated western Europe, no provision was made to keep the Wehrmacht fighting in cold weather. There were other factors that led to defeats, such as changing objectives and Hitler shifting panzer divisions around, creating delay. But the real mistake was not expecting another quick victory, but rather preparing for the invasion only under the assumption that all of Russia could be conquered in the few months before the notoriously fierce Russian winter arrived. That overconfident oversight meant that the German army could not fight at anywhere near its best level in the cold weather. It also cost the Wehrmacht tens of thousands of unnecessary casualties from frostbite or worse. Making the mistake of preparing only for the best of outcomes pretty much guaranteed the worst. If the German army had been properly equipped and prepared to continue fighting during the cold weather, they might well have captured Moscow and forced Russia to seek peace on Hitler's terms.

||||||||||||||||||||||||||||||||||||||||||||||||||||||||||||||||||||||||||||

76

IGNORING A
WARNING

Intelligence Failure

1941

||||||||||||||||||||||||||||||||||||||||||||||||||||||||||||||||||||||||||||

There are many questions about what exactly caused the disaster that occurred at Pearl Harbor on December 7, 1941. By December 8, the questions as to who made what mistake and who failed to do what were being asked. After more than sixty years and dozens of books, the questions are still being asked. The result of this great mistake is simple to define. The U.S. fleet and U.S. Army air corps airfields were not ready for the attack. They were set up in such a way as to be almost as vulnerable as possible. Unless a lot of people wanted to see the U.S. Pacific fleet slaughtered, and they did not, a mistake occurred that ceded control of the Pacific for months.

The commanding officer of the Pacific fleet was Admiral Kimmel, and General Short commanded the army air bases. The air force was not yet a separate branch of the armed services. On Sunday, December 7, 1941, as the map shows (see page 291), the Japanese struck both the fleet in harbor and the air bases. The attack totally surprised everyone in Hawaii. In many cases, only skeleton crews manned the ships and ammunition for antiaircraft guns was locked away. That did not need to have happened. Someone made a very great mistake that affected the entire war in the Pacific. The failures were there, but not the ones most people expect.

To begin with, let's eliminate any thought that there had not been sufficient warning. Three communications sent days earlier pretty much ruled that out. While Pearl Harbor was not directly threatened, the tone of the communications showed that war was close and inevitable. The only question was where it would start. Read them for yourself:

FROM THE NAVY DEPARTMENT, NOVEMBER 27, 1941

This dispatch is to be considered a war warning. Negotiations with Japan looking toward stabilization of conditions in the Pacific have ceased and an aggressive move by Japan is expected within the next few days. The number and equipment of Japanese troops and the organization of the naval task forces indicates an amphibious expedition against either the Philippines, Thai or Kra Peninsula or possibly Borneo. Execute an appropriate defensive deployment preparatory to carrying out the tasks assigned in WPL 46 [the navy's war plan]. Inform district and army authorities. A similar warning is being sent by the War Department.

In 1941, the air force was a part of the U.S. Army.

FROM THE DEPARTMENT OF ARMY, NOVEMBER 27, 1941

Negotiations with Japan appear to be terminated to all practical purposes, with only the barest possibilities that the Japanese Government might come back and offer to continue. Japanese future action unpredictable, but hostile action possible at any moment. If hostilities cannot, repeat cannot, be avoided, the United States desires that Japan commit the first overt act. This policy should not, repeat not, be construed as restricting you to a course of action that might jeopardize your defense. Prior to hostile Japanese action you are directed to undertake such reconnaissance and other measures as you deem necessary, but these measures should be carried out so as not, repeat not, to alarm civil population or disclose intent. Report measures taken. Should hostilities occur, you will carry out the tasks assigned to Rainbow Five [the army's war plan] so far as they pertain to Japan. Limit dissemination of this highly secret information to minimum essential officers.

FROM THE CHIEF OF NAVAL OPERATIONS, DECEMBER 3, 1941

Highly reliable information has been received that categoric and urgent instructions were sent yesterday to Japanese diplomatic and consular posts at Hong Kong, Singapore, Batavia, Manila, Washington and London to destroy most of their codes and ciphers at once and to burn . . . confidential and secret documents.

So four days before the Japanese attack on Pearl Harbor, both commanders knew that the Japanese diplomats were preparing for war. The only surprise was that the attack came at Hawaii.

If you had commanded the only U.S. Navy fleet in the Pacific or the main Pacific air base, what action would you have taken? Admiral Kimmel and General Short decided that, even with war imminent, there was no concern for an attack on Pearl Harbor since the various intelligence branches had not specifically mentioned one but did see signs of other attacks (which also happened). So on the basis of this, and perhaps personal and racial egotism, they did nothing to prepare for such an attack. The island was not even on alert, and crews were allowed to leave all the docked ships. Obviously Kimmel did not see his fleet as being at risk.

This mistake becomes even less understandable when you realize that less than a year earlier, obsolete British aircraft attacked and sunk a good part of the Italian fleet while docked in the similarly shallow and protected Taranto harbor. Or that by November 16, the bulk of the Japanese fleet and all its major carriers had simply disappeared. The United States had no idea where the main fleet was of a nation it knew was preparing to attack them. Yet the commanding officers in Hawaii had their bases in a very low level of alert.

This attitude, and the low alert level, led to more minor mistakes that made things worse. When the new radar unit spotted the approaching first wave of attackers, the operator told his commander, and the officer commanding the radar station assumed it was six army bombers that were expected that morning. Ships radioed warnings when the Japanese flew overhead, but these were still being processed in a lightly manned communications center when it was too late. Reports of periscopes also failed to bring the bases to a higher level of alert. Despite the situation, the sightings, and the unknown location of the Japanese carrier fleet, from the commanding officers on down, nothing was done in time to stave off disaster.

Actually *nothing* is not correct: Both American commanders had taken some recent actions. They were, however, very bad decisions that made the situation worse. Based in Pearl Harbor were eight battleships, three aircraft carriers, and numerous supporting ships. Even docked, if on full alert and warned, this was a powerful antiaircraft defensive force. Unfortunately, the fleet was at a very low level of alert, which meant that on a Sunday morning most of the crew was ashore. When the Japanese attacked, there were not even enough sailors to man all of the guns. Those who were on the ships in the harbor woke to explosions and sirens. Many never made it to the deck or their stations before their battleships were sunk. Even unprepared, the navy and army defenders shot down twenty-nine planes from the two waves of more than 350 attacking.

The army air force was equally badly prepared. The few men on the base were surprised at breakfast. Ammunition lockers were locked, and when the first wave attacked, barely a quarter of its machine guns, and only four of thirty-one antiaircraft batteries, were fired. General Short had been much more concerned about sabotage by spies hiding among Hawaii's large Japanese population than about the chance his air bases would be bombed. As a result, he ordered all of the aircraft to be lined up in straight rows in the open on the runways. This way they all were far from the fences, and it allowed the MPs to keep a good eye on them. This setup also made them perfect targets for bombing and strafing attacks. The Japanese attackers simply flew along the tightly packed lines of American aircraft and were able to destroy several

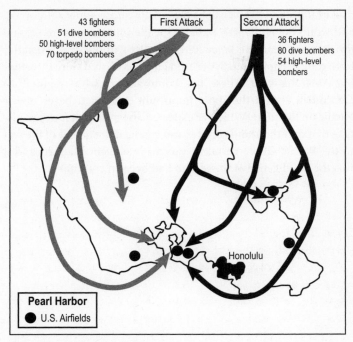

43 fighters
51 dive bombers
50 high-level bombers
70 torpedo bombers

First Attack

Second Attack

36 fighters
80 dive bombers
54 high-level bombers

Honolulu

Pearl Harbor
● U.S. Airfields

The attacks on Pearl Harbor

planes with each pass. Virtually none of the army aircraft made it into the air, not even an hour later when the second attack wave hit.

When the second wave had finished, five battleships and two destroyers were sunk or so badly damaged that they couldn't be used for the rest of the war. Four more battleships and five cruisers were damaged. The army air corps lost almost 200 of 350 planes with most of the rest damaged. More than 2,400 veteran sailors, marines, and soldiers died. Only the coincidence that all three U.S. carriers were at sea prevented total disaster.

The mistake made by Admiral Kimmel and General Short was not to be prepared. Another was to ignore the intelligence they had been given. If the American Pacific surface fleet had not been effectively neutralized on December 7, 1941, then the Japanese expansion and successes in 1942 might well have been much less.

The Philippine Islands might have been successfully reinforced, and so no Bataan Death March. But the mistake was made, and for the next year, the Japanese expanded without real resistance until they occupied much of the Pacific Ocean and were threatening Australia itself. These two commanders, who resigned on December 8, had the most important American bases in the Pacific on low alert. With war expected any moment, it was a mistake that cost thousands of lives and changed the nature of the war in the Pacific. There certainly was an intelligence failure, and it was the intelligence of those who had been in command.

77

SELF-DEFEATING VICTORY

Pearl Harbor Redux

1941

The Imperial Japanese Navy's December 7, 1941, surprise attack was not only an intelligence and tactical disaster for the United States; it was also the worst strategic action taken by Japan in all of World War II. To understand this you have to look at why Japan went to war against the United States. There was never a thought in Tokyo that Japan could actually defeat and conquer the much richer and more populous North America. From the beginning, the intention was to force the United States into a peace agreement on Japan's terms. Those terms were, generally speaking, designed to leave Japan in control of Southeast Asia and a sphere of islands in the Pacific.

But remember that before the Pearl Harbor attack there was no state of war between America and Japan. Nor were there any American plans in motion to start a war. The United States was protesting diplomatically the Japanese treatment of China and had cut off oil and scrap metal shipments, but that was very far from declaring war. President Roosevelt was on record as wanting the country involved in the war, but he wanted involvement in the war in Europe, not in the Pacific. Even after the attack on Pearl

Harbor the president pushed for and ensured that the U.S. war effort was concentrated on Europe.

It has often been maintained that Japan was sure its attacks on British and French territories in Indochina would bring the United States into the war, but that was hardly a guaranteed response. The strong isolationist feeling the majority of Americans held kept the country out of war while France itself fell, the Battle of Britain was fought, and the Nazi invasions of Norway and other neutral countries came about. It was far from definite that invading Vietnam and Burma was going to force America to defend the colonies of nations that America had not gone to war to defend when the homelands were attacked. So the very basis of claiming there was a need for an attack on the United States was and is questionable.

What the surprise attack in Hawaii did create was a diplomatic disaster that should have been easily foreseen. After all, a beneficial negotiation was the goal, with Japan dictating from strength, but to have that, the other party has to be willing to negotiate. And this was only to get the United States to accept Japan's extended conquests on the other side of the world. So here is the mistake. In an attempt to force the Americans to make a beneficial treaty with Japan, they started a war in a way that was guaranteed to enrage virtually every American. Its actions in attacking Pearl Harbor pretty much guaranteed that no moderate compromise with the United States would ever be possible.

If you want to reach an agreement with someone you are arguing with, then sucker punching him or her is probably not the best technique. Worse, the attack had a second effect, having aroused the need for revenge in a nation with ten times the industrial capacity; the Japanese were forced to push hard for some sort of dramatic victory. Having angered an industrial giant, they had to win fast. This then forced the Japanese into aggressive and eventually militarily disastrous battles such as those on the Coral Sea and at Midway. But no matter how many battles the Imperial Japanese Navy won, from the beginning, forcing such a negotiated victory was no longer possible. The American public simply would not have accepted one. Nor would that always "decisive victory" have been decisive. The U.S. Navy was able to make up all its losses from Pearl Harbor and go on to become a force that put hundreds of warships off Okinawa just a few years later. Unless the American morale broke, and there was little chance of that after what President Roosevelt described in his radio announcement of the attack as "a day that will live on in infamy," not one or even several naval victories could force the peace Japan started the war to obtain.

War is often said to be an extension of diplomacy. Yet by attacking Pearl Harbor before war was declared, the Japanese instead excluded diplomacy as a means of resolution. It was a mistake they paid dearly for making.

|||||||||||||||||||||||||||||||||||||||||||||||||||||||

78

SHORT-RANGE THINKING

Double Betrayal

1941

|||||||||||||||||||||||||||||||||||||||||||||||||||||||||||||

On December 7, 1941, the Japanese attacked Pearl Harbor and started a war with the United States. The wisdom of that decision was itself dubious, but the mistake made by Adolf Hitler a few days later easily equaled it in dire consequences. It had been a good year for Hitler and the Third Reich. The German army had conquered most of Europe and the only setbacks had seemed minor. The British had managed to repel the air offensive and so avoid an invasion of their island. In Africa, Erwin Rommel had been stopped short of Cairo in what was really a minor sideshow. The war with Russia had gone brilliantly with almost 2 million Russian soldiers killed or captured and vital parts of that country occupied. For years, Hitler had cultivated the Japanese leadership in expectation that Japan would attack Siberia, providing a second front against Russia. The German foreign minister, since Operation Barbarossa, had suggested to Japan that mineral-rich Siberia was theirs for the taking. Hitler personally had seen the damage having to fight on two fronts did in World War I to Germany. He was anxious for Russia to suffer the same fate.

When Adolf Hitler heard about Pearl Harbor, he was recorded

as being visibly happy. Based on what he did next, there must have been an expectation that Japan, who had already declared themselves an ally of Germany and Italy, would join in attacking Russia. What he did not know was that months earlier the Japanese had decided to concentrate on the United States and had no interest in attacking Russia. Worse for Germany was the fact that Russia had been informed of this by a spy in Tokyo. This security breach served both Japan and Russia well. It allowed Stalin to begin pulling the elite Siberian battalions west immediately after the Germans invaded. With most of the Russian divisions gone, Japan did not need to station significant forces on the Russian border either. By October 1941, the Russians and Japanese had actually signed a nonaggression pact. The loser was Germany. But four days after Pearl Harbor, on December 11, Adolf Hitler declared war on the United States in support of Japan. That he did so based on a false assumption is clear from his remarks at the time. He expected Japan to attack Russia. Also, after seeing the effect American units had when they finally joined in the Great War, he certainly wasn't anxious to see them in Europe again. It was his expectation that Japan would distract America, leaving Germany free to complete what seemed to be the inevitable conquest of Russia and to force a peace on Britain. Of course that was not how it worked.

But there was another factor beyond unrealistic expectations that made this declaration one of the worst mistakes the German Führer ever made. The American public simply did not want to get involved in a second war. Isolationist candidates had won many elections. For more than two years the American president, Franklin Roosevelt, had been lobbying for the country to be more involved in the war in Europe. His often-stated opinion was that if the Nazis were able to use the wealth and manufacturing power of an occupied Europe, they would pose a deadly threat next to the Americas. But on December 10, 1941, the Americans were not angry with Germany. On December 8, Congress had declared war only on Japan. The military, and the people, wanted revenge for that day of infamy. But by declaring war on December 11, Hitler made Germany appear part of the conspiracy. It gave Roosevelt an opening to do what he wanted, where he wanted. Only after Hitler declared war was the American declaration expanded to include Germany. Almost immediately, the power generated by the surprise attack was channeled into Roosevelt's Europe First policy. America began to mobilize and plans were made to send the bulk of the new army to England, not the Pacific. The shipments of trucks and weapons to all of the European Allies were dramatically increased as the United States went on a wartime footing.

It is likely that eventually the United States would have joined the war in Europe. But without Hitler's declaring war first this might have happened months later. The Asia First movement was strong even after Hitler's declaration. It is notable that, in his December 9 fireside chat, Roosevelt did not call for a declaration of war on Germany. He blamed them for having goaded Japan into attacking but stopped short of widening the war. Had he done so, he might well have lost the amazing unity caused by Pearl Harbor and become more susceptible to the growing attacks he was under for his failed domestic policies. So without Hitler doing it for him, Roosevelt would likely have had to wait months before declaring war on Germany, perhaps longer. Those months of delay could have been decisive. In a scenario that does not include the massive number of trucks, tanks, aircraft, weapons, and ammunition that the United States sent to Russia and England during those months, the German army might well have been victorious in Russia in 1942. Without the American armed forces in Europe and a resilient Russia, the defeat of Germany, if possible at all, would have taken years longer.

Rarely has a wartime leader been so completely wrong. In declaring war on the United States on December 11, Hitler accomplished exactly the opposite of what he expected. It gained Germany no assistance against Russia and enabled Roosevelt to shift the emphasis of the American war effort to Europe. Hitler's declaration of war may have actually served Japan well, but only because it allowed Roosevelt to send fewer forces to the Pacific and more forces to Europe. An emphasis on Japan would have meant that the war in the Pacific would have ended earlier. Instead, by declaring war on the United States at a crucial time when American anger was just crystallizing, that Nazi act of solidarity helped both to hasten and to make inevitable the defeat of Germany.

79

||||||||||||||||||||||||||||||||||||||||||||||||||||||||||||||||||||||

NOT LEARNING
FROM HISTORY
Full Speed Alone
1941

||||||||||||||||||||||||||||||||||||||||||||||||||||||||||||||||||||||

I t is impossible to discuss what mistakes Japan made in World
War II without including some mention of how they ignored
2,500 years of naval tactics and paid a high price for doing so.
The convoy system for protecting merchant ships goes back to
when warships were first invented. When the Persian emperor
Xerxes' triremes lost the sea battle of Salamis, he was forced to
withdraw most of his invading army from Greece. This was not
because they were under any threat, but because his army needed
to be supplied by merchant ships crossing the Adriatic Sea. With
the loss of most of his triremes, Xerxes no longer had enough
ships to convoy those merchants and protect them from Greek
raiders. That, combined with a fear of losing his escape route
across the Bosphorus, is why the Battle of Salamis won both the
land and naval war for the Greek city-states.

In time of war during the age of sail, the practice of convoying
groups of merchant ships with warships was the established policy
for all of Europe. The English sea dogs always lay in wait for the
Spanish plate (as in silver plate) fleet, which consisted of armed
merchant vessels protected by Spanish warships. The English navy
itself formed convoys during almost every war. A British convoy

crossing the Atlantic during the Napoleonic Wars might contain as many as 100 merchants and be protected by as many as five frigates and often a ship of the line.

The British were slow to institute convoys in World War I, waiting until 1917. When they finally did, there was a nearly 50 percent drop in merchant ship losses. During that period, most of the coal used in France had to be transported to them across the English Channel. Initially, German submarines wreaked havoc with the slow cargo haulers. But once a strict convoy system was implemented, the total losses to submarines for the next year was a negligible four ships out of hundreds of sailings.

In World War II, the Royal Navy instituted a convoy, beginning on September 6, 1939. That convoy consisted of thirty-six ships sailing in four rows of nine each with an escorting warship front, right, and left. The first major assistance given to Britain, at Roosevelt's insistence under the Lend-Lease Act, was not cannons or tanks, but fifty destroyers and fifty-four destroyer escorts. These were all used for the convoy duty of protecting Britain's Atlantic shipping from U-boats. All British ships crossing the Atlantic during World War II were required to sail in convoy. After Pearl Harbor, a combination of the U.S. Navy instituting convoys in May 1942 and technical advances broke the U-boat offensive a few months later. By February 1943, with aircraft and even small aircraft carriers acting as escorts, the German navy lost forty-three U-boats and sunk only thirty-four merchant ships. Well-escorted convoys could overcome even the highly sophisticated tactics of Doenitz's U-boats. Lone ships never had a chance. When Russia joined the war, convoys of weapons and ammunition were instituted to sail from Britain, past occupied Norway, to Murmansk.

Which leads to the question of why did Japan, the other major island nation engaged in World War II, fail to ever institute a convoy system? A large part of the reason may have been the attitude of those in command. Warships were meant to fight battles, not protect merchants. This strategy worked at first after the Philippines and Wake Island fell. Distances were too far for American submarines to spend much time in the major Japanese shipping lanes and subs were too few. But as the war progressed, the Japanese merchant fleet was subjected to ever greater losses with no reaction by the Imperial Japanese Navy other than to tell them to sail faster and zigzag. In December 1941, the Japanese lost only twelve merchant ships out of hundreds. In January, as the American bases in the western Pacific were lost, the number dropped to only seven ships lost. By that February, only two were sunk all month. Similar numbers prevailed until the end of 1943. This success without convoys meant dozens of destroyers could act as escorts to carriers, transport troops, or bombard enemy islands, and so the Japanese felt that their strategy worked.

But then losses began to mount, and rather than institute convoys, the Japanese reacted to the increased sinkings by announcing that more merchant ships had to be built. This "solution" was stunted by the limited shipbuilding facilities available and the competition for those same spaces by the Imperial Navy. By 1944, the Japanese merchant losses more than doubled, ranging from a low of sixteen to more than forty ships lost each month. Oil tankers particularly suffered. The amount of oil reaching Japan went from 1.75 million barrels in August 1943 to 360,000 barrels in July 1944. This was an intolerable level and far below the needs of either their industry or military. When the world's largest battleship, the *Yamato*, made its final sailing, it had on board only enough fuel to reach the American fleet and not enough to get back to Japan. There was no more to spare for even the possibility that the great ship might survive to fight on. It didn't.

Many in the U.S. Navy submarine service waited and even trained for dealing with Japanese convoys. They never had to. By November 1944, fifty-nine Japanese ships were sunk, mostly merchants or transports. By the end of the war, an amazing 54 percent of the total Japanese merchant capacity had been sunk. Most of the rest cowered in port. For a nation that totally depended on imported metals, oil, and even food, the fact they never instituted a simple policy that had been consistently successful for more than 2,000 years and had just proven amazingly successful for their opponents in the Atlantic is a mistake almost beyond understanding.

Japanese production and even the development of weapons was slowed dramatically by a continual lack of resources. The Imperial Air Force was crippled not only by a shortage of new aircraft due to a lack of metals, such as aluminum needed to build them, but also from an aviation fuel shortage so severe that pilot training was curtailed from weeks to a matter of hours. No matter what the bushido reasoning for the Japanese failure to institute convoys, the mistake allowed the American and Allied submarines to effectively destroy the very lifeline carrying the raw materials Japan needed to carry on the war. With more surviving merchant ships, the Japanese might well have slowed the American advance to the home islands and may even have negotiated something other than total surrender.

80

OBEYING ORDERS
TO A FAULT

He Who Hesitated

1942

The Battle of Midway Island is often considered the turning point in World War II in the Pacific. It took the Japanese several mistakes to bring this about, including one in planning by their great naval genius Isoroku Yamamoto. But his was not the error that changed the nature of the entire Pacific theater in 1942. That one specific mistake was left to the commander on the scene.

A little more than six months after their attack on Pearl Harbor was a heady time for Japan and the Imperial Japanese Navy, often referred to as the IJN. Victory seemed automatic, with armies surrendering at Singapore and Bataan and the quick capture of islands all over the Pacific. They had challenged the mighty United States and seemed to be winning. Morale in the navy and among the Japanese people had soared, and the militarist leaders found themselves popular. Then all that joy came crashing down, due to the daring bombing raid by Jimmy Doolittle and sixteen B25s on Japan itself. It was not that the raid did any real damage or that several of the bombers were not shot down, but rather it was the sheer fact that the home islands were bombed. When the war had been both successful and distant, it was one thing; when the Japanese saw their home islands attacked for the first time in centuries, it was a shock and an embarrassment.

Something had to be done to restore the prestige and face lost by the raid. The decision was to accomplish this and more by invading Midway Atoll. Yamamoto's real hope was that the much stronger IJN could draw what remained of the American navy into a decisive battle and destroy it. This was actually a good strategy. If Midway fell, it would be almost impossible for the U.S. Navy to protect the Hawaiian Islands. If the atoll was occupied, hundreds of land-based aircraft from Midway would be able to support an IJN attack on Hawaii. The Pacific fleet would have to move to San Francisco. With the U.S. Navy gone and the air base at Midway in Japanese hands, the Hawaiian Islands were as good as lost. So the Japanese knew correctly that the American navy had to react to any attack on Midway.

At this point in the Pacific theater, the U.S. Navy was definitely not in a strong position. The IJN was correct in thinking they had almost every advantage. The odds were against the Americans, who had so few surviving large ships that a surface battle was inconceivable. This allowed two fast battleships to be assigned to protect the Kido Butai, the main carrier force. Those two ships alone had more heavy gun firepower than the U.S. Navy had in the Pacific. But the Japanese also had another major battleship force a day behind the Kido Butai, and that force included the *Yamato*, the world's largest battleship. Added to this was the painful fact that at this point in the war the Japanese surface ships were newer, often faster, and all better armed than their U.S. Navy counterparts.

The Japanese also had more than twice as many fleet aircraft carriers in the Pacific, with eight IJN to just three U.S. carriers. Worse yet, there were three only by including the badly damaged *Yorktown*. After the Battle of the Coral Sea, this carrier was in such poor condition that when she sailed out of Pearl Harbor toward Midway, a number of frantically working repairmen were still on board.

The U.S. Navy had one very real advantage. The surprise attack on Midway was not a surprise. The cryptography division on

Hawaii, under Commander Joseph Rochefort, had managed to break the IJN's code. While the United States could not read all of every message, they were able to determine, and then use a ruse to confirm, that Midway Atoll was the target and when it would be attacked. This allowed what remained of the Pacific fleet to sail days sooner than a just-reacting fleet would have left Pearl Harbor. The U.S. Navy also could ignore a real but unimportant attack on two islands off the Alaskan coast, Attu and Kiska. Even so, the odds remained four highly experienced fleet carriers and a light carrier to the U.S. Navy's three carriers. And there was the Japanese massive dominance in surface combat ships.

After the war, the Japanese attempted to understand why their admirals acted as they did in the attack during the battle for Midway Atoll. The eventual conclusion was what they called "victory disease." By this they meant overconfidence and disdain for your opponent based on past victories. This was a concept that might well have been studied almost thirty years later by the U.S. military leaders who confidently expected to overwhelm the Vietcong in weeks. What directly resulted from this attitude was an overly complicated battle plan that split the IJN into several parts. Then, even though he wanted a decisive victory, the Japanese admiral chose this time to split off two of his eight fleet carriers to support the unimportant Alaskan invasion whose sole purpose was to—unsuccessfully, thanks to Rochefort—distract parts of the U.S. fleet. Then he sent away two more carriers to Japan for needed, but not vital, repair and refurbishing. So by plan and before a bomb fell, half the IJN's aircraft carriers were not where the planned decisive battle was to take place.

But that overly ornate battle plan—the splitting of forces and the overconfidence shown by the Japanese navy at every level—was not the mistake that made all of the difference. The error that ended the IJN's dominance of the Pacific and halted the Japanese empire's expansion was made not by Admiral Yamamoto, but by the commander of the Kido Butai carrier force itself, Admiral Chuichi Nagumo.

Now, the character of the carrier fleet's commander was a major factor. Unlike the innovative Yamamoto, Nagumo was a competent but by-the-book officer. When your strategy is work-ing and you have serious superiority in numbers, this is not a problem. But what you don't learn when you command by the book is how to make vital decisions quickly when disaster looms. But Yamamoto had given his carrier commander detailed orders on what to do in a range of situations. That made Nagumo's con-sistent obedience to his orders a positive thing because Yamamoto could count on him to do what he was told. But his elaborate plan meant that the brilliant and decisive IJN commander was hun-dreds of miles away and under radio silence during the entire Battle of Midway.

The Japanese invasion plan followed a proven pattern that had been successful many times. The carrier force, the Kido Butai, would lead the attack, neutralizing any land-based airfields and sinking any ships in the atoll. If the first wave of bombers and fight-ers didn't do the job, there was plenty of time for a second wave to finish it. This plan assumed that it would take the U.S. Navy at least two days to steam to Midway from Pearl Harbor once they heard about the attack. That would leave plenty of time for Nagumo to thoroughly pummel the atoll before help could arrive. With Mid-way's airfield and major defenses bombed into ruin, the battleships would arrive and further bombard the island into submission. By the time the elite assault force landed, resistance would be minor and uncoordinated. By the time the U.S. Navy arrived, the island would be in Japanese hands.

So the first wave of Japanese attack planes went in, but thanks to the broken code they were not able to surprise the island. Every plane at the air base was already in the air when they hit and every weapon was manned and waiting. The air base was damaged, but heavy ground fire prevented the Japanese bombers from com-pletely wrecking the atoll's defenses. At about the same time the IJN aircraft had brushed past the obsolete U.S. fighters to attack Midway, the heavy bombers, dive bombers, and torpedo planes from Midway had attacked the four carriers of the Kido Butai. While bravely delivered, not a bomb or torpedo struck, and most of the American attackers were shot down.

The need for a carrier aircraft second attack on Midway was

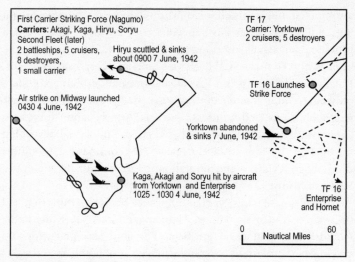

The Battle of Midway

one of the contingencies in the fleet commander's orders. Nagumo prepared to recover the first attack wave's aircraft and got a second attack ready to bomb the island. Everything was going according to the plan. Then a radio message arrived that changed everything. One of the IJN scout planes had spotted the *Yorktown*. This was not part of the plan; there weren't supposed to be any American carriers in the area for days yet. He had been assured just hours before, by a line of scout submarines, that no major ships had been spotted leaving Pearl Harbor. Thanks to Rochefort, the American ships were already gone when the Japanese subs got into place to watch for them.

The information that a U.S. Navy carrier was nearby meant that Chuichi Nagumo was torn between two conflicting orders. One order was to follow the plan and finish off Midway. To do this he had to launch his aircraft at the island again. But he also knew that the intent of the whole plan was to draw out the American carriers, and now one was within attack range. But it was days early, and the IJN battleships were not yet even close. His aircraft would have to take care of the carrier. To go for the *Yorktown*, Admiral Nagumo had to order the removal of the explosive and shrapnel bombs, which were almost finished being attached to the second wave of aircraft, and the loading of armor-piercing bombs and torpedoes. Only that type of weaponry was capable of damaging an armored carrier and its escorts. But the change would take at least an hour. This was not part of the plan he had been given by Admiral Yamamoto. Nagumo's orders did not tell him what to do in this situation because the confident Japanese had never considered that the U.S. Navy would not react how and when they expected. And with radio silence, Nagumo could not even radio Yamanoto and ask him what to do.

So Admiral Nagumo, whose strength was carrying out the plans of his brilliant superior, had to take the unusual step of deciding for himself. Did he disobey the orders for the invasion to go for the carrier and risk allowing the Midway air base to be repaired and perhaps new defending aircraft flown in from Hawaii? Or did he ignore the carrier and obey his original orders as written? And here is the mistake that changed the war forever: For a number of minutes, Nagumo did nothing. This hesitation, his inability to decisively disobey an order, even when the situation he was in was unforeseen, changed the entire war in the Pacific.

Doing nothing in war is often a mistake, and in this case the loss of all four carriers and the initiative resulted. If Nagumo had launched the aircraft against the atoll or had gotten them rearmed in time and launched against the *Hornet*, the war's history would be very different today.

While only one had been spotted, there were actually three American carriers in range to attack the Kido Butai. So eventually Admiral Nagumo made what was likely the best decision for the new circumstances and ordered a rapid change of the armaments on all of his aircraft to antiship weapons. But the time spent deciding what to do and the chaos of the weapons change meant that not only were the aircraft almost all still on the decks of all four carriers fueled and armed when the American aircraft attacked, but that the land attack bombs, which had been removed, were also still stacked near them. As a result, when the IJN fighters were off chasing the few survivors of two American torpedo groups, aircraft from two groups of U.S. Navy dive bombers were able to hit three of the highly vulnerable Japanese aircraft carriers. The bombs and fuel in the aircraft on the decks of the three ships exploded and greatly increased the damage. Within minutes all three carriers were beyond repair and covered in flames.

Nagumo continued to fight with the remaining carrier, sinking the *Yorktown* just as his last carrier too was lost. Then his last carrier was sunk, and the entire IJN force had to retreat. The powerful battleship fleet and Admiral Yamamoto never even got close to the island. Midway was saved. Admiral Chuichi Nagumo's hesitation and a lot of luck on the American side meant that the massive IJN superiority in carriers in the Pacific was lost in a matter of hours.

81

NO RETREAT

The Stalingrad Disaster

1943

Winter of 1942 had belonged to the Russians. In the snow and freezing weather, they had held the Germans and, in places, had even driven them back. But by spring 1943, a bruised but still unbeaten Nazi army prepared for another series of war-winning attacks. While pressure was kept on Moscow and Leningrad, the real German effort would be in the south.

There were a number of good reasons for the shift. The open steppes and dry plains of southern Russia were more conducive to the Blitzkrieg and massive pincer movements that had served the Wehrmacht well in 1941. The area was much less well fortified and more thinly populated. So southern Russia offered a much better opportunity to break through or capture major elements of the resurrected Soviet armed forces. But perhaps the most compelling reason for the move against southern Russia was that the Reich desperately needed the oil that was on the other side of the Caucasus Mountains.

Two vast attacks were planned. One was to sweep south and grab the oil. The other was to move east and capture the most important city on the Volga River. The Volga was the key route for the Russian north and south transport. It also had to have appealed to Hitler that to control the vital Russian supply line of the Volga River, the city Stalin had named for himself, Stalingrad, had to be occupied.

The original plan to capture Stalingrad was not a mistake. The city was the key to controlling the southern Volga River. It was also one of Russia's premier weapons manufacturing centers. Perhaps even more than this was the propaganda value of capturing the former Tsaritsyn, named now after the Soviet dictator and Hitler's greatest nemesis, Stalin. Even the strategic plan started well. Army Group A, under Paul von Kleist, broke through line after line of Russian defenders, crossing Russian defense lines set up on river after river. Army Group B, commanded by Hitler's favorite general, Friedrich von Paulus, also punched its way through several Russian armies until, by August 23, 1942, the two panzer armies in it had reached the banks of the Volga and were approaching their objective, the city of Stalingrad.

It's at this point that a series of mistakes doomed half a million German soldiers and changed the momentum of World War II irrevocably. All of these mistakes were made worse by Hitler's choice of commander for the Sixth Panzer Army, von Paulus. The general had been chosen not because of his battlefield experience but because he got along with the testy Adolf Hitler. And in Nazi Germany that qualified you for anything, even command of one of the few elite panzer armies. In 1941, Friedrich von Paulus had shown himself to be an excellent administrator and planner. He was the chief architect of Operation Barbarossa and was known for his skill at staff work. The problem was that von Paulus as a field commander . . . well, he was a very good staff officer. He did a competent but unimaginative job and obeyed orders, Hitler's orders, to the letter.

As Army Group B approached Stalingrad, Hitler personally ordered half of its armored strength, Hoth's Fourth Panzer Army, to hurry south and join up with Army Group A. It was to assist in the final lunge for the Caucasian oil fields. The decision was a mistake that cost both army groups the use of that armored formation for weeks while it changed direction and moved south.

Still, even with his Sixth Panzer Army alone, von Paulus began to successfully attack Stalingrad.

The city of Stalingrad in 1942 had grown in a long strip along the Volga River, ten miles long and from a few to five or six miles deep. Most of the large buildings and factories were located near the river. Even at half strength, the power of a panzer division was great, and soon the Sixth Panzer was grinding into the city from north, west, and south. To the east was the Volga River, and herein was a continuing mistake the unimaginative von Paulus made. He never attempted to cross the Volga, and so he was never able to completely surround or cut off Stalingrad.

The Volga was able to act as the route for reinforcement and supply throughout the battle for the city. By never even attempting to cross the Volga, the Germans provided the city's defenders with a safe base from which hundreds of thousands of reinforcements were shuttled into the city. The east bank also provided a safe location for masses of artillery, which later constantly punished the Germans. Such an attack certainly was possible, especially early in the battle for the city, and was a much better use of the highly mobile armored units in a panzer army than was house-to-house urban warfare. So von Paulus failed to surround a city he was attacking and left the enemy a secure and unmolested base just a few hundred very wet yards away from it.

From September on, the Germans drove the Russian defenders back against the Volga. By December, the defenders no longer could maintain a continuous line. Only pockets of fierce resistance remained. But those pockets were constantly reinforced. In one such pocket was the now-famous Dzerzhinsky Tractor Factory. The plant had been converted to manufacturing T34 tanks and continued in production even when completed tanks, often showing mostly unpainted metal, would roll off the line, be armed, manned, and find themselves in combat as they pulled out of the factory's doors.

Often the Germans would occupy a part of the city after hand-to-hand fighting during the day and then would have to pull back to their bases for supply. The Russians would reoccupy the ruined buildings that night. The next day, the Nazis would have to retake the same building again. Russian soldiers, many ill trained, were poured into Stalingrad by the tens of thousands and died in equally great numbers. The sewers under the city also became the scene of a surreal parallel battle where the dead and wounded simply disappeared into the muck. By the time cold weather arrived, the Sixth Army controlled nine-tenths of the city. Their own casualties had been high, but the Russians' casualty numbers were much higher. It was von Paulus' stated hope that he was punishing the Russian Sixty-second Army so badly they soon would have to give up the city. He was wrong. On November 8, Luftflotte 4, a good portion of the Sixth Army's bombers, had to be withdrawn. They were needed in North Africa. Just as the Russians had been forced into a strip less than a thousand yards deep, the German pressure began to ease.

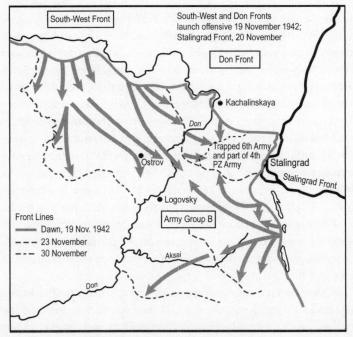

The Battle for Stalingrad

On November 19, everything changed. For months Marshal Zhukov had been accumulating fresh Russian armies and just waiting until winter and enough troops arrived. Now he had both. The Battle of Stalingrad itself had taken the efforts of the entire Sixth Panzer Army. With the Fourth Panzer Army gone, von Paulus had to use whatever else he had at hand to defend the flanks of the salient that ended in Stalingrad. The flanks north and south of the city were held only by thinly spread Romanian divisions and backed up by virtually nothing. These underequipped and often reluctant Romanians could see and hear the buildup as two tank armies and eighteen infantry divisions prepared to attack in just the north. They begged for reinforcements, but von Paulus had no one to send and was focused on completing his conquest of the city. At sunrise on the nineteenth, Russian Operation Uranus began when overwhelming numbers of Soviet tanks and infantry easily shattered the Romanian divisions north of Stalingrad. Two days later in the south, the Romanian IV Corps received the same treatment. The Romanians who were not killed or captured were forced into Stalingrad. Within days, both attacking Soviet armies had met and closed the trap. This time it was the Germans who were encircled. More than a quarter of a million men in the Sixth Panzer Army and allied formations were trapped in Stalingrad.

The German high command wanted to order an immediate breakout. But a month earlier Hitler had told a crowd of thousands in the Berlin Sports Palace that the German army would never withdraw from Stalingrad. He would not take back his promise. He instead met with Hermann Goering, head of the Luftwaffe. Goering promised that his flyers would be able to deliver 750 tons of supplies per day into the city. Unfortunately, the reality was far different. To haul 750 tons, the Luftwaffe needed every transport and most of the bombers on the eastern front to fly four supply missions each day. The trouble was there was not enough daylight for four missions, or often even two. Nor was there ever enough aircraft available. The most tonnage that was ever actually flown into the trapped army, in one day, was 289 tons on December 19. The average, though, was only ninety-four tons per day, or an eighth of the amount needed. Each day, the trapped soldiers had less ammunition and less to eat. By the end of the airlift, in January 1943, the Luftwaffe had lost almost 500 aircraft. One out of every two planes had been shot down or crashed trying to fulfill Goering's promise. But Hitler himself ensured that the pilots' efforts were all in vain.

After they had joined up, the Russian armies formed a defensive position facing both Stalingrad and the Germans outside to the west. They formed lines of circumvallation, whose design would have looked familiar to Caesar's legionnaires at Alesia. Unfortunately for the trapped Sixth Army and von Paulus, this worked just as well for Zhukov as it had for Caesar. Arguably the best commander the Germans had was sent to deal with the problem of saving the Sixth Panzer Army. This was Erich von Manstein. He mounted a counterattack using Hoth's Fourth Panzer. It penetrated to within thirty-four miles of Stalingrad against determined Russian opposition. Again, the German high command asked for permission for the Sixth Panzer Army to break out and join up. Again, Hitler refused, and von Paulus, knowing that this decision likely doomed his army, obeyed. Facing overwhelming numbers of Russian tanks, Hoth eventually had to withdraw. A few weeks later, the Soviets launched an offensive named Winter Storm. This attack almost trapped all of Army Group South and forced a general withdrawal of more than 100 miles. The Sixth Army in Stalingrad was now separated by almost 150 miles from the new German defensive line.

Supply flights, having to cross even more unfriendly territory, became less frequent and suffered higher losses. German soldiers on the lines in Stalingrad literally starved when they did not die of exposure first. Ammunition was rationed and medical supplies virtually gone. Then the airstrip was overrun, and the last German plane to land took off again carrying wounded and a few officers on January 23.

By the middle of January, the Sixth Army became a formation that was broken into pockets. The Russians then approached von Paulus with an offer. If he surrendered, his men would be treated well, receive medical help, and be guaranteed repatriation after the war ended. Seeing no chance of escape or victory, von

Paulus asked Hitler for permission to surrender. This was Hitler's reply:

> *Surrender is forbidden. 6 Army will hold their positions to the last man and the last round and by their heroic endurance will make an unforgettable contribution towards the establishment of a defensive front and the salvation of the Western world.*

General von Paulus obeyed and turned down Zhukov's offer. On January 30, having doomed the army and its commander once more, Hitler promoted von Paulus to field marshal. The Führer then informed the hapless commander that no German field marshal had ever surrendered. Finally, the former staff officer acted on his own. Though by this point the only action left to him was to surrender. He did this, including the men defending his pocket, the next day. Two-thirds of the Germans trapped in Stalingrad had died. The remaining 91,000 had all surrendered by February 2. Of those men, less than 5,000 ever returned alive to Germany, most many years after the war had ended.

Hitler's mishandling of the Battle of Stalingrad, from appointing a personal favorite but untested commander to twice refusing to allow the army to save itself, cost Germany half a million soldiers. Half a million veteran soldiers would have made France impregnable to an Allied landing or delayed the Russian advance on Berlin for months. The men of the Sixth Panzer Army would be desperately needed as the Soviet war machine pushed west, but they were all lost because of Adolf Hitler's mistakes.

82

||||||||||||||||||||||||||||||||||||||||||||||||||||||||||||||||

TOO LITTLE,
TOO LATE

The Salient Question

1943

||||||||||||||||||||||||||||||||||||||||||||||||||||||||||||||||||||||||||

The strategy of pinching off a salient, or bulge, created by the last surge of the Soviet army's central front's winter offensive was not a bad one. Some action that would punish and slow the relentless advance of the Soviet army was a necessity. Since Stalingrad, the Wehrmacht had been reacting to the Russian army, and they knew that their first priority had to be to get the initiative back. Russian tank production was beginning to peak at so many tanks per month that that German high command did not believe the figures. Worse yet, German production had hit a snag. They had stopped some of the production of their workhorse panzer IVs in favor of building the Panther and Tiger models. A problem was neither of those tanks could be produced in numbers sufficient to replace the Mark IVs lost. In the month that the German tank industry changed over to producing the two new and much more powerful tanks, only twenty-five Tigers were manufactured. The Panthers also continued to have such severe reliability problems that, as Heinz Guderian bluntly noted in his memoir *Panzer Leader*, they were "simply not ready for the front yet." But Hitler, seeing the war effort crumbling on every side, put inordinate faith in his new "super weapons," among these the Panther and Tiger tanks and the ME262 jet fighter/bomber.

There were really only two choices for the German army. Many of the most experienced field commanders, including Erich von Manstein and Heinz Guderian, master of the Blitzkrieg, wanted to continue as they were. This was to use the superior tactics and skills of the German forces by forming mobile reserves that responded to and destroyed every Soviet army penetration. If they could crush enough tanks and their supporting infantry, both the numbers and the skill level of their opponents would fall. Just as in World War I, when the Russian soldiers felt they were being wasted, they revolted.

The chief of staff, General Zeitler, had a more ambitious plan. He wanted to return to the sweeping encirclement of 1941. His idea was to draw the Russian army in and destroy them in one large battle. This was, not surprising, a form of the decisive battle fallacy found all through history. He felt that he had found the ideal location for such a confrontation. The Russians had pushed forward into the German position and formed a deep bulge located in almost the center of all of the German positions. On one flank of the penetration, the Wehrmacht held the city of Orel, and on the other, Kharkov. Both cities were major rail centers and so ideal locations for the buildup of forces needed to pinch off the salient. The German armies would encourage the Soviets to place, in or near Kursk, as many tanks and soldiers as possible. Then they would pinch it off by converging on Kursk in the center, trapping so many Russians that their offensive capability would be crippled. This plan is shown on the map (see page 320). The reality would have much shorter lines for the German advances: barely showing in the north and half as long in the south.

Hitler wanted a decisive victory, and one at Kursk both would be dramatic and had a better chance of knocking Russia out of the war. So on May 4, 1943, Hitler decided on Zeitler's plan, dubbed Operation Citadel, and ordered it be implemented. At this point, it became his plan and so it was sacrosanct and unchangeable by anyone else. The war was going badly on all fronts. Hitler

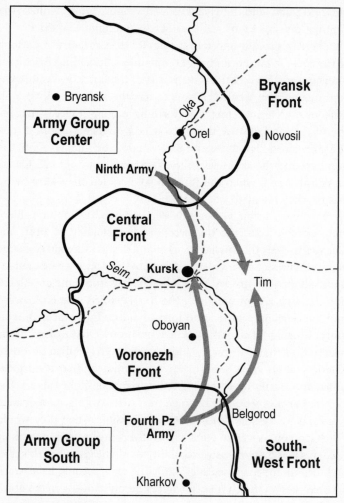

The Battle of Kursk

had become, at best, unstable and tended to irrational screaming fits or worse. Just telling him what he did not want to hear was risky. He was still the absolute dictator of the Reich.

Two problems appeared immediately. The first was that the Russians were already preparing a defense in depth of the salient. Line after defensive line was being prepared with antitank guns, machine guns, and fortifications. The Russian tanks, which were the target of the exercise, were being placed farther back. This meant that before there could be Blitzkrieg, the German panzers would have to slug through miles of fixed defenses. Experienced panzer general von Mellenthin saw the aerial photos of those defenses and correctly described the attack as being a "Totenritt," a death ride. Field Marshal Guderian tried to get Hitler to cancel the attack. According to Guderian, the Führer admitted that thinking about the plan made his stomach turn, but he refused to cancel it. Hitler wanted a decisive victory that would change the war and give him the victory he thought he had in 1941.

The second problem was there simply were not enough of the new Tiger tanks to guarantee a victory. The T-34 and KV-1 Russian tanks had sloped and thick frontal armor. The 75mm cannon on the Mark IVs had difficulty penetrating it. The 88mm gun on the Panthers and the Tigers cut through the Russian sloped armor and were effective at twice the range of the guns on the Soviet tanks. Hitler counted on his secret weapon tanks to counterbalance the far superior numbers of Soviet armor. But there were far fewer than 100 Tigers ready on May 4, when the plan was agreed to. Optimistically, assuming that the incredibly slow production of the new tanks would accelerate given time, Hitler solved this problem by delaying the attack until July 4.

This delay ignored two realities. To break through and encircle the Russians west of Kursk, the panzers had to fight through the defenses being prepared. The two-month delay benefited both sides, but the Russians more. Waiting for enough Tigers meant allowing two more months of Russian construction on the defenses. The delay also gave the Soviets two more months of tank and assault gun production. According to *Jane's World Armoured Fighting Vehicles*, the Soviets were manufacturing almost 2,000 tanks and a few hundred assault guns each month in 1943. This compared with no more than 1,000 a month for the Germans, with only a small percentage of those being the Tiger. So the longer the battle was delayed, the greater the German inferiority in the number of tanks grew. There were also an estimated 44,000 tanks the Americans and British built in 1943. Time was not on the Nazis' side, but still Hitler ordered a delay of two months. It is no wonder that thinking about the battle for Kursk upset Hitler's stomach.

Just to make sure things went badly, there was also a Russian spy network, code name Lucy, that extended all the way up into the German high command. It made sure Stalin was apprised of the plan and any changes right up to and during the battle itself. It also allowed Stalin and Zhukov to know the numbers and plans for Citadel. It is significant that, knowing all this, they actually waited for the German Kursk offensive and even held out large formations from that battle for counterattacks once it failed. It seemed everyone but Hitler knew his offensive was doomed to failure. But Hitler was the only one who could stop it.

At midnight on July 4, two hours before Operation Citadel's scheduled jump-off time, a massive Soviet barrage hit the German assembly areas on both flanks. This put every Wehrmacht soldier on notice of what their commanders already knew. There would be no surprise for the long-planned and -prepared attack. Within the Kursk bulge, the Russians had placed 20,000 artillery pieces, many of them antitank guns grouped by the dozens and protected by earth and concrete defenses. Inside or near the salient were 3,600 tanks, 2,400 aircraft, and 1.3 million soldiers. Every square mile of the bulge had been saturated with more than 5,000 land mines evenly split between personnel and antitank. Civilians drafted from the nearby cities had dug thousands of miles of trenches and ditches deep enough to slow or trap a tank.

The two German attacks consisted of 10,000 guns, 2,700 tanks, 2,000 airplanes, and 900,000 soldiers. These men all came from the best-equipped and most-experienced veteran divisions left to the Wehrmacht. Even with the loss of surprise and knowing about the defense they faced, the sheer size of the attack force gave the German commanders some degree of optimism. General Mellenthin stated, "No offensive was ever prepared as carefully as this one."

The two prongs of the German attack took some time to recover from the disruption caused by the surprise Soviet barrage. At 4:30 AM, rather than 2 AM as scheduled, both armies began their attack. At first the Germans, at high price, managed to break through the defenses. But it was slow going, with losses mounting. In the north the Ninth Army was able to push forward only six miles at the cost of two-thirds of its tanks. The Ninth's losses after six days were 25,000 men and 200 tanks. In the south, the Fourth Panzer had more men and tanks and was comparatively more successful. But by July 12, the only way to continue their attack had been by committing all of the German reserves to it. By that day, the southern attack had lost half its tanks, and to continue attacking, it gathered the 600 tanks that remained into a single force.

Marshal Zhukov realized that the northern penetration had been stopped and that the Germans were just about played out. He released his reserve, the Fifth Guard Tank Army, in an attack on the massed German tanks, which were still spearheading the Fourth Army's attack. The two tank forces met about fifty miles from Kursk. The day was foggy and the tanks had intermingled by the time the Fourth Panzer was aware of the 1,500 Russian tanks. A wild melee followed, with some tanks fighting literally barrel to barrel. The Germans lost more than 300 tanks, and by nightfall, the Fifth Guard Tank Army was torn and in ruins. But those German tank losses made it impossible for the offensive to continue. The Battle of Kursk was over.

Within days, Russian offensives on both sides of the Kursk bulge began. These really did not stop until Berlin. By betting it all on a "decisive battle" that even he must have realized his army could not win, Hitler completely ceded the initiative to Russia for the rest of the war. Germany was never again able to make up for the tanks and trained crews lost attacking Kursk. Had the limited counterattack plan, which was the alternative, been chosen, the Wehrmacht might have retained enough tanks and planes to slow or stop the Soviet army. Without those lost tanks, even the most valiant and brilliant tactics could do no more than cause local delays. The Battle of Kursk was a mistake that sealed the defeat of Nazi Germany and guaranteed the Soviets control of eastern Europe.

83

OPINION OVER REALITY
Asleep at the Switch
1944

Erwin Rommel knew that he had to stop the Allies on the beach when they invaded France. This was mandated simply by the dominant air superiority the British and Americans had. The field marshal had seen, in North Africa, what damage the aircraft could do to any column of troops or formation of tanks. If the Allied army got a foothold on the French coast, they might well be able to reinforce it quicker and in greater numbers using ships from Britain than he could transport over what remained of the French highways and railroads. History is to show that he was correct. Part of Rommel's reaction to this reality was to pour money and labor down the drain of the West Wall. His other efforts were spent attempting to ensure that there would be enough men, tanks, and artillery near where the Allies landed to throw them back into the sea.

Erwin Rommel's opinion was not shared by everyone. Having seen the damage ships' guns could do at Salerno, Field Marshal Gerd von Rundstedt wanted to let the Allies land and then chew them apart on a line that was just out of the range of the naval weapons. Hitler, as always, did not want to give up an inch of French soil and pushed to make the beach defense of the West

Wall so strong that the landing craft never made it to shore. But he also encouraged the competing views of both of his field marshals.

A chart of the actual command situation in France in 1944 would resemble a plate of spaghetti, with lines of command and responsibility that bore little resemblance to those on the charts on the walls of the high command in Berlin. The high command (OKW) ran the war in the west, but Hitler personally could, and often did, override their decisions. These changes could be quite painful for the staff and OKW generals: By this time, the Führer was disposed to screaming fits and loud lectures. Just telling Hitler something he did not want to hear could be hazardous to your career; and explaining why any order or demand he made was wrong could have fatal consequences. Often these consequences involved a long train ride to the Eastern Front.

While Field Marshal Wilhelm von Keitel was in overall command of France, he did not have control of the Third Air Fleet, which Goering held tightly, or Navy Group West. The navy group had few ships, but it did control most of the heavy guns built into the West Wall. So the man in charge of defending France was not in control of much of his shore artillery and none of the aircraft in the theater. The ground forces in France and the Low Countries were commanded by von Rundstedt. He controlled, when his orders were not countermanded by Hitler, fifty-eight divisions, including seven panzer divisions. Also in France were almost totally independent panzer units controlled by the SS. The SS were responsible directly to only Hitler or their own headquarters in Berlin.

Preparing to meet the Allied landing as it moved inland, von Rundstedt located a strong reserve force, including most of the panzers available, near Paris. Erwin Rommel felt that with Allied air superiority, any unit not close to the front would be unable to get there until it was too late to matter. So he lobbied to have the best units, including most of the tanks, stationed near the beach. He even went over his commanding officer's head, talking Hitler into giving him control of all seven of the panzer divisions in France. Needless to say, Field Marshal von Rundstedt was upset to be overruled and went himself to the Führer. So Hitler reversed himself and gave control of the panzers back to von Rundstedt. But both men continued to bicker, and eventually Hitler made a compromise by assigning three of the panzer divisions to Rommel and four to von Rundstedt for the OKW reserve. This was a mistake since now neither field marshal had a large enough force to be decisive.

Complicating the scenario for the Germans even more was the question of where the Allied landing would be. For a range of reasons, which included excellent deceptions in England to the opinion that the V1 and V2 rockets were so effective that they had to be the Allies' first target, Hitler and many of his generals were sure the real landing would be at the Pas-de-Calais. It also sat across the narrowest part of the Channel. There was even a lot of chatter and messages from Nazi spies who had turned into double agents that the landing at Normandy was really a diversion and no more than a large raid. Every effort was made to reinforce the defenses based on this mistaken assumption.

Because of the complicated command structure, the rivalry between the German field marshals, and the expectations of Hitler, when 75,000 British, Canadian, French, and American troops landed on four beaches, only the three panzer divisions under Rommel reacted. And he was proven correct about one thing. Even the nearby panzers had problems moving short distances by day due to attacks by the Allied airplanes. And the four panzer divisions commanded by von Rundstedt? They sat and waited. Not just for Hitler to wake up in the morning and approve an order to move, but for Hitler to wake up and realize Normandy was the real landing. Then when the tanks of OKW reserve finally began to move toward the fighting, they soon found out just how much Rommel had been correct. Harassment by the Allied air forces slowed or simply prevented them from moving at all during daylight. More than half the German panzers took no part in the fighting during the first and most vulnerable days of the landing.

Hitler made the mistake of splitting the best weapon Germany had to meet the Allied invasion with: its armored units. By doing so, he ensured they could not all join in a truly decisive counterattack. Then because of Hitler's mercurial nature and his holding on to the belief that the real Allied invasion was still going to be at Pas-de-Calais, there was a delay in committing more than half of his panzer divisions until it was too late. By the time they arrived, the landings were a success, and Germany's defeat in France almost assured.

On D-Day in Normandy on June 6, 1944, the first wave that landed on Juno Beach suffered 50 percent casualties. On Utah Beach, things were just as bad. The assault went so badly on Omaha Beach that General Omar Bradley almost pulled the troops back off when they bogged down with massive casualties only a few yards onto the sand of the beach. At any one of these beaches, the addition of a panzer division to the initial defense might well have wiped out or driven off the landing. If each beach had one additional division, the entire invasion would have been in shambles. With only two beachheads left, the flanks of both would have been open to the very type of attack the panzers excelled at. In addition, if the fourth reserve panzer division had been in the area where the paratroopers landed, this would have meant their total destruction.

With intense naval bombardment and massive air support, the Allied armies might well have gained and expanded their five D-Day beachheads. If Eisenhower had been willing to endure the casualties, there would have been enough men waiting offshore to reinforce what beaches were held, even in the face of momentous losses. D-Day most likely still would have succeeded, but only at a terrible cost in lives. The loss might have been so great that the breakout and conquest of France might well have been delayed by weeks or longer. So by personality, purposely muddled command, and a decision made as a compromise, Hitler himself made the key mistakes that guaranteed the success of the Normandy D-Day landing.

84

THE HIGH PRICE OF
RACISM

Liberators Lost

1933–1945

Y ou can talk about what battlefield mistakes Germany and
Japan made that lost those nations World War II. Taking
an overall strategic view, both nations were basically overwhelmed. The Japanese lost because they simply could not compete with the industrial strength of the United States. No matter
how valiantly Japan fought, going it alone against a nation that
was launching one fleet carrier and at least another jeep carrier
each month, they were going to lose. The Germans not only
shared being overwhelmed by the sheer mass of manufacturing
that poured out of the United States, Britain, and Russia but also
were swamped by the manpower of their opponents. If it weren't
for a fundamental mistake—a tragic flaw, more accurately—by
both of the Axis powers, this would not have been the case.

The problem was the irrational and self-destructive racism
that was so heartily embraced by both nations. Racism first cost
Germany much at home. Hitler and the Nazis did not need to
bash the Jews to get elected in 1933. The fear of the communists
and economic collapse gave them that victory. But Hitler and his
henchmen were so sold on their Aryan superiority that they overlooked what they denied Germany by banishing or killing off that

nation's Jews. The group that contributed a higher percentage of volunteer soldiers than any other in World War I was the German Jews. Their patriotism was widely recognized during that war. In science and manufacturing, they had always contributed far beyond their numbers. Many of the world's top scientists were German Jews. Almost all eventually fled the country. Among those who fled to the United States was Albert Einstein. Out of the 6 million Jews who died in the Holocaust, if the same percentage had instead been left alone and served in the Wehrmacht in World War II, this would have added at least ten more divisions of highly educated soldiers. Ten more divisions might have taken Moscow.

Nothing portrays the cost of Aryan racism more than footage of Nazi units "liberating" towns in Ukraine. The Soviet Union had conquered Ukraine. It was never part of Russia culturally or politically, and it is adamantly not today. Ukraine had actually been part of Germany itself for much of 1918, having been sold out by the Bolsheviks as part of their peace agreement with the kaiser. When Germany collapsed, Ukraine became an independent nation with a population equal to that of Poland. Eventually, through betrayal, Ukraine was absorbed by the Soviet Union. Always too independent and resistant to communism, Ukraine was punished by Stalin in every way he could manage. In the years before the second war, 9 million Ukrainians were killed by Stalin either directly or by consciously created famines. So when the Germans arrived, they were treated like lost brothers and liberators. Wehrmacht officers helped open churches and were feasted and flirted by the local population. These millions of people were ready to work for and fight for Germany. Within weeks, the SS began implementing secret orders for occupied Slavic territories. The order included the elimination of all Jews, leaders, priests, teachers, and military officers. The stated eventual goal of the SS plan was to depopulate large parts of Ukraine and enslave the survivors. The then-empty Ukraine was to be settled by German overlords.

A supportive Ukrainian population could have provided up to a million additional soldiers to fight against Russia. This would have replaced all the losses taken at Stalingrad in the winter of 1942 to 1943. But because of the Aryan myth and the sheer sadism of the SS, three months after the Germans were welcomed in Ukraine, its forests were full of guerrillas. Instead of tying up tens of thousands of soldiers with occupation duties, Ukraine should have provided hundreds of thousands of soldiers fighting alongside the Germans. The story was the same for the Balts, the White Russians, the Tartar, the Mongolian, and even the German Balts. They were a ready source of support and recruits for the manpower-poor German army, but the Nazi leadership could not get past their extreme racism and wasted this great potential asset. The final result was that as the formerly hated Soviets recaptured Ukraine and its neighbors, the surviving men often volunteered to join the ranks of the Red Army. German racism turned a literal army of peoples that hated the communists into their willing recruits.

Germany did not have the monopoly on racism in the 1940s. The Americans put tens of thousands of Japanese Americans into camps for no more reason than they looked Japanese. The heroic combat record of the Nisei division in Italy shows the fallacy of that action. There was also the treatment by the army of black soldiers. Many were allocated to noncombat roles and denied promotion on no other basis than their skin color. It wasn't until twenty years after the end of World War II that the last Jim Crow laws disappeared. But anything any of the Allies did paled compared to the sheer barbarism of the Japanese toward other Asian peoples and everyone else during the war.

In places such as Indochina and the Philippines, it had not been that long since British, French, and American troops had been battling with local independence movements. One of the reasons the Thompson machine gun was developed was to knock down machete-swinging Philippine rebels who were impervious to pain because of the druglike effects of the plants they chewed. Certainly as soon as the Japanese left, all of Vietnam went right back to trying to throw out the French. Each of these countries had millions who would and did embrace a pan-Asian philosophy. But the Japanese soldiers were indoctrinated to treat everyone not Japanese as inferior and not really human. This attitude was so pervasive that all over Asia it was rare to see any non-

Japanese assisting them in combat. This contrasts with the tens of thousands of Indian and Malaysian troops that joined with the British to repel the Japanese. In almost every country where Japanese had been welcomed for throwing out the European colonial master, within days, powerful resistance movements had sprung up.

The Japanese had a habit of shooting or beheading anyone who annoyed them, even their own soldiers, without as much as a hearing. This behavior reflected the barbarism that permeated all of their behavior. Officers treated their men with disdain, and the common soldiers passed on that hate and brutality with enthusiasm. The Japanese made it clear to all other Asians that they were held in contempt and were unworthy of respect. Americans rarely remember that 80 percent of those who died on the Bataan Death March were Philippine. The Philippine people never forgot, though. By actually acting like they promised to with their coprosperity sphere, Japan might have been able to recruit literally millions of new soldiers. They could have much more effectively tapped the resources of Indochina and might even have had enough soldiers to complete the conquest of China. The entire war in China and the Pacific would have been far different and an Allied victory far from assured.

The mistake and cost of racism were obvious even at the time. But like the Confederacy being asked to recruit former slaves as soldiers, the Imperial Japanese and Nazi Germans found that acting against their prejudices was inconceivable. They had every reason, and hard necessity, to treat potential allied peoples well and always failed to do so. Simple racism, more than any strategic blunder, doomed the fascists.

85

||||||||||||||||||||||||||||||||||||||||||||||||||||||||||||||||

STUCK TO A BAD
BARGAIN

Stopping at the Elbe

1945

||||||||||||||||||||||||||||||||||||||||||||||||||||||||||||||||||

At the time of the Yalta conference, World War II in Europe was almost over. By February 1945, the Germans' last gasp, the surprise attack at Ardennes, had failed. There was no further chance of a serious German counterattack. The three leaders who met there, Roosevelt, Stalin, and Churchill, knew this. Germany had no more left, and Japan, while still dangerous defending their islands, had no offensive strength left. The discussions and agreements were more about the shape of postwar Europe than about the ongoing war. There were actually two major areas of agreement at Yalta. One was to confirm the formation of the United Nations and its structure. The other laid out who would occupy what parts of Germany and the fate of the rest of occupied Europe.

Poland was to be clearly under the Soviet thumb. Russia had not done well against invasions coming out of Poland since the Red Army almost lost the 1920–1921 Polish–Soviet War. They were taking no chances of that happening again, even if it meant occupying Poland forever. There were details, but Stalin publicly agreed that most of eastern Europe would get elected governments within a year or so. History has shown the Soviet dictator had no intention of keeping his word on any free elections, but the United States wanted his help if it became necessary to invade the Japanese home islands, so they accepted this. Any invasion of the homelands was going to be vicious and generate a lot of casualties. A million or so hardy Russian soldiers joining in could make the conquest a lot easier. Also there were Japanese soldiers in Asia—mostly in China, Korea, and Mongolia—who needed pressure kept on them.

Between February and late April, the Allied armies pushed into the heart of Germany. By late April, the question was more one of what areas would be occupied rather than of defeating those remnants of the Wehrmacht that were still fighting. There was also concern about rumors of a guerrilla army forming in the south German mountains. These turned out to be false, but it was a worrisome possibility. The big question was, where would Eisenhower push? To the frustration of Patton and other commanders, the decision was made to turn away from Berlin and to actually reverse any penetrations into eastern Europe. This was ordered even as it became more apparent that Stalin had no intention of granting any real elections or giving up one ounce of control in any part of the nations Russia occupied. Word came down from Roosevelt, and the U.S. Army was effectively ordered to concede eastern Europe to the Soviets. The mistake here was not agreeing to the terms at Yalta. The mistake was not being concerned about a final guerrilla retreat in the mountains that never existed. The Americans' real mistake was adhering to their parts of the treaty when it was already apparent the communists had no intention of honoring any of it.

Had the U.S. president and army been prescient enough to foresee the Cold War, as Churchill did, would Eisenhower have ordered a continued push? His divisions could have gotten to Berlin first, considering how resistance had collapsed. It would have been possible for the highly mobile American mechanized divisions to reach Austria, Berlin, Albania, Bulgaria, and maybe Czechoslovakia. Would, as Patton expected, or maybe hoped, this have resulted in a shooting war between the former allies? It was a war that neither side would have been guaranteed to win. But Russia was a nation as tired of war as the others.

There is no way to know what the world might have looked like had Roosevelt and then Truman risked war and stood up to Stalin. What America did instead was stick to the terms of a treaty that had become meaningless. This mistake resulted in tens of millions of eastern Europeans being condemned to fifty years of communist repression.

||||||||||||||||||||||||||||||||||||||||||||||||||||||||||||||||||||||

86

MISQUOTED

What Sphere of
Influence?

1950

||||||||||||||||||||||||||||||||||||||||||||||||||||||||||||||||||||||

A diplomat's tool is words, and it is reasonable to assume someone who has risen to be the top diplomat for the United States means what he says. So when Joseph Stalin and Kim Il-sung invaded South Korea, they were shocked and honestly amazed at the vehement reaction from the United Nations (UN) and the United States. They had every right to be, since effectively they had been given permission to attack by the U.S. secretary of state.

Secretary of State Dean Acheson, on January 12, 1950, made a speech to the National Press Club. This was a policy speech and not casual remarks. It seemed likely that the speech was intended to act as a warning to the now-antagonistic communist Russia, China, and their satellites. In this speech, Acheson described the American post–World War II sphere of influence as it extended all over the world. The problem came when he described the U.S. interest in the Pacific and mentioned Japan, but not Korea. Imagine Kim Il-sung's joy when he heard that coveted South Korea was not protected by the United States.

The problem of mixed signals on Korea was also complicated by politics. President Truman was a Democrat, and the Congress was controlled by the Republican Party. And the Republicans did not like many of Truman's foreign policies. As a result, when Truman requested $60 million in aid for South Korea, Congress refused to pass it. Then a bill that would finance 500 advisers and training personnel to assist in equipping the South Korean army with modern weapons was defeated in the House by the close vote of 193 to 192. Those in power in Moscow and Pyongyang saw a clear message. America was abandoning South Korea.

An action taken by Truman on April 25, 1950, might have cleared up the matter and put the North Koreans on notice. This was National Security Directive 68, which committed American resources to counter any communist aggression "anywhere in Asia." It was a strong and clear statement and could have been an equally clear warning. The problem was national security directives are classified top secret.

 A public statement by John Foster Dulles, Truman's special envoy to Asia, likely was intended to put the communists on notice. Unfortunately, he worded his statement in typical diplomatic terms, obscuring the message. The closest Dulles came to a definitive statement was in his speech to the South Korean Assembly. He said that America was "faithful to the cause of human freedom and loyal to those everywhere who honorably support it." Not exactly fighting words to warn off an aggressor.

North Korean troops poured over the thirty-eighth parallel on June 17, 1950. The poorly armed and disorganized South Korean army was incapable of serious resistance. The few American units in Korea were quickly forced to retreat south. Then the world responded to the invasion.

After all they had heard, it was likely that both Stalin and Kim Il-sung found the adamant reaction by the United States a shock. Had the Soviet Union or China actually expected a military response from Truman, it is likely that they would have not allowed Kim Il-sung to attack. Certainly they would not have let the invasion happen while they were boycotting the Security Council. Because the Russians were not attending the UN Security Council meetings, the council was able to pass a resolution calling for strong military force to support and restore South Korea. Before the conflict ended, 50,000 UN soldiers, mostly Americans, were killed along with many times that number of North Koreans and then Chinese. It was a high price to pay for what was effectively just sloppy language.

||||||||||||||||||||||||||||||||||||||||||||||||||||||||||||||||||||||||||||||

87

EGO OVER WISDOM

MacArthur and the
Chinese

1950

||||||||||||||||||||||||||||||||||||||||||||||||||||||||||||||||||||||||||||||

T he mistake that changed the Korean War and cost more than 10,000 American lives was caused by ego. Not just the ego of one man, though there was a man whose ego was as enormous as his reputation. That man was General Douglas MacArthur. It also involved a bad attack of victory disease by the chief of staff and a good bit of racial prejudice. The problems that resulted from this mistake are still in the news.

It all began because the North Korean Army (NKA) attacked South Korea. (The diplomatic mistakes that caused this are discussed on pages 335–337.) In the first few weeks after their surprise attack, the NKA forced the few South Korean and American divisions into a small area in a southern corner of the Korean peninsula that became known as the Pusan Perimeter. Then, on September 5, in a bold move, MacArthur landed 70,000 men at Inchon. The successful landing was above and behind the bulk of the North Korean Army. Within days, the Americans had taken back Seoul and fought their way across Korea. At the same time, United Nations forces in the Pusan Perimeter broke out and swept north. Cut off from retreat, not to mention food, ammunition, and fuel, while pressed from two sides, the NKA simply collapsed.

North Korea was a communist country, and it was known that it got support from Red Premier Mao's China. When it was apparent that there were no longer substantial North Korean forces left to even slow MacArthur should he push above the old border at the thirty-eighth parallel, the Chinese asked the Indian ambassador to notify Washington that it would be considered an unacceptable threat to the People's Republic of China for North Korea to be occupied. This was tantamount to a public promise to attack. Unfortunately, the CIA designated the ambassador as an unreliable source and ignored China's message.

There were no aircraft overflying China and Manchuria. MacArthur and his staff had been in the habit of depending on the radio intelligence of the Armed Forces Security Agency (AFSA) to keep them informed about the Chinese. But the signal intelligence agency was unable to break the Chinese codes and were reluctant to admit so. What intelligence did come in, before MacArthur's troops continued north, came from the CIA. Unfortunately, what they provided was more analysis that conformed to their own general beliefs instead of real intelligence. By their own later analysis of their efforts in 1950, they reported, "While full-scale Chinese Communist intervention in Korea must be regarded as a continuing possibility, a consideration of all known factors leads to the conclusion that barring a Soviet decision for global war, such action is not probable in 1950."

So while the Chinese felt that they had publicly warned the United States to stop, no one got the message. Regardless, the Chinese communists had put the world on notice, and not responding strongly would have been a terrible loss of face for Mao's relatively new government. Former admiral and the Japanese ambassador to the United States, Kichasaburo Nakamura, warned the Truman government that China would be required to react strongly if MacArthur continued, but again, the message was ignored. Nor would such a warning have been welcomed. Buoyed by his Inchon victory, MacArthur's attitude might be characterized as: They wouldn't dare.

MacArthur, urged by the South Korean leader Syngman Rhee, launched his two corps north, sending the Ten Corps up along the southern coast and the Eight Corps to land at a port 100 miles north of the thirty-eighth parallel. Both forces then advanced against little resistance. The operations could be best characterized as a cleanup. As both corps approached the Chinese border, they began to capture first individual and then entire Chinese units. Still everyone on the U.S. side refused to believe the Chinese would attack.

The CIA had information that they simply refused to believe as of October 13. It correctly placed 498,000 Chinese combat troops and 370,000 additional security and support troops on the Korean border. Daily summary reports were issued by the CIA. Their report for October 13 said that "China had no intention of entering the war in any large-scale fashion." The three-quarters of a million soldiers were explained as being on the border within miles of the invading UN forces "to protect the hydroelectric plants along the Yalu River that provide power to the Manchurian industrial area."

On November 24, the CIA stated that even though they had identified twelve Chinese divisions inside Korea and that China did have the capability for a large-scale offensive, they did not appear to be preparing to launch one. Before this CIA analysis could reach MacArthur's headquarters, his two corps were under attack by 300,000 Chinese. The Eighth Army took 4,000 casualties as it made a fighting retreat and the Tenth Corps First Marine Division was surrounded and survived only by making one of the most heroic fighting withdrawals in history.

The Chinese had told everyone they were going to attack. Then they stated that, having done so, they had to attack if MacArthur's offensive continued. Next they left a half million men along the border for weeks. Then the Chinese sent smaller units into Korea that were seen, and some Chinese soldiers were captured by the advancing American forces. And still no one of authority from MacArthur to the CIA analysts believed that, even after they had repeatedly said they would, the Chinese would actually attack. The cost of this arrogance was two more years of war, tens of thousands of UN casualties, and perhaps a million Korean dead. There is still no peace treaty between North and South Korea.

88

DIRTY TRICK

Staying Clean

1953

Scientists at 3M in Minnesota were trying to make a better formula for synthetic rubber. The rubber shortages of World War II had made such research important even into the 1950s. As sometimes happens, one of the lab assistants spilled an ounce or so of one of the many compounds onto the tennis shoe of scientist Patsy Sherman. Trying to redeem himself, the lab assistant worked hard to remove the substance from the shoe. Nothing worked, not soap, alcohol, or water. In fact the stained area repelled everything he tried. Sherman and another researcher, Sam Smith, began working with the spilled substance. Between them, they refined the chemical and, in 1956, 3M began selling Scotchgard.

89

MYTH OF THE
DECISIVE BATTLE

Cards, Spades, and the
High Ground

1953

One of the most socially and militarily traumatic events in American history was the U.S. involvement in Vietnam. The failures there left scars that affect military decisions even into the twenty-first century. The United States had to and did make a lot of mistakes to lose their part of that war, but the real mistake that started it all wasn't one any American made. It was made by a Frenchman. A French general to be exact. His name was Henri Navarre, and he hated to lose. Normally that is a good trait in a general, but in this case it led him to make a mistake that cost thousands of French lives and later ensured there would be tens of thousands of American and Vietnamese dead.

General Navarre was in charge of the pacification of Vietnam after World War II. When that war had ended, the French returned to their former colony of French Indochina after the defeated occupying Japanese departed. There was some expectation by the French who returned that things would go back to normal when the French plantation owners and managers returned home. But times had changed. There was no normal to return to.

The Japanese had not only defeated but also embarrassed the European nations, taking away the entire subcontinent with impressive ease. During the war, the Allies had encouraged local guerrilla movements to resist the Japanese, training a few and arming many. The communists joined in this, fielding their own resistance movements. When the French returned, the Vietnamese refused to trade the new master for the old one. The French resisted. After nine years of insurrection, the French government accepted that they were not going to turn back the clock. Also, until Navarre made his mistake, there was a good chance that Võ Nguyên Giáp, leader of the Viet Minh, would accept a coalition government or similar compromise so long as it gave Vietnam self-rule. Though the Viet Minh likely had a further expectation of taking over once the French were gone.

It was a fact that both sides had started talking and that actually spurred General Navarre to look for his own victory. He may even have seen the talks as a sign of his failure. His job had been to reassert total French control and that had not happened. He had not done his job. Navarre certainly realized that once the diplomats had reached any agreement, there would be no way for him to retrieve the situation. But a major victory that dramatically broke the rebellion would not only vindicate his efforts and the sacrifices his soldiers had made already but would also ensure a favorable settlement. What Navarre wanted is a phrase that has appeared before: He sought a decisive battle that would win his war. Unfortunately, to quote a cartoon squirrel popular at that time, "that trick never works."

The problem with fighting any insurgency is how to bring them to battle. Navarre needed the Viet Minh to fight him in a standup battle. But they had so far been wiser than to do that. With air support, artillery, and tanks, there was every expectation that the French would dominate any conventional fight. But the French general thought of a way to force just such a battle. And he was correct: The plan worked and the battle occurred, just not how and when he expected.

The idea was to set up a target that was such a challenge and so enticing that Giáp had to take the bait. To offer this, the French established a base near the town of Dien Bien Phu. This was in the far western part of Vietnam, near nothing except the Laotian border and across trackless jungle from just about anything else. Then, to sweeten its appeal as a target, Navarre built his base in a valley surrounded by steep mountains and did not occupy the mountains. Then Navarre moved most of his army there.

This location seemed to so favor the Viet Minh that they had to attack or lose credibility. Navarre also thought that it really favored him. He saw the battle in his mind and was sure how Giáp would react. Since the French flew in all of their supplies and reinforcements, it wasn't too inconvenient to be far from everyone else. But the French general's expectation was that the dense jungles and distances would limit Giáp to troops armed with only what they could bring with them. This would be men with rifles and little else. It was a long walk.

The Vietnamese had shown a liking, as they later did against the Americans, for human wave attacks. Navarre expected Giáp to rush thousands of his rifle-armed guerrillas in suicidal charges at the base to be slaughtered by his planes, tanks, and artillery. Then, once the strength of the Viet Minh had been wasted, Navarre's army could easily pacify the rest of the country. His decisive battle would win the war, retrieve French honor, and provide an ideal position for the negotiators. And it would work if Giáp did as expected.

But of course Giáp did not do what Navarre wanted. He did summon every Vietnamese he could muster, but not for suicidal attacks. For months, the French would get glimpses of the guerrillas in the mountains around them, but they would vanish before the French airplanes could be called in for a strike. Viet Minh snipers regularly took shots into the camp, most at maximum range. But other than harassment, nothing happened for months at the French base in Dien Bien Phu.

What General Henri Navarre did not see was that during all those months of seeming inactivity, tens of thousands of peasants and guerrillas were hauling on their backs ammunition, artillery pieces broken down into parts, and everything else needed to win a modern battle against the arrogant French in the valley. Villagers would put one artillery shell weighing seventy or eighty pounds in a sling and spend weeks carrying it along jungle paths, which were invisible under the trees, to deliver them to caves cut into the mountains. Finally, the heights on every side of Dien Bien Phu were covered with dug-in artillery and mortar positions. Shells were stockpiled, and when the rainy season arrived, Giáp was ready.

With the rain came the clouds. The clouds were so constant and thick that the French airplanes could not be used effectively. And the rain came on like a monsoon, because it was one. Soon the French tanks could not even move in the deep mud. Everything rusted and had mold. Then the Viet Minh attacked. The French camp was first subjected to a round-the-clock barrage. Thousands of artillery shells were fired. French casualties mounted, and the survivors began shooting blindly into the mountains. There was nothing Navarre's men could do. After several days of bombardment, the human wave attacks did begin. Yes, the Viet Minh losses were high, but the attacks succeeded. Section by section, building by building, the French perimeter contracted. Brave French Foreign Legionnaires attempted to parachute into the diminishing French-controlled area by jumping blindly through the clouds. This was before the era of controllable parachutes, and almost all of those volunteers were either killed or captured. When the airstrip was lost, there was no more hope. A short time later, the French command bunker was overrun. The decisive battle was over with a decisive result. The French had lost, and lost badly.

The peace talks had stalled for months, awaiting the results of the battle at Dien Bien Phu. Once it was apparent just how greatly the Viet Minh had won, they were able to drive a hard bargain. The French agreed to split the country, ceding the northern half to the Viet Minh and setting up a friendly government in the south. The North Vietnamese waited to unite the country under their control.

The Viet Minh were communists and so Western nations began to support and assist the South Vietnamese government even as the Viet Minh, now known as the Vietcong, began an insurgency. Had Navarre not lost at Dien Bien Phu, the settlement might not have split Vietnam. A more peaceful resolution might have been reached: one in which the two halves of Vietnam were actually joined under a single government.

The Western fear was that Vietnam would become a Chinese satellite. But we know now that the Vietnamese were never willingly going to become pawns of the Chinese. After the United States pulled out, and the country was united, Vietnam and China fought three little-publicized but vicious wars. Relations even today are chilly.

But in the name of containing communism, America sent some "military advisers" and began their involvement in Vietnam. And whole books have been written about the mistakes made by the United States. But the entire mess started because a brave French general wanted a decisive battle so badly that he was willing to put his army in a position from which it could not win. Had he not, there would have been no American Vietnam War.

MARKETING
DISASTER
The Ford Edsel
1957

||||||||||||||||||||||||||||||||||||||||||||||||||||||||||||||||||||||||

In "We Didn't Start the Fire" by Billy Joel, he quips that the "Edsel is a no-go." He was referring to a colossal flop by Ford Motor Company in the late 1950s that incurred heavy financial losses for the company and served as a negative example for future endeavors by Ford and other companies. The Edsel was such a failure that on the fiftieth anniversary of its unveiling, *Time* magazine made a list of the fifty worst cars of all time in its honor.

Numerous factors combined to make the Edsel a colossal failure. Described frequently as "the wrong car at the wrong time," it was a large, gas-guzzling car at a time when consumer preferences were shifting toward smaller cars. Sales trends in the years preceding its release suggested that the automobile market had nowhere to go but up. With the onset of a recession in 1958, the Edsel's release was hardly opportune; only two cars saw an increase from 1957 production in that year. Moreover, the Edsel was released in September, a time when most dealers were discounting 1957 models. In 1958, Ford first released its most inexpensive model of the Edsel, the Citation, causing its later-released model, the Corsair, to seem excessively expensive by comparison.

A certain mystique surrounded the Edsel's release as a result of an intense advertising campaign by Ford. The car was billed as a revolutionary design, and in some ways it was: Its self-adjusting rear brakes and automatic lubrication were unprecedented features. However, leading up to its release, the Edsel was presented as a car of the future. All ads featured only blurred images of the car or pictured only its hood, stating, "The Edsel is coming." As vehicles were shipped to dealers, the dealerships were required to keep the cars covered with tarps. Ford created a television program called the *Edsel Show*, featuring big-name celebrities like Frank Sinatra. Ford advertising heralded the day the car would be unveiled as "E-Day." Consumers expected an auto that could drive on water and brew coffee; they got, in their view, a rehashed version of other Ford models. Members of the media derisively referred to the vehicle as "an Oldsmobile sucking a lemon" or "a Pontiac pushing a toilet seat." While many people flocked to dealers to see for themselves what this new model looked like, few bought the car. Internally projected to sell 200,000 vehicles, the Edsel sold only about a third of that. The company lost about $250 million, equivalent to more than $2.25 billion today. The only possible silver lining was that technological advances in the Edsel were incorporated in future Ford vehicles. Moreover, on the strength of other sales, Ford still maintained a profit in the years the Edsel was in production.

Problems existed beyond Ford's marketing strategy, however. By establishing a new division for the Edsel, Ford would use brand-new dealerships rather than relying on dealerships that had already delivered for the company. Unfortunately, Ford did not establish new manufacturing facilities for the Edsel. The Edsel division had to rely on manufacturing facilities for other divisions, such as Mercury. There was no incentive to ensure quality in Edsel vehicles, since the division benefited from selling its own vehicles; in fact, there was some interdivisional competition, which resulted in deliberate sabotage of Edsel vehicles. Cars would arrive at Edsel dealerships with parts missing or the brakes not working. Another problem was a complicated "Tele-touch" gear-shifting mechanism that many drivers and mechanics had difficulty understanding. Design flaws such as a poorly secured hood ornament also became a hazard that gave Edsel a bad reputation; at speeds of about 70 mph, the ornament on the original model was known to fly off the hood.

Other issues stemmed from internal disputes at the top of the Ford food chain. Robert McNamara (later secretary of war), a prominent figure in the company, was generally unsupportive of the endeavor and was instrumental in getting the Edsel nixed in 1960; his argument was that the Edsel was bleeding the company dry. There were even intense disputes about the name. In the early 1950s, Ford had become a publicly traded company, no longer exclusively owned by the Ford family. While Henry Ford II, the original Henry's grandson, was president, his will was not inviolable. Though he was opposed to the automobile being named after his father, a meeting from which he was absent resulted in the decision to dub the new car the Edsel. Numerous studies and surveys by Ford to determine what name should be used yielded no conclusive results. The company even hired a prominent poet, Marianne Moore, to offer input; her suggestions, including "Utopian Turtletop" and "Mongoose Civique," were rejected. Though Edsel was settled on, it was learned after its release that consumers associated the name with negative phrases such as "weasel," "dead cell," and Edson (a tractor), which tempered demand for the car. Moreover, many thought the designers' attempts at making the car physically distinguishable from others merely resulted in an ugly vehicle.

The Edsel's legacy exists as the archetypal flop. Though it is a collectible for some, a stigma is still attached to the car. In the early 1990s, Saturn Corporation used Edsel's failure as an example of what not to do when developing and marketing their flagship car. Rumor has it Skip LeFauve, former president and CEO of Saturn, distributed books about the Edsel to his executives and had them underline everything Ford did wrong. Some described Saturn as "the next Edsel." Evidently they were wrong, considering the company's success.

It is unclear whether there ever will be a "next Edsel" because pains have been taken to avoid that dubious distinction. Regardless, the Edsel will forever be memorialized as a huge disappointment to the car-buying public, a huge embarrassment for the company, and a huge lesson for corporate America.

91

INDECISIVE LEADERSHIP

Bay of Pigs

1961

The original plan for the Bay of Pigs invasion was for a small group of rebels to land near the mountains in Cuba. They were to be the seed from which an insurgency that would overthrow Fidel Castro grew. This was modeled on a very successful CIA program that had overthrown a left-leaning government in Guatemala a few years earlier. Much of the same team worked on both. Both plans were the brainchild of Richard Bissell, the chief of covert operations for the CIA. Bissell was both brilliant and proven. From the moment he took on the project during the Eisenhower administration, everyone was sure Castro was doomed.

This project ran parallel to other less than brilliant moves by the CIA, including hiring the mob to stage a hit on Castro. Still it got strong support from the vice president and the likely next president, Richard Nixon. But John Fitzgerald Kennedy won instead. This had two effects. The first was that Bissell had to sell the program to the new president. Kennedy was young and had a lot to prove. He was facing increasing pressure from the hawks in both parties (yes, there used to be Democratic hawks, really) and was inclined to support anything that made him look tough on communism. Using half-truths and not explaining too much, Bissell got a busy JFK to agree.

The second effect of Nixon losing was that Bissell no longer was working with any real supervision. Nixon had been active in the planning. Kennedy was too busy. Thus many things changed. The small group became a small army. A sneak landing became an amphibious attack. More than 2,000 disgruntled Cubans began to train in secret Central American bases.

Kennedy continued to agree, but only on the basis that the entire plan be secret and that the United States have deniability. It could not look like the U.S. government was involved at all. It was unclear who else he expected the world to blame for an amphibious landing and B26 bombing raids on its island neighbor. That summer the *Miami Herald* found out about the training camps. They were pressured to kill the story and did. At the end of October 1960, a Guatemalan newspaper ran a detailed story about Cubans training in their country. On January 10, 1961, the story about the Guatemalan training camps was featured on the front page of the *New York Times*. But the CIA and Bissell remained confident.

By February 1961, the Bissell invasion plan involved the U.S. Marines, two bomber wings of the U.S. Air Force (USAF), numerous U.S. Navy destroyers, and his intrepid Cubans. Strangely, there was no clear plan about what to do if the invasion did overthrow Castro. There was no government in exile or any one group ready to inspire the Cuban masses and form a friendly government.

Kennedy balked at the sheer size of the plan, and despite the CIA's best efforts, he demanded it become a solely Cuban project without any direct involvement by the American military. Undeterred, Richard Bissell presented on March 11, 1961, a new plan confirming the president's desires. This plan now called for a few thousand men to land, rally the Cuban people, and defeat the 200,000 soldiers of the Cuban army. The landing location was moved to a better beach, but one that was sixty miles from the mountains and safety if anything went wrong. A confident Bissell assured Kennedy that the plan would be a 100 percent Cuban affair and would almost assuredly succeed. Kennedy agreed and then was distracted by other affairs, one of them with Marilyn Monroe.

With less than a month to go, one element had to be added. With Kennedy pulling the USAF out, the invasion would need air cover and support. The Cuban air force was a joke by modern standards, but it had enough prop-driven aircraft to disrupt the landings unless neutralized. What the CIA devised was a wing of B26 bombers manned by quickly trained Cuban "volunteers." No provision was made to explain how the Cuban rebels obtained a complete wing of heavy bombers.

At this point, the Pentagon got involved and examined the final plan. They were less than impressed, giving the landings alone a 30 percent chance of succeeding. But, not wanting to antagonize the new administration or the CIA, the Joint Chiefs officially reported to the White House that the plan had a "fair" chance of succeeding. Then the PR element of the CIA went into action, and press releases from a fake "Cuban Leadership Council" began to appear.

At the beginning of April, the 1,500 Cubans trained in Guatemala were shipped to Nicaragua and boarded a number of rusty freighters, which were later dubbed the "Cuban Navy" in the Cuban Leadership Council's press releases. At this point, it also became apparent to all but the most unobservant that U.S. deniability was gone. A "defector" flying a B26 that was supposedly from the Cuban air force was put on display in Miami. But the man was not a Cuban airman. It was quickly noticed by some newsmen that, judging from what he did not know, he could not have been in the Cuban air force, and that the model B26 he had "stolen" was one not in use by Cuba. Castro certainly knew something was up. Kennedy, realizing this, gave orders canceling the bombing mission that was supposed to isolate the beach where the Cubans were to land.

Everyone seemed to know that the bombers would not show except the Cuban rebels on their ships. But even then, the Cuban rebels' morale was so bad that the CIA handler in charge of the landing went ashore on April 17 along with the scuba divers who were to secure the beach. Onshore he found no defenders except a bogota full of partying locals.

The CIA agent radioed for the Cubans to land. Before they reached the beach, a single Cuban army jeep on patrol appeared and swept the beach with its spotlight. Likely, this was a standard procedure and as yet there really was nothing to see. But the CIA man opened up with his Thompson machine gun. The jeep fled and with it any chance of surprise.

When the boatloads of Cuban rebels reached the beach, it was noticed that no one had been appointed to command the landing. Once more, CIA personnel substituted for officers and directed the whole thing. When the escaped jeep reported the invasion, Castro was notified. He immediately ordered the nearest armed units to drive off the invaders. The units happened to be from the Cuban Military Academy. The cadets were armed and dispatched to the beachhead. One working airplane, a World War II Sea Fury, flown by the top pilot in the Cuban air force, Enrique Carreras, also scrambled and was soon strafing the beach. Pinned down by the cadets and the Sea Fury, the 1,500 Cuban expats and their CIA handlers dug in. More Cuban troops arrived, and soon it was difficult to run ammunition from the boats to the beach. By afternoon, the Cuban rebels' ammunition was already running low. There was not going to be enough for a breakout from the beach. There was barely enough to maintain a defense.

That evening Bissell pulled President Kennedy from a formal reception. He explained to the president that the situation was dire. The only way to save the invasion was to release the fighters and bombers from the carrier *Essex* located nearby. It was at this point, after having approved every action taken so far, that Kennedy lost his nerve. He refused permission because he did not want the United States involved. The navy chief of staff who attended the meeting is said to have pointed out that it was already involved, but Kennedy refused permission. He suggested that the Cubans flee to the mountains as planned, but Bissell pointed out that the landing location had been changed and those mountains were now sixty miles away and on the other side of an increasing percentage of the Cuban army.

The fighting became more intense as more units of the Cuban army arrived on the eighteenth. Still the Cuban rebels held out on the beach. They had nowhere else to go. Kennedy did finally agree to one bombing raid by the "volunteer" Cubans in the B26s. American jets could accompany the bombers to discourage them being attacked, but were not to engage any ground targets. Unfortunately for deniability, the Cubans who were to fly the bombers refused to do so. They had seen how their comrades had been abandoned and were not willing to trust that the American fighters would be released to defend them. Eventually, the raid did occur. The bombers were being flown by that well-known Cuban unit the Alabama National Guard, dressed in their National Guard uniforms and operating on U.S. radio frequencies. Making things worse was that the rebel Cuban pilots were right. Someone forgot that the backup bombers in Nicaragua and the fighters in Florida were in different time zones. Four of the National Guard bombers were shot down when the fighters never appeared.

By April 19, it was apparent that the landing was a failure and that the rebels could not hold out much longer. The CIA handlers had gone back to the boats of their "Cuban Navy," which were waiting offshore and loaded with ammunition and weapons. One attempt was made to get to the beach with the needed ammunition, but the convoy turned back when the leader of the 1,500 rebel Cubans surrendered before the first boat arrived. The Cuban army rounded up 1,189 invaders and found 114 dead. A year later, President Kennedy ransomed the survivors from Castro for a payment of $59 million.

The failure of the Bay of Pigs landing was likely inevitable given the changes to the plan. So perhaps the greatest mistake, among the many, was Kennedy simply approving the landings at all or Bissell proposing it. Kennedy's had been a political decision, and he paid little attention to the military concerns. Certainly when JFK refused to support the landings with any American forces, he eliminated any chance of success or even survival by those Cubans who were risking their lives and freedom at the CIA's behest.

Had this been handled differently, there would have been a good chance that, if shown a viable alternative, the Cuban people would have thrown an increasingly more repressive Castro government out. The inaction by Russia during the entire drama demonstrated their unwillingness to get involved. But the plan did fail, and Cuba in 2009 remains one of the last communist regimes. Another consequence of this failure was a near-nuclear war. The Russians were emboldened by the stumbling reactions of President Kennedy, and they then felt free to establish nuclear missile bases in Cuba. Kennedy, having learned his lesson on being faint-hearted, took a strong stand regarding the Cuban-based Russian missiles, and many experts say that both superpowers were just a few misunderstandings or missteps away from complete mutual atomic destruction. Had the plan worked as it had in Guatemala, the Western Hemisphere would be very different. A capitalistic Cuba may have discouraged many communist insurrections in Central and South America. Would there be a Hugo Chávez today if Kennedy had not lost his nerve?

92

PUT UP WITH THIS MISTAKE

Sticky Problem

1968

|||||||||||||||||||||||||||||||||||||||||||||||||||||||||||||||||||||||||

I n 1968 a scientist at 3M named Spencer Silver decided to work on improving one of the most successful of that company's products, adhesive tape. What was needed was a better glue that held more firmly, but still allowed the tape to be removed. By 1970, he had instead developed something very different, but of no use to adhesive tape. What Silver had managed to produce was a glue that was easy to remove but had only weak sticking power. Interesting, but seemingly a failure if there were no commercial uses for it. Four years passed, and then a colleague of the scientist commented that he was frustrated that the small sheets of paper he used to mark that day's songs in his hymnal would fall out. The friend didn't want to use tape because he was worried about harming the book's pages. Finally there was a use for the weak glue that had been a mistaken result four years earlier. By 1980, the Post-it note was found in offices all over the world.

93

||||||||||||||||||||||||||||||||||||||||||||||||||||||||||||

UNNEEDED RISK

Watergate

1973

||||||||||||||||||||||||||||||||||||||||||||||||||||||||||||||||||

Mired in a political scandal that threatened to destroy his presidency, Richard Nixon famously declared, "I am not a crook," in a televised Q and A session with 400 Associated Press managing editors in November 1973; while he never recanted such words, the enormity of evidence suggesting he was a crook left a permanent blemish on Nixon's presidency. As a result of the Watergate scandal, Nixon became not "the president who ended Vietnam" or "the president who oversaw large-scale racial integration" or even "the president who helped take America to the moon." Nixon instead became "the president who resigned to avoid being justifiably impeached."

The scandal initially looked like a mere robbery. On July 17, 1972, a security guard at the Watergate Office Complex—where the Democratic National Headquarters was located—noticed that tape was covering several doors to keep them unlocked. He removed the tape and continued his shift, but when he noticed that the doors had been retaped, he phoned the police. Five men were arrested and later indicted, along with two others, for conspiracy and burglary. The burglars had on their persons and in their hotel rooms thousands of dollars of cash that could be traced back to the 1972 Committee to Reelect the President, a fund-raising organization for the Nixon administration that was given the pejorative acronym CREEP by his opponents. This connection between the committee and the burglary earned the burglary considerable media attention. The scandal became the subject of an investigative journalism project spearheaded by *Washington Post* reporters Bob Woodward and Carl Bernstein, who relied largely on anonymous sources. Their correspondence with a source referred to as "Deep Throat" (revealed in 2005 to be former FBI Associate Director William Mark Felt) suggested that the burglary and its coverup had ties to the FBI, the Justice Department, and even the White House. This fueled a broader investigation that did not end with the burglars' convictions. It was not long before Nixon asked for the resignation of some of his closest aides implicated in the scandal, H. R. Haldeman and John Ehrlichman. He also fired White House Counsel John Dean, who would later become a witness against Nixon.

Hearings held by the Senate garnered substantial media coverage; the majority of Americans saw some segment of the hearings between May 17 and August 7. It was learned during the hearings that all conversations held inside the Oval Office were recorded. Archibald Cox, a special counsel in the Justice Department charged with examining the Watergate scandal, subpoenaed the tapes; Nixon refused, citing executive privilege and issues of national security, and ordered Cox to withdraw the subpoena. Nixon offered Cox a rigged compromise: John C. Stennis, a famously hard-of-hearing Senator from Mississippi, would review the tapes and summarize them for the special prosecutors. When Cox refused, Nixon forced the resignation of Attorney General Elliott Richardson. The attorney general had been appointed just two months before, and he refused to comply with Nixon's demand to fire Cox. Richardson was replaced with Robert Bork. Bork reluctantly dismissed Cox and replaced him with Leon Jaworski, who picked up where Cox left off. It was this incident, dubbed by the press as the "Saturday Night Massacre," that led Nixon to assert he was not a crook.

Jaworski did not give up. His efforts caused Nixon to attempt a compromise, releasing transcripts of the tapes with information pertinent to national security redacted. Controversy stemmed from an almost twenty-minute gap in one of the tapes. In July 1974, the Supreme Court mandated that full access to the tapes had to be granted. That same month, the House Judiciary Committee voted to recommend three articles of impeachment against the president: obstruction of justice, abuse of power, and contempt of Congress. In August, a tape was released that was deemed the smoking gun of the affair, an irrefutable piece of evidence that destroyed Nixon politically. It detailed a 1972 conversation between Nixon and Haldeman in which Haldeman described a plan to cover up the burglary by having the CIA obstruct an FBI investigation into the affair; Nixon approved the plan. That conversation, along with charges that Nixon paid blackmail money to hush conspirators, sounded the death knell for Nixon's presidency. Nixon's own lawyers abandoned him, and many who had been reluctant to impeach him declared that they had changed their minds.

Though Nixon never admitted to being involved in Watergate or its coverup, he did declare that he regretted not handling the scandal correctly. After being informed that there were enough votes in Congress to impeach him, he resigned on August 8, 1974. His successor was Vice President Gerald Ford, who a month later fully pardoned Nixon to protect him from criminal prosecution. Such an action drew accusations that a deal had been made between Ford and Nixon in which the latter would be pardoned for handing over the mantle of the presidency, though no evidence of such a deal has ever surfaced. Many attribute Ford's defeat in the election of 1976 to the Watergate incident.

The political landscape in the decades following Watergate had been irrevocably altered by the political consequences of Nixon's actions. Initially, the Democrats gained substantial ground in congressional elections as a result of the subterfuge of a Republican organization devoted to getting Republicans elected. The practice of recording conversations in the White House ended. Many new laws came into existence with the ostensible purpose of encouraging ethics in government.

Our language now shows just how deeply Nixon's Watergate mistake affected the nation. Any public scandal is defined with the "-gate" suffix. These are across-the-board issues ranging from sports to pop culture: Spygate (a football controversy involving the New England Patriots spying on the New York Jets); Monica-gate (Monica Lewinsky's ill-fated relationship with President Bill Clinton); and, more recently, Kanye-Gate (singer Kanye West publicly humiliating another singer during a televised awards ceremony).

Nixon oversaw many positive political developments during his tenure. He had significant foreign policy successes, such as his historic visit to China in 1972, which opened up diplomatic relations with them. He also initiated the Anti-Ballistic Missile Treaty with the Soviet Union, and he signed a cease-fire with North Korea, effectively ending American involvement in the Vietnam War. He made significant advances on the domestic front, implementing many of the most progressive social reforms of the 1960s. During his presidency, the Environmental Protection Agency (EPA) was created, and Nixon signed the Clean Air Act and supported extensive conservation measures and environmental reforms. He was also the first president to take up the issue of welfare reform. He signed important legislation prohibiting gender discrimination and implemented the first significant Affirmative Action program. Perhaps most notable, he was pivotal in desegregating Southern public schools.

When the Watergate was broken into, Richard Nixon was up almost twenty points in the polls. He had a lead that was beyond insurmountable and won easily. Watergate was just not necessary on any level. This one mistake meant that his other achievements have been completely overshadowed by scandal. Perhaps the most negative consequence of Watergate was the rise in public cynicism toward politicians. So many investigations went on after Watergate—often initiated primarily to destroy political opponents—that the public became jaded. In the decades since Watergate, public apathy for important political issues has risen. Politicians and their political agendas are often looked at with deep skepticism. This mistake changed how we view our leaders. The fallout has reverberated across the decades, ushering in a new era of public cynicism, apathy, and partisanship that continues to this day.

94

INCOMPLETE RESEARCH

Marketing Madness?

1985

I n 1985, Coca-Cola created what many consider to be one of the biggest marketing fiascos in history by replacing the old Coca-Cola formula with a new version of Coke to compete with a sweeter-tasting Pepsi. Public outrage was so great that Coca-Cola was forced to reintroduce the old version just seventy-nine days later. Six months after New Coke was launched, Coke was back on top, with sales increasing at more than twice the rate of Pepsi's. So was it really a colossal marketing failure or a stroke of marketing genius?

Right after World War II, Coca-Cola enjoyed a 52 percent share of the cola market. But in the fifteen years before the introduction of New Coke, sales were slipping, while Pepsi's continued to grow. By the early 1980s, Coke's market share had dwindled to 24 percent, primarily because Pepsi was beginning to outsell Coke in supermarkets and other venues. In the 1960s, Pepsi had successfully targeted the youth market, which seemed to prefer its sweeter taste. Executives at Coca-Cola were convinced they had to take drastic action to stay ahead of the competition. So in 1983, Coca-Cola launched Project Kansas (named after a famous photo of a Kansas journalist sipping a Coke) to come up with a sweeter, better-tasting formula. They began conducting top-secret research and taste tests.

Why would Coca-Cola tinker with the legendary secret formula that had been so successful for almost 100 years? It primarily came down to the perception that Pepsi tasted better than Coke. Taste tests conducted by both cola rivals showed that most people preferred the taste of Pepsi. And later taste-test results went even further to validate the idea that Coca-Cola should reformulate its flagship beverage. Not only did consumers express a preference for Pepsi over Coke in those taste tests, but they also preferred the New Coke formula (dubbed Kansas) over both old Coke and Pepsi.

However, three serious research and marketing problems emerged, which were not fully understood by the company until after New Coke was launched. The first problem had to do with the taste tests themselves. The tests used small samples the participants were supposed to sip. While many people preferred the sweeter taste of Pepsi in small amounts, they didn't care for the soda in larger amounts, like those found in a typical can. In fact Coke is often preferred in larger volumes because it is less sweet.

The second problem is what is called "sensation transference." First coined in the late 1940s, the phrase is used to describe the phenomenon of tasters unconsciously responding to the drink's packaging, and that product packaging can change the perceived taste. In the case of Coke, people responded to the red color of the can with its distinctive script when tasting the beverage. Many marketing experts think it may be impossible to separate the taste of the product from its brand name and distinctive package.

The third problem was that the company underestimated the sentimental value attached to the original Coca-Cola, which many people considered an integral part of American culture and tradition. When the initial taste-test results came back favorable toward New Coke, the executives decided to conduct surveys and focus groups to help decide if they should get rid of old Coke altogether or keep both old and new formulas. However, because of the intense secrecy surrounding the prelaunch marketing research, they never asked a key question: Do you want us to replace the old Coke with a new version of Coke? Instead, they asked people if they would purchase and drink Kansas if it were called Coke instead. Only a small percentage of people completing the survey said they would not purchase the Kansas drink if it were renamed Coke. However, the executives chose to ignore 11 percent of those in focus groups who stated that they would stop drinking Coke altogether if the Kansas choice was called Coke. And this segment of the focus group population was an exceedingly vocal and angry minority, ultimately influencing others in those Kansas test groups indirectly and causing the negatives to jump way up.

The executives ultimately decided that keeping both the old and new Cokes would divide their own share of the soda market and the result would be that Coke would no longer be the number-one-selling cola in the United States. Pepsi could then claim not only that more people prefer the taste of Pepsi over Coke but that more people drink Pepsi than Coke. The last thing the company wanted was to wage a cola war between two competing versions of Coke. Fearing a marketing nightmare, Coca-Cola replaced old Coke with New Coke, instead of introducing New Coke as another soda option.

They timed the release of New Coke with much fanfare and to coincide with the company's hundredth birthday. New Coke was launched on April 23, 1985, and production of the original version was halted that same week. Sweeter and smoother, New Coke tasted much more like Pepsi than an improved version of the original Coke.

The public backlash was immediate. People began hoarding old Coke. Many likened it to trampling the American flag. Protest groups were formed, such as Old Cola Drinkers of America, which boasted more than 100,000 recruits trying to bring back old Coke. Even Coke bottlers were concerned. They wondered how to promote a drink that had always been marketed as "The Real Thing" now that it had been so dramatically changed. There was noise made that the bottlers themselves might follow consumers and boycott the product. But public protests, boycotts, and the dumping of bottles into city streets were just some of the company's problems. Company headquarters was bombarded with more than 400,000 calls and letters. Coca-Cola hired a psychiatrist to listen in on phone calls to the hotline. The doctor reported to executives that some of the callers were so distraught over losing their beloved old Coke it was as if they were talking about the death of a family member.

On July 11, the company announced the return of old Coke to store shelves. The news was so big it made the front page of every major newspaper in the United States, and two major networks interrupted their regular programming to break the news as it occurred. Some likened it to "the second coming." Phone calls and letters again flooded headquarters, this time expressing profound gratitude. "You would have thought we cured cancer," one company executive said, describing the joyous response. The company president, Donald Keough, explained the entire fiasco this way: "We did not understand the deep emotions of so many of our customers for Coca-Cola."

The crucial failing on Coca-Cola's part was that they never asked Coke drinkers themselves if they wanted a new version of their beloved soft drink at the expense of losing the old, familiar drink. Their mistake at least changed the soda-drinking habits of millions all over the world. Coca-Cola ended the fiasco having lost several percentage points of the soda market when people, avoiding New Coke, found other flavors from other companies that they liked. That was tens of millions of shoppers putting something else in their carts all over the world.

As for the theory that Coca-Cola orchestrated a brilliant tactical move by temporarily pulling old Coke to generate overwhelming demand, Donald Keogh may have put it best: "Some critics will say Coca-Cola made a marketing mistake. Some cynics will say that we planned the whole thing. The truth is we are not that dumb, and we are not that smart."

|||||||||||||||||||||||||||||||||||||||||||||||||||||||||||||||||||||||||||

95

OPEN SAYS A ME

A Real Press Release

1989

|||||||||||||||||||||||||||||||||||||||||||||||||||||||||||||||||||||||||||

The man most responsible for the collapse of the East German government and the reunification of Germany was a communist bureaucrat. The mistake, and the change it initiated, came in relation to the Berlin Wall. That wall had been put up to stop a hemorrhage of refugees traveling from East Germany to West Germany. The best and most-trained East Germans also had the most to gain by crossing to the West where wages were often ten times as much as in the socialist economy. First the border was closed. Most of the border between the two German states was either fenced, hard to reach, or both. So closing it was more a matter of instructing border guards than of engaging in construction. This left the anomaly of West Berlin. Sitting in the center of East Germany, the city was part of West Germany due to the agreement of the Yalta Conference between the Allies during World War II. When the rest of the border was closed, East Germans began to pour across the dividing line down the center of the city. To stop this exodus, the East German government built the notorious Berlin Wall. The wall was actually a series of obstructions and guard towers culminating in a high concrete wall or bricked windows. In the years that followed, almost 300 East Germans were killed and hundreds more wounded attempting to flee across the wall's barbed wire and other obstructions. It became a visible symbol of Soviet repression.

By 1989, the German Democratic Republic, the most repressive of the Soviet satellites, had eased some restrictions on their people. It was a trend actually encouraged by the new Soviet prime minister, Mikhail Gorbachev. After months of unrest and riots, the East German Krenz government had agreed to allow East Germans to travel through newly independent Czechoslovakia to West Germany. Trainloads of East Germans were soon taking advantage of that liberalization. So many that they were overwhelming the few crossings used in this program.

So by November 1989, the East German Politburo and leadership had been working hard to create new regulations that eased this pressure while still maintaining a comfortable level of control. The normal communist procedure for such a relaxation of rules was to do it in small, carefully controlled steps. This ensured the government would remain in control of all aspects of whatever was liberalized and prevented a domino effect of increasing expectations and reactions from the population. Simply put, because the GDR leaders significantly held down and controlled their people, the East German government feared relaxing that control too quickly or visibly. The sure result they feared was what did happen. Once a breach in repression appeared, there was no way, short of violence, to keep it from being torn open even further. Moscow, working itself toward what a few years later was the end of communism, would neither allow nor support sending in the tanks, even though this had been a common Soviet reaction to unrest in the 1950s.

Finally, plans and regulations for lowering restrictions on all border crossings were completed late in the day on November 9. They were to begin taking effect on November 17. Just after these plans were completed, a spokesman for the Politburo, Günter Schabowski, held a televised press conference to answer questions from the Western press corps. He was handed a note that said East Germans would be allowed to cross directly into West Germany. It said that further instructions would be available the following day after the border guards could be informed of the procedures and instructions. No more details were included, since the regulations and procedures had just been finalized a few hours earlier. Schabowski read the note out to the assembled reporters, which meant he was reading it aloud on the state television network. Then an Italian journalist asked him when the regulations were to go into effect. The note seemed, incorrectly, to infer that the change was to take effect that day. All that was needed was for the guards to be informed. It said nothing about gradual change to ensure government control. The spokesman answered, "As far as I know, effective immediately, without delay." He went on to assure the journalists, and so the German people, that the new regulations included the crossings into West Berlin.

Within minutes, the crowds near the crossing points in the Berlin Wall were flooded with cheering East Germans. The border guards, who hours earlier were sworn to shoot anyone crossing without very specific paperwork, had no idea what to do. Everyone, including many of those who had been watching television, was sure the regulations had been relaxed. Without orders, the guards kept the crossing closed peacefully the rest of that evening. But the East German government had been caught off guard. No orders were ready to instruct the border guards what to do. Finally that night, as the crowds continued to grow at one crossing after another, the guards simply opened the gates. Crowds of cheering East Germans flooded into West Berlin. Many were chanting, "Gorby, Gorby," correctly assuming any change had to have come from the top.

Once open without restriction there was no way to close the borders again. Within months, the wall began to be torn down. It no longer served any purpose except to be a reminder of an embarrassing failure. By July 1, 1990, there no longer were two German states. The Stasi, the East German secret police, was disbanded, and both the economies and the governments merged. The genie had been let out of the bottle by Günter Schabowski's mistaken announcement, and all of Germany, and Europe, was changed forever.

96

||||||||||||||||||||||||||||||||||||||||||||||||||||||||||||||||||||

UNDERESTIMATING
EVIL

The Price of Oil:
Invasion of Kuwait

1990

||||||||||||||||||||||||||||||||||||||||||||||||||||||||||||||||||||

I t was the widespread belief among President George H. W. Bush and many of his officials that Iraqi president Saddam Hussein had no intention of invading Kuwait in the summer of 1990. It was the widespread belief of Hussein and many of his officials that when they invaded Kuwait, George Bush wouldn't care. Both were wrong. Despite numerous aggressive actions by Hussein's regime during that summer, Western intelligence agencies regarded his behavior toward Kuwait as mere saber rattling. Such an error inflated Hussein's confidence and ushered in a violent invasion, known as the First Gulf War, which eventually led to Western military intervention and numerous avoidable casualties.

The roots of the conflict lay in economic disputes. Saddam Hussein's Ba'athist regime considered itself the natural leader of the Arab world in the wake of the Iranian revolution. In 1980, Hussein initiated an eight-year conflict with Iran, which depleted the resources of both countries and ended with no clear winner in terms of territorial gain. Hussein had relied heavily on loans from Saudi Arabia, Kuwait, and others during the Iran-Iraq War. In the wake of the conflict, Hussein characterized Iraq's actions as a valiant defense of the Arab world against a Persian onslaught; such an assertion was coupled with pressure on its neighbors to waive debts incurred by Iraq during the war. Kuwait was resolute in its opposition to such a concession—this apparent ingratitude irked Hussein greatly. At an OPEC meeting in the wake of the war, Iraq sought to greatly increase the price of oil to pay off war debts. Kuwait was opposed to such an endeavor, and its efforts to keep oil prices lower was regarded by Hussein as an act of economic warfare.

In addition, Hussein accused Kuwait of "stealing" billions of dollars' worth of oil via its drilling in the Rumaila oil field, even though the southern tip of the field lay in Kuwaiti territory. Numerous attempts at wringing concessions from Kuwait were fruitless, and Iraq began resorting to more strong-arm tactics. Hussein delivered speeches describing Kuwait's efforts as a type of warfare that would earn an equivalent response. He deployed 100,000 troops along the border between Iraq and Kuwait. Despite this, British and American intelligence agencies believed it was a bluff by Hussein and did not condemn the military buildup.

Such a conclusion seems strange in the context of Hussein's brutal history. Hussein had no qualms about attacking other nations in pursuit of economic and military hegemony in the region, as demonstrated by Iraq's participation in the longest war of the twentieth century against Iran. His violent treatment of the Kurds in northern Iraq should have also concerned the West. Hussein had a history of pursuing weapons of mass destruction; his use of chemical weapons against the Kurds and his attempt at shipping in triggers necessary for nuclear weapons clearly demonstrated this. Yet it was concluded that Iraq, with its fourth-largest military in the world, was principally concerned with deterring its neighbors—Israel, in particular.

This is not to say that the West was completely complacent. Various media outlets and an array of American politicians condemned Hussein as a barbarous villain whom the West would inevitably have to confront. However, attempts at economic sanctions or formal condemnations of the regime were hijacked by the State Department and the Bush administration. While the United States did not hesitate to declare its disapproval of the invasion after it occurred, its actions in the weeks leading up to the invasion emboldened Hussein. Despite unease about Hussein's endeavors, Washington continued to assure Hussein that it viewed the dispute as an Arab conflict that America had no place in. A Voice of America broadcast, decrying the regime, upset Hussein; Washington's response was to distance its position from the editorial and to remove members of the government who had expressed their concerns to the media. U.S. Ambassador April Glaspie told Tareq Aziz, Iraq's foreign minister, that "It is absolutely not U.S. policy to question the legitimacy of the government of Iraq." Shortly thereafter, she met with Hussein. A recorded transcript of the meeting revealed that Hussein candidly admitted a conflict could result with Kuwait, and he demanded that the United States remain uninvolved. Glaspie told Hussein that the United States had no opinion on "Arab-Arab conflicts, like your border disagreement with Kuwait," a tidbit of 1930s-style appeasement that apparently allayed Hussein's fears of American reprisal.

Compounding the problem was America's evident prioritization of securing stable oil supplies over preserving the sovereignty of smaller nations. Such a policy had its foundations in the Carter Doctrine, a policy that officially stated foreign intervention in the Middle East would be regarded as a threat to American economic interests. While such a threat had dissipated with the fall of the Soviet Union, American concern over oil had not. Such a concern was made extremely apparent in the wake of the invasion when the State Department reiterated its standing policy of remaining "determined to defend the principle of freedom of navigation and to ensure the free flow of oil through the Strait of Hormuz." Oil was America's predominant concern, and Iraq did not fail to notice that. Although the department issued an addendum stating that territorial integrity also mattered, it was obvious where its priorities lay.

On August 2, 1990, Iraq invaded Kuwait and took over the country in hours. Most of the important government officials escaped, but Iraq had achieved its goal. British intelligence agencies admitted outright their failure to account for this scenario; American intelligence agencies frantically pointed fingers and revealed their incompetence in assessing Hussein's motives. Hussein himself declared that there was no shortage of signs in the weeks leading to the invasion. Nonetheless, Hussein had made a mistake in underestimating the international response to his actions. Within days, the United States formed a coalition to officially condemn Iraq's aggression. Long-standing allies, like France, no longer supported the regime.

The West marginally compensated for its grievous errors in calculating the likelihood of invasion by a swift response in the aftermath. Nevertheless, the United States was a firm response away from deterring a brutal Iraqi invasion into Kuwait. This serious miscalculation set the stage for the subsequent U.S.-led military intervention and America's continued involvement in Iraq into the twenty-first century.

||||||||||||||||||||||||||||||||||||||||||||||||||||||||||||||||||||||||

97

STOPPING SHORT

Saddam Stays

1991

||||||||||||||||||||||||||||||||||||||||||||||||||||||||||||||||||||||||

At the conclusion of a stunning display of American military might, President George H. W. Bush had Saddam Hussein in the palm of his hand. In the wake of Iraq's 1990 invasion into Kuwait, months of diplomatic stalemate had yielded minimal results. Military engagement in January and February of 1991 put the United States in the position to supplant the brutal dictator, but inaction allowed Hussein to maintain control of Iraq. Had Bush Senior not been so timid, the current global landscape would be dramatically different. While it's difficult to conclusively determine what would have resulted, it is likely that the catastrophic civilian casualties resulting from the continuation of Hussein's brutal regime would have been avoided. It is also likely that if Hussein would have been ousted during the First Gulf War, the subsequent 2003 U.S.-led invasion into Iraq, resulting in the first major war of the twenty-first century, would have also been averted.

In the months leading up to the First Gulf War, miscalculation was the name of the game. Western intelligence agencies grievously miscalculated the probability of Iraq invading Kuwait; Hussein grievously miscalculated the probability of Western reprisal. Hussein's murderous tendencies were well-known in his treatment of Kurds in northern Iraq. Tales of horrendous actions by the Iraq army in Kuwait unsettled many Western politicians. Months of diplomatic wrangling won small concessions from Iraq; in December 1990, Hussein released hostages whom he had been using as insurance against an invasion. Nonetheless, Iraq was resolute in its opposition to what Hussein declared as "flagrant Western imperialism." This period was later to be described by Bush as his attempt at "giving peace a chance."

A UN resolution, championed by Margaret Thatcher, issued an ultimatum to Iraq—withdraw by January 15, 1991, or "all necessary means" would be justified against Iraq. Buoyed by oft-embellished descriptions of atrocities committed in Kuwait and the opportunity to assert American dominance in a new era of unipolarity, President Bush narrowly earned authority from Congress to use military force against Iraq shortly before the deadline. On January 17, 1991, Operation Desert Shield, the five-month military strategy of defending Saudi Arabia against aggression by Iraq, became Operation Desert Storm.

Operation Desert Storm was a remarkably one-sided affair. The U.S. military deployed 1,700 planes in the first assault, losing only one. The air attack (including planes from the United States, Britain, France, Italy, Kuwait, and Saudi Arabia) focused on destroying weapons facilities (such as nuclear, biological, and chemical), communication centers, air bases, and bridges. Hussein's palace was bombed, though he had fled to a residential area. Vietnam-era strategies of ignoring civilian casualties had been discarded as the recipe for a public relations disaster; consequently, with few exceptions, the coalition avoided striking areas where civilians were at risk. Iraq lashed out against neighbors Israel and Saudi Arabia with Scud missiles, though most were shot down by U.S. forces. Israel's desire to retaliate was tempered by the United States, which feared Israeli participation in the war would alienate predominantly Muslim countries of the coalition.

In mid-February 1991, the ground assault began after Iraq ignored another ultimatum to withdraw. Iraq's army continued to set oil facilities to fire in Kuwait and did not withdraw. General

Colin Powell convinced General Schwarzkopf to begin an assault into Iraq, which began in full force on February 24. Iraq's troops surrendered in droves and various tank skirmishes had lopsided results. Baghdad radio announced on the twenty-sixth that Iraq would comply with UN demands. The coalition had suffered a mere 379 deaths, half of them due to friendly fire or accidents. These numbers were far lower than preinvasion predictions; the military effort was regarded as a great success.

It was at this critical juncture that President Bush committed a grave error. While encouraging popular revolt via leaflets distributed by planes across Iraq, he committed no military effort to guarantee the success of such a revolt. Demands of Iraq after the war included withdrawal out of Kuwait and release of hostages, but there was no insistence that Hussein stand trial for his crimes. Bush presumably believed the political defeat Hussein suffered would make his downfall inevitable; however, Hussein's firm control of the military prevented an internal coup. The Intifada, a popular uprising against Hussein in the wake of the war, was brutally suppressed. U.S. military forces observed the slaughter without providing aid. Many members of the Intifada have since stated that they did not require American troops to fight but merely desired military supplies to help finance their efforts; reports have since suggested that the U.S. military refused such assistance and, in some instances, directly frustrated rebel efforts. America had called for a rebellion and seemingly changed its mind about such a rebellion's desirability. Tens of thousands of Shiites were slain in the conflict, often via chemical weapons that the United States had specifically condemned. However, the media were largely unaware of such actions as Bush exultantly declared to Congress and the public that the war was over. Fear for American soldiers and coverage of the "Highway of Death" (U.S. bombing of a retreating Iraqi military convoy that was widely deemed unnecessary) made continued U.S. involvement in the Gulf unpalatable to many.

Margaret Thatcher, no longer prime minister in Britain, was appalled at the coalition's decision to leave Hussein in power. She declared, "Half measures never work, you've . . . got to do the job properly and show the world you're serious so they better not let it happen again." She was right—in the decade that followed the war, atrocities continued to be committed by Hussein's regime. It was not long before Hussein was again shunning the West, hijacking domestic attempts at democracy, and ignoring international demands to investigate Iraq's potential weapons of mass destruction (WMDs) facilities.

After 100 almost casualty-free hours the coalition troops stopped. This left Hussein in control of the core of his country. Why the attack was stopped and he was left in power has been explained many ways. The official explanation was that the UN had said to free Kuwait, and the troops stopped once that was ensured. However, this does not explain occupying half of Iraq and enforcing a no-fly zone over those areas even after the UN forces pulled out. The pundits said that it was because there would be a power vacuum left in Baghdad, which could be bad. This power vacuum was apparently a worse alternative than keeping a psychopathic dictator in power—a man who gladly dropped nerve poison on his own people a few years later. Or maybe the United States just didn't want to upset Iraq's neighbors by completing the conquest. The improvement in the relations between the United States with Iran and Syria had not really occurred. Or maybe George H. W. Bush did not want the problems of occupying the country once we had it. Perhaps that reasoning makes the most sense, though he might have mentioned this to his son and saved a lot of trouble later.

History since has shown that whatever the potential problems, the job should have been finished. Why? Because the United States did it all over again twelve years later. Had the UN and America taken a more courageous stand, tens of thousands of Iraqis might not have had to die in another war and thousands of Americans might not have died in both the second invasion and the subsequent occupation. The problem of Iraq could have ended in 1991. But it did not, and the reverberations of that mistake have negatively affected the U.S. economy, foreign policy, reputation, and social order ever since.

98

|||||||||||||||||||||||||||||||||||||||||||||||||||||||||||||||||||||||||||||||

BELIEVING THE
WRONG PEOPLE

The Hunt for Weapons of
Mass Destruction

2002

|||||||||||||||||||||||||||||||||||||||||||||||||||||||||||||||||||||||||||||||

In 2002, Vice President Dick Cheney charged that, "Simply stated, there is no doubt that Saddam Hussein now has weapons of mass destruction [WMDs]." It was not long after the United States invaded Iraq in 2003 that it became clear that the only thing that could not be doubted was that Cheney had been dead wrong. President George W. Bush later called the intelligence breakdown the biggest regret of his tenure. The invasion of Iraq became a fiasco, a reflection of poor military planning and careless intelligence gathering. The Bush administration erred in such an egregious way that the repercussions are still being felt years after the initial 2003 invasion.

The history of Saddam Hussein and weapons of mass destruction seemed, on the surface, to support the administration's charge that Iraq was pursuing such weapons. Hussein had used deadly chemical weapons against the Kurds in northern Iraq, against Iran during the Iraq-Iran War, and to suppress revolts in the immediate aftermath of the First Gulf War; moreover, attempts at securing nuclear triggers and establishing purportedly civilian nuclear facilities in the 1980s were thwarted by British customs officials and Israeli missiles, respectively. Hussein's rhetoric leading up to the First Gulf War certainly seemed to point to the fact that he regarded possession of WMDs as a crucial measure for preserving Iraq's security against Israel and other aggressors.

Nonetheless, considerable amounts of Iraq's arsenal were eradicated by precision strikes during Operation Desert Storm in 1991. The United States and its allies forced conditions upon Iraq in the aftermath of the war. The United Nations Special Commission on Weapons (UNSCOM) was established to carry out weapons inspections in Iraq; the International Atomic Energy Agency (IAEA) was tasked with examining the possibility of Iraq developing nuclear weapons.

UNSCOM regularly inspected Iraqi facilities from 1991 to 1998. During that time, evidence of past attempts at creating chemical and biological WMDs in Iraq was revealed. Confessions by "Dr. Germ" (Iraqi biologist Rihab Rashid Taha) indicated that she had overseen numerous experiments with the intent of weaponizing pathogens. Iraq remained tight-lipped about its previous endeavors. UNSCOM discovered evidence of continuing research at Al Hakam, a facility Taha described as a chicken feed plant. The plant was destroyed in 1996; Charles Duelfer, UNSCOM's deputy executive chairman, retorted to Taha's claims by quipping that, "There were a few things that were peculiar about this animal-feed production plant, beginning with the extensive air defenses surrounding it."

Iraq became increasingly uncooperative, and in December 1998, the United States and the United Kingdom initiated Operation Desert Fox, a four-day bombing campaign of various suspected weapons sites. UNSCOM officials left shortly before the campaign and later reported they were 90 to 95 percent convinced that Iraq's weapon capabilities had been eradicated; shockingly, Hussein did not embrace the inspectors back with open arms. For the next four years, Iraq was no longer subject to regular inspections. This understandably created anxiety among Western analysts, who estimated that Hussein could swiftly restart any weapons program in the interim. Hussein publicly stated that Iraq was not pursuing weapons of mass destruction, though this did little to allay fears when he sandwiched such rhetoric with claims of the justifiability of Iraq pursuing any weapons necessary to defend itself against its enemies.

In the months leading up to the 2003 invasion into Iraq, President Bush spearheaded efforts to force Iraqi compliance with its disarmament obligations; this manifested in the passage of Resolution 1441 by the UN Security Council, which demanded just that. Hussein accepted the resolution on November 13, 2002. Inspections by the IAEA and the UN Monitoring, Verification and Inspection Commission (UNMOVIC) yielded no evidence that Iraq had resuscitated any of its old weapons programs, nor was there evidence of new attempts at developing weapons. UNMOVIC stated that months would be required to completely verify Iraqi compliance with Resolution 1441; evidently that was too long for President Bush, who invaded Iraq shortly thereafter.

The Bush administration based its strategy off of various reports that the CIA had deemed unreliable. Despite the dubious nature of the source, the conclusions of the report were presented as fact to the American public and to Congress. Charges were made by Andrew Gilligan that British documents had been embellished to justify the invasion. Two trailers, heralded as evidence Iraq possessed mobile weapons facilities, were later deemed innocuous; discoveries of decayed chemical weapons were discounted by experts due to their nonlethal nature. The Iraq Survey Group, headed by David Kay, swiftly determined, in the wake of the invasion, that Iraq's WMD pursuits had been crippled in 1991 and never revived.

The absence of WMDs was a public relations disaster for the Bush administration. Many on the left charged that documents were deliberately falsified to justify intervention. Others attributed the invasion to sheer incompetence. Regardless of motive, the lack of success in replacing Hussein with a stable democratic government has marred whatever legacy Bush might have hoped for. As evidence of the administration's error surfaced, the president and his cohorts shifted strategy. The war became one aimed at removing an ally of Osama bin Laden from power, though no evidence of a relationship between Hussein and bin Laden has ever surfaced. The war then became one designed to foster democracy in the Middle East. These shifting justifications became fodder for criticism by Democrats. Many who protested the conflict attributed the war to economic concerns over oil or an Oedipal desire to finish what his father started. In an interview in 2003, former Deputy Secretary of Defense Paul Wolfowitz stated that, "For bureaucratic reasons, we settled on one issue—weapons of mass destruction—because it was the one reason everyone could agree on."

Six years after the invasion, the United States remains mired in Iraq, with numerous failures to contend with. Democracy is still tenuous; thousands of American troops have perished, and countless more Iraqi civilians have died; the search for WMDs has long since been abandoned. Ignoring evidence suggesting the lack of WMDs in Iraq before the invasion was a grave error committed by George W. Bush, and many others affiliated with his administration. Whether he sincerely believed they existed in Iraq at that time or whether he used that issue simply as a pretense to remove Hussein for other reasons, George W. Bush's legacy will be forever tainted by using a seemingly unprovable and possibly false reason for invading Iraq.

99

DESIGNED TO FAIL

Floodgate

2005

On July 31, 2006, The Independent Levee Investigation Team released the results of their investigation of the cause of the August 29, 2005, New Orleans levee failures during Hurricane Katrina. It would be satisfying to blame those failures and floods on crooked politicians or the Army Corps of Engineers. But the reality is that the original mistake that led to all the other failures came long before and was a simple mistake. The levees were designed using a model storm to test their strength and survivability. This mathematical testing of the levee designs was called the Standard Project Hurricane. That was the problem. The testers used only standard hurricanes. The model was simplistic and missed some of the effects of the storm. Worse yet, the math used to determine the power of the standard hurricane excluded the data on the most extreme storms. So it is not hard to understand why levees that were designed using the standard model failed when faced with a much stronger than standard storm. Perhaps the math should have also taken into account that the chances of a 100-year hurricane occurring any year are the same for next year as they are for 100 years from now. Such storms can come anytime.

Had the math worked and the assumptions made proved correct, 2,000 people need not have died and tens of thousands would not have been made homeless. The failures made before, during, and after Katrina affected the entire United States. There were many mistakes made on every level, but the one that started it all was made by a mathematician in some quiet design and testing office years before.

100

IIIIIIIIIIIIIIIIIIIIIIIIIIIIIIIIIIIIIIIIIIIIIIIIIIIIIIIIIIIIII

THOSE WHO DO NOT
STUDY HISTORY

Are Doomed to Repeat
the Mistakes of the Past

2008

IIIIIIIIIIIIIIIIIIIIIIIIIIIIIIIIIIIIIIIIIIIIIIIIIIIIIIIIIIIIIIIIII

J ust about every person in the world in 2008 suffered from
the collapse of the stock markets and total implosion of the
world's banks. The entire disaster came as a great surprise
to almost everyone, as we'd been raised hearing the mantra that
the U.S. financial system had so many protections that a 1929-
type depression could never recur. And perhaps in 1980 that was
true. But as it was so painfully demonstrated, protection so carefully constructed in the 1930s and 1940s failed.

Well, actually it did not fail. The problem was that the protections created out of the economic pain of a generation didn't really
fail, because they simply weren't there anymore. In the name of
modernization and just outright shortsighted greed, the protections and restrictions had been removed one by one. The details
of what is discussed here are complex and fairly Byzantine. An
eighth-century Byzantine emperor who was busy manipulating
markets and neighbors while debasing his currency would probably have felt right at home with the U.S. Congress.

The best example of what happened is the 1999 repeal of the
1933 Glass-Steagall Act. Note that it was 1999 during the Clinton
administration, and its repeal was strongly supported by the

White House. The Glass-Steagall Act was written in reaction to abuses by the finance houses and major banks. They had created a financial bubble that burst in the crash of 1929. Back then, companies such as Goldman Sachs created investment funds that sold and were valued at more than $1 billion in a single year. None of them was supported by even a small percentage of real value. To get money to invest in the highly profitable markets, banks sold mortgages to just about anyone who seemed vaguely qualified. They would be able to pay, or, if they could not, the repossessed buildings could be sold at a profit, since property values had gone up steadily for a decade. Either way, the banks profited. So the Glass-Steagall Act was created to prevent such gaming of the system as had been done by the Morgans and Rothschilds and for which, when the bubble burst, the entire nation paid the price.

Is any of this beginning to sound familiar?

Move the clock ahead to the late 1990s. The tech boom was booming, and there was money everywhere. The stock market had jumped from a Dow Jones of 1,000 in 1970 to near 14,000 in 2007. On paper, a lot of people were a lot wealthier. So Congress and President Clinton finally succumbed to decades of demands by the financial businesses to remove the "onerous" and "unnecessarily restrictive" regulations of such bills as the Glass-Steagall Act. In 1999 they did. Forgetting that the bill was there because of what greed and short-term thinking had done to the nation seventy years earlier, legislators promised a new era of prosperity. After all, that was a long time ago, and we haven't had a collapse like that since. The part of that equation the politicians and money handlers missed was that we hadn't had such a collapse because the very laws they wanted repealed had forced moderation and protected Americans against it. It wasn't even as if some of the leaders didn't understand what they were doing.

Senator Byron L. Dorgan was quoted in the *New York Times* in 1999:

> *I think we will look back in 10 years' time and say we should not have done this but we did because we forgot the lessons of the past, and that that which is true in the 1930's is true in*

2010 . . . I wasn't around during the 1930's or the debate over Glass-Steagall. But I was here in the early 1980's when it was decided to allow the expansion of savings and loans. We have now decided in the name of modernization to forget the lessons of the past, of safety and of soundness.

The representatives who repealed Glass-Steagall and other related laws knew what they might be doing. Short-range profits and campaign contributions promised to be generous, and if it kept the boom going awhile longer, then the repeal must be a good idea. It just seemed that they could not help themselves.

With Glass-Steagall repealed, there was no limit on how big a financial company might become or what it could be involved with. A major trophy on the wall of the office of billionaire Sanford Weill was the pen that President Clinton used to sign the Glass-Steagall repeal. Weill went on to build Citi—we're too big to fail; give us $45 billion please—group, which includes Citibank.

As a side note, those mega companies that we considered so vital to the economy that we had to bail them out with billions of taxpayer dollars were only really about a decade old. Almost all of the good times and economic expansion was done without them. Which rather begs the question of whether they were really that important.

With Glass-Steagall gone, the financial sector lobbied for and got further relaxations of those nasty restrictions that had been passed because of the Depression. These allowed for the massive rise in subprime mortgages, the trading in the same subprimes, hedge funds, and unsupported debentures. These were bought and sold by just about every institution that had to be saved with taxpayer dollars and increases in the national debt.

The Federal Reserve Bank changed its approach from depositor protection to profit protection and in doing so guaranteed the subprime mortgage would someday explode. One of the greatest offenders in these practices was Goldman Sachs, and the head of that investment firm, Lloyd Blankfein, showed he was very clear on what was happening in a Goldman Sachs profile run by the *New York Times* in June 2007:

We've come full circle, because this is exactly what the Rothschilds or J. P. Morgan the banker were doing in their heyday. What caused an aberration was the Glass Steagall Act.

After the repeal of Glass-Steagall, the big banks and financial houses—there being little distinction between them anymore—succeeded in getting reversed just about all of the protections put in place after the Great Depression. The constant refrain was that those laws were no longer necessary. Then of course the bubble burst, and we all found out that those exact same things can, and did, go wrong again. Sometimes they had new labels, but the abuses and results were the same. It took more than a decade and a world war to break the economic malaise of the Great Depression. It is possible that the baby boomers, some of whom were in their sixties in 2009, may not live long enough to see a full economic recovery. All because, even when it is clearly spelled out, the politicians of the world once more did not learn from history and so made the same mistakes.

Those who cannot learn from history are doomed to repeat it.
—GEORGE SANTAYANA (1863–1952)

Of course George Santayana also said:

History is a pack of lies about events that never happened told by people who weren't there.